Managing
Criminal Justice

Managing Criminal Justice

John W. Raine and Michael J. Willson
University of Birmingham

HARVESTER
WHEATSHEAF

New York   London   Toronto   Sydney   Tokyo   Singapore

First published 1993 by
Harvester Wheatsheaf
Campus 400, Maylands Avenue
Hemel Hempstead
Hertfordshire, HP2 7EZ
A division of
Simon & Schuster International Group

Printed and bound in Great Britain by
Biddles Ltd, Guildford and King's Lynn

British Library Cataloguing in Publication Data

A catalogue record for this book is available from
the British Library

ISBN 0-7450-1530-1

1 2 3 4 5   97 96 95 94 93

This book is dedicated to our children,
Lucy Miles Willson (and her cat Obo);
Owen-John, Bryony and Edwyn Raine.

Contents

Acknowledgements

We wish to thank the many people who have helped us shape our ideas about the management of criminal justice. We are particularly grateful to the magistrates' clerks and probation officers with whom we have worked in recent years and who have provided us with the opportunities to observe, listen and learn about the realities of managing in criminal justice. We also wish to mention the students of criminal justice management on the Public Service MBA and MSoc Sc Programmes at the University of Birmingham who inspired this book.

Next we want to mention a few names and express special appreciation; to Clare Grist, our commissioning editor at Harvester Wheatsheaf, for her faith in our project; to Elaine Bentley for the cover design and illustration; also to David Allam, Rena Smith, Cedric Fullwood and Eileen Wright, who have variously advised and reassured us in what we have tried to say.

Finally, this has been a truly joint project and we owe each other a very special acknowledgement.

Michael Willson and John Raine

Managing criminal justice

This book is concerned with the importation of the principles and practices of management into the criminal justice process. The focus of the book is upon the courts; the fulcrum of what is commonly described as the criminal justice system.

Managerialist values and practices have been increasingly emphasised in the courts, particularly over the past ten or fifteen years, as indeed they have in other parts of the public and private sectors. In many respects, the focus on management was to be welcomed. The traditional judicial and administrative culture of the courts had earned them a reputation in many circles as anachronistic bureaucracies, out of touch with modern-day values and priorities, seemingly organised and run more to suit the expectations of an elitist judiciary than the punters who would have to present themselves before the Bench. But in other respects the arrival in the courts of the new managerialist approaches was to prove problematical, not least because the new concern with economy, efficiency and effectiveness would challenge the traditional professional values of the court. In addition, there was the problem that the whole edifice of the courts, together with all their legal and administrative processes, had been established within a context of a judiciary that is constitutionally separate from the executive arm of the state. Thus the advent of the new managerialism, essentially a child of the executive and government, would inevitably provide a very special set of challenges and difficulties to be addressed.

This, then, is the context for our book, which has been written, not merely to describe the problems, but also to help direct thinking towards their resolution. The key point is that the courts have had to embrace new managerialist values and methods which have in many respects proved to be at odds with the conventions and expectations of the justice process. The three main questions which we therefore want to address are these:

1. What have been the effects and consequences for the courts and for justice of the pressures for a more management-oriented approach?
2. How have the courts as institutions coped and what dilemmas and problems have been raised along the way?
3. How do we judge the impact of managerialism upon the justice process?

Our book takes as its empirical centrepiece the criminal court structure of England & Wales, which is composed of the Crown Court and the magistrates' courts (the higher and lower courts respectively). However, most of the key issues on which we focus are by no means confined to the English & Welsh context alone. Quite the contrary. They are relevant to judicial systems in all countries where the new managerialist values and methods have found favour. This is certainly true of all the developed countries, but particularly, perhaps, of the USA, European states and Australasia. It is also true of many developing countries. Indeed, there is a fascinating international commonality about the managerial responses that have been made to what, on closer consideration, are very similar problems facing different criminal justice systems around the world.

Our aim is to present an analysis as to what might constitute good management within the context of the courts and justice. This might serve to help establish an agenda of priorities for the institutions most closely associated with the criminal justice process as they face continuing pressures of resources, workloads and expectations and all the uncertainties about future organisational arrangements which seem to have gone hand in hand with the managerialist values. Although the hey-day of managerialism was the 1980s when 'New Right' thinking was in the ascendancy, the full effects may take time to become apparent. This book is therefore as relevant to the future as to the past and present.

The book is organised into four main parts. Part I, 'Context and models', explores the changing perspectives on criminal justice in England & Wales. Some of the main pressures and changes affecting the courts over the past ten or fifteen years are examined, and different models of the criminal justice process and of management are considered with a view to enhancing understanding of what has been happening.

Part II, 'Strategies and consequences', focuses on the pursuit by government of enhanced accountability, reduced idiosyncrasy and greater efficiency in the courts. The various strategies pursued to these ends are explored. The consequences, some planned, others unintended, are considered.

Part III, 'Questions of balance', explores some of the difficult issues which confront management in criminal justice and on which careful balancing of competing interests and priorities has to be undertaken. Three such issues which arise in this context for the courts are considered in some depth. The first concerns the workload of the courts and the way it is scheduled. The difficult problem here is for the administrators to balance the conflicting objectives of minimising delay, conveniencing the various parties involved in cases and using court resources efficiently. The second issue concerns the relationship between the courts and the other criminal justice agencies. Here the challenge for the courts is to strike an appropriate balance between, on the one hand, the requirement for 'inter-dependence' with other agencies and, on the other, the constitutional imperative of judicial 'independence'. The third issue concerns relations between professional staff and the laity and the difficulty of achieving balance between the demands and expectations of the two groups.

Part IV, 'Consolidation', considers the future management of criminal justice. The argument is that the courts, and indeed other agencies in the criminal justice process, must adopt a more mature perspective on management and that this requires a clearer sense of purpose and recognition of the relevant underlying values.

PART I

Context and models

CHAPTER 1

The courts under pressure

'The double whammy.'
Chris Patten MP, 1992.

1.1 INTRODUCTION

The courts of England & Wales have been facing growing pressure through a period of significant change over the past fifteen or so years. In particular they have experienced the twin pressures of:

1. *Rising work pressure*
   resulting both from increasing numbers of criminal cases and increasing complexity so far as the law, legal procedures and practices are concerned.
2. *Tight resourcing*
   reflecting decisions taken about public expenditure by central and local governments in the context of political and economic policies.

The combination of these two pressures has provided much of the impetus for a stronger emphasis on management in the administration of justice. The Government's argument was that the key to meeting these pressures was better management. Managing the caseload more efficiently and using the judicial and administrative resources more effectively, it was stressed, would create the capacity to respond to the extra workloads without requiring a proportional increase in resources. However, the emphasis given to such management values, as opposed to the values of traditional and stable administration, itself created further pressure upon the courts since it challenged established values and practices and demanded the adoption of philosophies and approaches which were novel to the judicial context.

A prime example of this was the high priority given by government in recent years to the idea of the courts belonging to a system of criminal justice. Increasingly, courts have been encouraged to regard themselves as just one part of such a system and are expected to work more closely with the other agencies in the system to ensure an efficient and effective performance overall. But might such an expectation threaten the traditional independence of the judiciary and all that that might imply so far as constitutional priorities, individual rights and expectations about justice are concerned?

Before considering answers to such a question, let us examine in more detail the twin pressures of rising workload and tight resourcing.

1.2 RISING WORK PRESSURE

In England & Wales, as in most western countries, the statistics on the number of recorded crimes reveal a dramatic rise over the course of the twentieth century. In the second half of the century in particular, the workloads of the agencies involved in criminal justice (the police, prosecuting authorities, courts, prisons and probation services) have greatly increased. Indeed, the number of crimes reported to the police in England & Wales has risen tenfold in the past 40 years and by 26 per cent in the five years between 1985 and 1990.

At first sight such statistics suggest a serious loss of social control and rising lawlessness. However, as criminologists are quick to remind us, the statistics require cautious interpretation, particularly since they tell us as much about the attitudes of the public towards the reporting of crimes, and about the diligence of the police in recording such reports, as they do about levels of criminality. Moreover, they also tell us as much about police attitudes to prosecution, as opposed to the maintenance of Law & Order through less formal means, such as 'clips round the ear' for juvenile offenders and threats of court or warnings for adults, as about levels of anti-social behaviour in society.

Nevertheless, few doubt the magnitude of the upward trend in criminality. From the British Crime Survey, indeed, it has been estimated that only about 26 per cent of offences are recorded (and that only about 3 per cent are subsequently cleared up and end in convictions (Mayhew, Elliott & Dowds, 1988)). As Radzinowicz comments, the trend in criminality seems to have shattered completely the contention that:

> 'It was only a question of time before the advance of civilisation would effectively eradicate crime as a mass phenomenon.' (Radzinowicz, 1991, p. 422)

Moreover it has also proved to be a serious challenge to the contention that demographic shifts, such as fewer births and longer life expectancy, would lead to a lowering of the crime rate in the population as a whole. As Radzinowicz (1991) further points out, this proved to be so only to a very limited extent and for a very short span of time. The dominant universal trend has been of a steady, substantial increase.

> 'It embraces all age groups, both sexes, fresh recruits as well as its hard core, the recidivists, the non-violents as well as the violent. It has ceased to be an almost exclusive phenomenon of great urban agglomerations and extends all over the country, though naturally with varying intensity, and it embraces virtually all the major categories of infractions.' (Radzinowicz, 1991, p 423)

1.2.1 Rising numbers of court cases

To the courts, this was certainly how it felt. For them, the absorbing debate among criminologists about the interpretation of statistics has been of secondary significance to the plain reality of the increasing numbers of cases to be heard. Figure 1.1 demonstrates the dramatic trend of rising work experienced in the courts since 1960. Meanwhile Table 1.1, which charts more recent the trends in the very serious cases, reveals a steady rise in most categories of offence, especially those involving violence against the person, sexual offences and robbery (even though the numbers of such cases are small compared with theft, burglary or criminal damage).

Moreover, the rise in numbers of cases coming before the courts in England & Wales would have been much greater over the past decade but for some important changes in prosecution policy. For example, during the 1980s an increasing number of minor offences were made subject to 'administrative penalties' (fixed penalties) as an alternative to formal prosecution in the courts. There was also a considerable increase in the resort to formal 'cautioning' of offenders (a warning procedure

Managing criminal justice

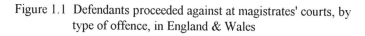

Figure 1.1 Defendants proceeded against at magistrates' courts, by
type of offence, in England & Wales

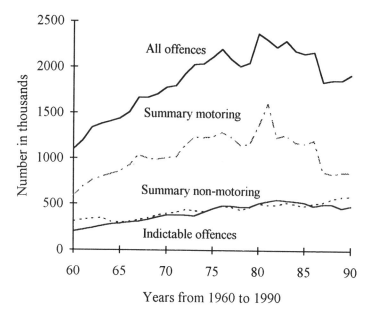

Table 1.1 Notifiable offences (000s) in England & Wales, 1985-1989

Offence	1985	1986	1987	1988	1989
Violence against the person	121.7	125.5	141.0	158.2	177.0
Sexual offences	21.5	22.7	25.2	26.5	29.7
Robbery	27.5	30.0	32.6	31.4	33.2
Burglary	866.7	931.6	900.1	817.8	825.9
Theft	1884.1	2003.9	2052.0	1931.3	2012.8
Criminal damage	539.0	583.6	589.0	593.9	630.1
Other	16.7	16.7	19.3	22.7	27.6

administered by the police), again to avoid the full implications of prosecution and court cases. In fact in England & Wales in 1990 some 269,000 people were cautioned as compared with 810,000 who were prosecuted and found guilty in the courts.

1.2.2 Greater legal complexity

But the general rise in numbers of cases coming before the courts, even after the changes in prosecution policy, does not reveal the full picture of the rising workload pressure of the courts. In addition the burden has been as much affected by two other factors. First was the changing nature of the caseload being dealt with, in particular the trend towards a greater proportion of the caseload being of a more serious nature, as Table 1.1 suggests. Second was the increasing complexity and demands of the legal process. In part this reflected the introduction of more judicial safeguards and the greater consideration afforded to the rights and interests of those at the centre of the process. But at the same time it also reflected a tendency of new legislation to be increasingly less clear and consistent, therefore giving rise to more potential points of dispute and to alternative legal interpretations. Talking, for example, of some of the problems for magistrates' clerks in advising the lay Bench about aspects of the Criminal Justice Act, 1991, Spencer (1992, pp 79-80) highlights a number of serious contradictions and concludes that:

> 'Whether or not we like the policies enshrined in...the Act, they are ineptly carried out in as much as the Act contains apparently self-contradictory provisions and does not say in clear terms how you are supposed to resolve the conflicts. If legislation does that sort of thing and fails to state clearly what it is supposed to do it is very difficult to give quality advice to lay justices or to anybody else about what the law is. We should not end up with legislation which is obscure and of which nobody can understand the purpose or the meaning.'

> 'It is not simply a question of getting the policies right, we need greatly to improve our practical efforts at translating those policies into comprehensible statutes about which justices' clerks are going to be able to give quality advice to their magistrates.'

Some evidence of the effects of complex, if not contradictory, legislation is provided in the statistics on the number of hours devoted to judicial hearings in magistrates' courts, which have risen at a far higher rate than that for the number of cases.

1.2.3 More trials

Another recent trend is that a greater proportion of defendants plead 'not guilty' to the charges brought against them, perhaps because some of the serious charges tend to be more disputable (for example, cases of assault are often harder to prove than, say, a case of a vehicle owner caught speeding by radar detector equipment) or perhaps because fewer people are as acquiescent as in the past, and more are prepared to challenge allegations made against them. As a result, more trials are requested, each of which requires more court time and other resources.

1.2.4 Increased legal representation

A larger proportion of defendants are now represented by a professional lawyer in court, even when the plea is 'guilty'. This often leads to a more searching and lengthier exposition of the defence case than would have been likely had the defendants themselves presented the arguments. In addition, the procedures by which court cases are conducted have been modified by Parliament, not only to protect and extend the rights of the accused, but to safeguard against injustice and to ensure that the procedures are as open and principled as possible. Welcome as it is, the extension of such rights and safeguarding procedures has increased the work of the courts. In England & Wales, for example, the introduction in 1986 of the right of the defence to disclosure of the prosecution's case in certain instances in advance of a trial reduced celerity, since additional time was required for the information to be provided by the prosecution. More important, perhaps, such additional time often required an additional hearing following an adjournment at the first occasion, and therefore more work for the court in organising and re-starting the case on a new date.

1.2.5 Increased civil caseloads

The workload of most courts involves more than the responsibility for criminal justice. In England & Wales, as in most countries, the same courts deal with civil as with criminal casework. In this context, the pressures of workload have been heightened by a general trend towards more litigation and use of the courts for the purposes of civil dispute resolution. Just as judges in the Crown Court may also hear civil cases in the County Court, so magistrates in the lower courts have a Family Court jurisdiction as well as their criminal caseloads.

Taken together then, a number of different factors have greatly changed the pattern and demands of the workload of the courts over the past couple of decades. This change has in turn created pressures upon judges, magistrates and court administrators alike to be more efficient in tackling the workload or else be swamped by it. The days are fast disappearing when courts can expect to commence their sittings at 10.30am, when the Bench can afford to retire for half an hour at mid-morning to take coffee, and when the judiciary can safely plan, say, a round of golf in the afternoon because the day's cases are sure to be completed by lunch time.

1.3 TIGHT RESOURCING

The other major pressure on the courts used by the Government to make the case for a more management-oriented approach derived from the financial context. Indeed, above all, it was the financial resource pressure that proved to be the catalyst for the new focus on management for the courts in England & Wales. On the other hand, the rhetoric of tight resourcing under the Conservative Government of 1979 onwards seemed to be contradicted by the same politicians' assertion of a large 'real terms' increase in funding for criminal justice in the period up to 1989. Thus we need to explore the realities of public finance and their impact upon criminal justice agencies, particularly the courts, in a little more detail.

1.3.1 The context of public finance

The public expenditure climate in the UK began to change significantly in the mid 1970s. The 1960s had been characterised as a decade of relative prosperity and economic growth, even though some of the symptoms of the country's post-war economic problems were beginning to show themselves in the form of persistent inflation. War in the Middle East in 1973 and a subsequent leap in oil prices prefaced a decade when economic problems and declining confidence seemed to compound one another with a relentlessness that undermined a Conservative and then a Labour Government.

The crisis came to a head in 1976 when the Labour Chancellor of the Exchequer was forced to seek large scale additional borrowing from the International Monetary Fund to finance a record public sector borrowing requirement (PSBR). The loan was agreed, but the main condition was that the Government should act to control its public spending. Thus began a period, not experienced before in the post-war years, of financial 'squeeze' and cuts in expenditure. Plans for many new capital projects were also put to one side. While there was some relief from the resultant gloom as the Labour Government, supported by the Liberals, prepared itself for a General Election in 1978/79, the preceding two years were the formative period for the ideas of the New Right in Britain, with its strong emphasis on tight control of both monetary policy and public expenditure and with an ideology that rested on lower taxation to increase incentives for the individual.

The theory of economics which supported this ideology was much influenced by the American economist, Milton Friedman, whose ideas also fuelled the new Republican political agenda in the USA under President Reagan. In the USA, where rates of taxation had always been relatively low and the extent of public sector activity relatively constrained, the main purpose of tight control of monetary policy and of public spending was to provide the platform to defeat inflation and achieve economic growth. However, in Britain, the argument under Prime Minister Thatcher went further, to propose that many of the roots of the malaise of the British economy lay in the large size of the public sector. The arguments here were persuasively expressed by two economists, Bacon & Eltis (1976), whose research pointed to an inverse correlation between economic performance and the proportion of the Gross Domestic Product (GDP) consumed in the public sector. Too much of the nation's wealth, they argued, had been pre-empted by the public services. This, they said, was creating too much of a burden upon a shrinking manufacturing and wealth-creating sector. Their conclusion was that the Government should act to cut public expenditure and thereby create more scope for the private sector to generate the economic activity by which the country might recover from its now endemic economic weakness.

The arguments seemed compelling to sufficient numbers of people at the polling booths in April 1979, particularly after a wave of public sector strikes and strife in the preceding months (the Winter of Discontent). The Conservatives were duly elected. Within a few months, a White Paper on Public Expenditure set out both the philosophy on which the new economic policies would be based and the prescription which was planned.

A couple of quotations from the White Paper reveal the position from which the new Government was to act.

'Public Expenditure is at the heart of Britain's economic difficulties.'

'Increases in taxes have made inflationary pressures worse...high government borrowing has fuelled inflation, complicated the task of controlling the money supply, raised interest rates and thus denied the wealth-creating sectors some of the external finance they need for expansion.' (HM Treasury, 1979. p. 1)

The initial aim was to cut public expenditure in absolute terms. Thus some immediate, but fairly limited, cuts were made in line with manifesto pledges, for example, in regional aid and public housing investment. But soon it was apparent to the Government that, because of continuing double-figure inflation, the bill for public expenditure as a whole would continue to rise unless reductions were made in the major spending commitments such as social security benefits, defence, education, health and policing. The Government's policy on public expenditure was thus modified to one which aimed to reduce state spending as a proportion of GDP. This essentially meant that increases in public expenditure would be permissible so long as economic growth provided the funds to pay for it, and so long as the private sector grew at a faster rate than the public sector. In fact, after 1989, and in the face of mounting economic difficulties, this objective too became difficult to sustain (without major political difficulties over funding of key public services). The policy was therefore modified yet again. This time it was changed to accommodate expanding public expenditure and a short-term expanding share of GDP, as long as a reduction was achieved in the medium or longer term, or 'over the life of the economic cycle' as the Treasury preferred to explain it.

1.3.2 Expenditure on 'Law & Order'

But what did all this mean for criminal justice? In the early years at least, the Law & Order programmes experienced few of the pressures felt in housing, transport and industrial support in particular. A manifesto pledge by the Conservatives in 1979 to increase expenditure on the police service was quickly implemented and police pay levels were increased significantly to encourage recruitment and restore morale. Partly as a result, by 1989, the Government was able to point to a 62 per cent increase in Law & Order spending over the decade in real terms (i.e. after allowing for inflation: see Table 1.2).

Table 1.2 Percentage increases in resourcing of criminal justice
agencies in real terms between 1985/86 and 1990/91

Police	+25%
Probation	+31%
Magistrates' Courts	+37%
Prisons	+54%
Criminal Legal Aid	+76%
Crown Court (1)	+30%
Crown Prosecution Service (2)	+32%

(1) excluding the costs of the full-time judiciary and
covering the shorter period 1986/87-1990/91
(2) covering the shorter period 1987/88-1990/91
(Source: Home Office Annual Report, 1992.)

1.3.3 Where did the resources go?

That impressive commitment should, however, be qualified in two important respects. First, the measure of the 'real terms' increase used by the Government was based on a calculation that adjusted actual spending to allow for the general level of inflation in the economy, as opposed to the inflation which was specific to the particular criminal justice agencies or, indeed, to the public sector as a whole. Since through the 1980s inflation in the public sector exceeded that for the economy as a whole, the value of the increased resources for Law & Order programmes was significantly less than the official statistics at first sight suggested. Second, as indicated, much of the extra cash which the Government committed to Law & Order was in the form of higher pay for the police. As Figure 1.2 shows, the police services absorb by far and away the largest share of the criminal justice budget so that any super-inflation pay awards in that quarter would inevitably account for much of any officially recorded 'real terms' increases.

Figure 1.2 Shares of criminal justice costs in 1990/91

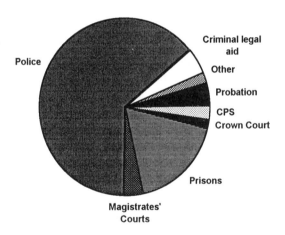

A rapid expansion took place in criminal legal aid costs, largely mirroring the workload trends discussed earlier. Besides this, however, increases in pay levels for police, court, probation and prison staff accounted for much of the extra funding provided to the Law & Order public spending programme. While this was, no doubt, regarded as good news by the staff concerned, it did not, of course, do a great deal in the way of affording extra staff to increase the capacity of the criminal justice services to handle their rising workloads.

On the other hand, throughout the 1980s, the Government did considerably increase its commitment to capital expenditure to replace older and inadequate court accommodation both for the Crown Court and for the magistrates' courts and to build new prisons. This, in turn, had the effect of squeezing still further the opportunities for affording extra staff because the costs of maintaining new buildings were generally much higher and therefore absorbed greater shares of revenue budgets. Much money was also invested during that decade in computerising the administrative systems of the criminal justice agencies, particularly those of the police and the courts. By the end of 1992, the general standard of court accommodation and the technical sophistication of the equipment available to, and linking, the criminal justice agencies had improved out of all recognition. The establishment of the Crown Prosecution Service (CPS) in 1986 also involved considerable investment in computerised administrative systems as well as staffing.

1.3.4 Symptoms of tight resourcing

Despite the investment and raised salaries, the policy of tight resourcing was certainly apparent. In particular, a firm grip was retained over the number of staff employed in criminal justice, much in keeping with the Government's broad policy of restricting the number of people on the public pay-roll. Except for the commitment to increase significantly the numbers of police officers (much of which, in fact, was achieved by filling existing vacancies rather than by increasing the establishment size of each force), and the initial staffing of the new Crown Prosecution Service, the number of new posts approved for judges, court officials, and probation and prison officers was strictly limited. To most people working in criminal justice, this meant that staffing increases were limited to levels well below the requirements of the increasing workloads.

By 1992 there had been several public expressions of concern from senior members of the judiciary about the shortage of judges and about the Government's reluctance to appoint many more. Indeed, the Lord Chief Justice, Lord Taylor, made critical reference to the problem in a televised lecture as follows:

'The persistent failure to appoint enough High Court judges has caused backlogs to reach unacceptable proportions and...unless more judges are appointed soon the arrears will become a national disgrace.' (Taylor, 1992)

Similar comments were made by a senior judge of the Commercial Court, where again delays reached an all time record in the early 1990s.

'We do not have enough judges to deal with the backlog that this term has brought, let alone with next term's list or the problems that next term will bring.' (Saville, 1992, p. 2)

Such comments demonstrated the effects of the pressure of tight resourcing in the higher courts. In the magistrates' courts, too, pressures were being experienced, but these tended to be of a rather different nature. Compared with its worries about the cost implications of recruiting additional salaried judges for the Crown Court, the Treasury showed little concern about recruitment of additional volunteer magistrates for the lower courts. The issue of administrative costs in the lower courts (for example, staffing, accommodation, equipment and other office resources) was, however, more sensitive. Here, a new and very significant financial pressure was exerted with the introduction of a cash-limited grant system in 1992.

1.3.5 Cash limiting

Like the police and other local agencies of the criminal justice system, the courts had been largely immune from the grip of cash limiting (placing ceilings on the amount of money that could be spent in each financial year) that government had imposed on local spending, notably in the health service and local government in the early 1980s. However, it was inevitable, given the Treasury's general dislike of 'open-ended' funding systems, that the case would eventually be made for this discipline to be extended to the Law & Order services.

In 1992, the grant support for the magistrates' courts and probation services was made subject to cash limiting. Despite the logic of cash limiting from the Government's viewpoint of controlling overall criminal justice spending, police expenditure initially escaped the constraint. However, it was announced a year later that cash limiting would in future be extended to policing. Before 1992, expenditure in magistrates' courts and in the probation services, as with policing, had been a matter essentially for local decision. Each year the local magistrates' courts' committees, the local probation committees, and the local police committees (the bodies responsible for resource management in their local areas) would decide their budgets in conjunction with the local authorities. The local authorities in turn were responsible by statute for providing the resources, though they had a right of appeal to central government if they did not agree with the committees' determinations. In practice such appeals were rarely made, partly because only a proportion of the costs had to be borne directly by the local authorities. In fact, central government had reimbursed local authorities to the extent of some 51 per cent of police expenditure and some 80 per cent of both magistrates' courts and probation expenditure. That meant, of course, that the local authorities had to finance just 49 per cent of police expenditure and 20 per cent of the other two services.

From April 1992, however, central government put a cash-limit on the total amount of specific grant payable nationally to the local magistrates' courts (and probation services) and adopted a formula approach for distributing that amount between the local committees. In effect, whereas each committee could previously determine the size of its budget, subject only to the approval of the local authority, now it was the Government's formula that would largely determine the resources available to the local services. Moreover, while the local authorities were expected at least to match the formula-based grant allocations with a corresponding 20 per cent contribution (as before), in practice, this did not necessarily follow. In many magistrates' courts' committee areas that were deemed to merit increased spending under the Government's formula, the local authorities declined to enhance their contribution because of other pressures on their own financial resources or because they did not see the justification for increasing expenditure on the courts. On the other hand, in areas where the formula implied reductions in grant, the local authorities were generally happy to cut their contribution to the courts' services in proportion to the Government's allocations, thus ensuring that immediate cuts in the courts' expenditure were made.

1.3.6 Legal aid

As part of the same policy of tight resourcing, the Government also became concerned about the public expenditure implications of increasing demands on the legal aid fund. Throughout the period from its introduction in 1945, but particularly in the period from 1970 to 1986, the cost to the Exchequer of legal aid had risen sharply. By 1991/92 the total bill amounted to nearly £1billion (Table 1.3), of which criminal work accounted for over half. The Government was especially concerned because of the problems of forecasting and controlling the costs of legal aid (Table 1.4), but the issue was politically delicate because of opposition by the legal rights lobby to any attempts to check 'access'.

Table 1.3 The cost of legal aid in 1991/92 (excluding contributions from clients and costs)

		£M
Criminal	Higher courts	186
	Magistrates' courts	210
	Police station advice	54
	Court duty solicitors	8
Civil	Non-matrimonial	161
	Matrimonial	115
	Interim payments	52
	Assistance by way of representation	22
Criminal & Civil	Legal advice	95
Administration	Legal Aid Board	41
TOTAL		944

Table 1.4 The cost of criminal legal aid

	Magistrates' courts	Higher courts	Cost to Exchequer (after receipts)
1982/83	£56.12M	£51.98M	£112.10M
1991/92	£212.03M	£187.47M	£472.44M

According to the Legal Action Group, an organisation campaigning for legal rights, eligibility to legal aid for civil cases was subtly reduced during the 1980s by changes in the rules about income, savings and capital (LAG, 1992). While the claim was initially refuted by the Government, shortly afterwards in November 1992, a formal announcement was made of reductions in eligibility as part of the strategy for controlling public expenditure and responding to rapidly escalating public borrowing (H M Treasury, 1992). The Government's estimate at the time was that about 7 million households would be made ineligible for legal aid as a result of the changes and that many more would have to pay an increased contribution.

So far as criminal legal aid was concerned, cuts in eligibility were also certainly made. Under the legal aid regulations of 1988, in order to be granted assistance, defendants had to face the loss of their liberty, reputations or livelihoods if found guilty. For some years, habitual offenders who were unemployed had generally been deemed by the courts in many areas to have neither livelihoods nor reputations to lose. Thus, for them at least, the key criterion for legal aid eligibility had been whether or not the charges were serious enough to imply the possibility of custodial sentences. In October 1992, however, certain provisions contained in the Criminal Justice Act, 1991, came into operation which were to affect access to legal aid. The Act allowed for a major extension of community sentences as alternatives to custody and, since the effect was to reduce the number of people likely to be jailed, it followed that the number of people eligible for criminal legal aid would also be likely to fall.

At the same time in 1992, the issue of access to legal aid in criminal cases was much affected by plans announced by the Lord Chancellor to terminate the practice of paying solicitors on an hourly rate basis for advocacy work in magistrates' courts and instead to institute a system of 'standard fees' (i.e. fixed fees for different categories of case). Behind the proposals, besides the clear aim of placing a stronger measure of control over the legal aid budget, lay the suspicion that solicitors had been inflating legal aid claims to make the work more financially attractive (perhaps to compensate for loss of their income in other fields of their work, for example, the reduction in house conveyancing business as a result of the recession). The view of the Law Society, the representative body for solicitors, was that any problem of inflated claims was small and that great harm would be done by introducing standard fees. The new financial regime, it was argued, would put pressure on solicitors to minimise the work done in preparing to represent defendants, and would encourage them to cut corners and threaten good professional practice. Many solicitors, indeed, stated their intention to withdraw from providing services under the legal aid scheme unless the new standard fee levels were set higher than initially proposed. Reduced access to legal advice and assistance seemed likely to follow from a reduction in the number of practitioners prepared to work under the legal aid rules. Once again, tight resourcing appeared to be placing pressure on the judicial system and, in this context particularly, upon access to justice.

1.4 THE PRESSURE FOR MANAGEMENT

The combination of rising workload pressures and tight resourcing represented a formidable double challenge for the courts which required considerable adjustment, adaptation and initiative by way of response. However, that challenge was amplified in the 1980s and early 1990s by the expectation of government that the criminal justice agencies, like the rest of the public sector, should adopt a much more managerialist approach towards their activities. While 'lip-service', at least, was paid to the argument that fairness and 'due process' should not be jeopardised as a result, the new priority for the 1980s and beyond soon became clear enough. It was to 'manage' the resources of criminal justice more efficiently and to demonstrate the effective disposition and use of resources, whether staff, buildings or equipment.

A key thread which stood out so far as the Government's objectives were concerned was that the criminal justice agencies, like other public service organisations, should become more business-like. The perceived attributes of the well-run private sector company (of high efficiency, of explicit accountabilities, of clear objectives, and of measured performance) should be the goals for management in the courts and other agencies. To this end, a whole range of initiatives and strategies, besides that of the tight resourcing policy, were pursued by the Government from 1979 onwards. The aim was constantly to seek out and implement methods for increasing the productivity of criminal (and civil) judicial administration. The 'three Es'; of economy, efficiency and effectiveness, became the new watchwords of court administrators in the Crown Court and magistrates' courts alike. The matter of 'value for money', too, had to be considered at every opportunity.

Much more attention than in the past was paid by the Government to the objectives of reducing delays in scheduling hearings in the courts, in completing the cases, and in collecting the fines levied. Attention was also increasingly directed at the manner in which the Bench and the administrators conducted themselves in undertaking their various responsibilities. The organisational structures, systems and processes of each of the agencies in turn came under close scrutiny. New responsibilities and duties were imposed on the agencies, for example, concerning the collection of more statistics and other performance-oriented data. Existing responsibilities were clarified, and in some instances reallocated. New methods and procedures were introduced to appraise and report on performance. In the 1990s, under the Citizen's Charter initiative (Cabinet Office, 1991), more attention became focused on the quality of service as well as on efficiency. Performance related pay schemes were introduced, as were fixed term contracts for senior staff, both as further ways of encouraging more emphasis on management performance.

But how might all this affect criminal justice? Would the pursuit of managerialist approaches with such apparent vigour achieve the fundamental changes which their proponents seemed to expect, or might they merely add a veneer on to essentially stable organisational forms and processes? Would criminal justice be better or worse for the injection of management principles and practices into the traditional administrative culture? Perhaps most important, how would the new managerialism help the courts' organisations to tackle the pressures of rising workloads, tight resourcing and changing expectations? These are some of the key questions to which we turn in Part II of this book. However, before this, let us bide a little longer in the context into which the new managerialism was thrust and consider some of the other circumstances and changes surrounding the courts. Let us also explore a little further the nature of the criminal justice process, the different models by which it might be understood, and the character of the new managerialism that came its way.

CHAPTER 2

Changing policy and developing practice

*'Change is inevitable. In a progressive country
change is constant.'*
Benjamin Disraeli, 1867.

2.1 INTRODUCTION

It was argued in the previous chapter that the combination of tight
resourcing and increased workloads had precipitated a pressure upon the
administration of criminal justice to which an answer was found in
management. The argument in this chapter is that, even without those
factors, other social pressures would have set in motion a review of the
work of the criminal justice agencies. Public and government
expectations of the criminal justice agencies were also changing.

The newly elected Government in 1979 was determined to release the
country from what it regarded as the stranglehold of the unions and the
suffocation of equally unaccountable professions and bureaucracies.
Further, the Government was committed to positive action on crime and
delinquency which were rising, seemingly out of control. However, the
performance of the professional agencies responsible for criminal justice
appeared idiosyncratic, piecemeal, unaccountable and often ineffective.
The situation could be simplistically characterised (the standard level of
analysis adopted by journalists and parliamentarians in this field) as
follows: the police no longer walked the beat and now rushed around in
squad cars, increasingly out of touch with the public who wanted their
reassuring presence nearby; the courts were archaic idiosyncratic clubs
in thrall to an unaccountable and eccentric judiciary which handed out
sentences in an entirely incoherent manner; the probation officers were

friendly but ineffectual social workers who tinkered around the edges but did not tackle the offending behaviour of their clients, most of whom were only minor felons anyway; the prisons absorbed large amounts of money but provided little more than the warehousing of offenders, many of whom needed rehabilitation, training, education, and therapy instead of colleges of crime. Meanwhile, the victims of crime got short shrift from the professionals and, in the absence of organisational accountability, monitoring or inspection, the treatment of the accused was always variable and sometimes dishonest.

The Government looked at the performance of the police, probation, prisons, and courts and decided that it was no longer acceptable that they should all work according to their own professional whimsy. With a manifesto pledge towards 'Law & Order', the Government decided to become active in promoting a coherent programme of crime control. It was going to fight crime and required the various agencies to play their part in a programme to this end which it would shape and lead. It would consult, listen and learn but, since the professionals drew their salaries and authority from the state, so they were expected to be accountable to the Government and to comply with government policies.

Over the next decade, despite a froth of fashion and platform politics, a coherent criminal justice system was to be created with the clear aim of a twin track of diverting offenders from criminal careers and the reservation of custody as a means of last resort for severely punishing those committing serious offences. This policy was given a statutory basis in the Criminal Justice Act, 1991.

As the Government involved itself in crime policy so did issues of criminal justice further enter into public consciousness. During the 1970s and 1980s, more and more information about criminal justice was brought to our breakfast tables and into our living rooms. From our newspapers, radios and televisions, we learned about overcrowding in the prisons, about new waves of criminality among the young, about the plight of victims of crime, about mounting delays in criminal cases coming to court, about inconsistencies in sentencing between courts, about discrimination in the treatment of black people and other minority groups by the criminal justice agencies, and about miscarriages of justice. This information was partial and often partisan but most people developed a greater awareness of the difficult issues of criminal justice. Further, the appreciation of criminal matters is always clouded by the response to anxiety that projects the bad onto others and introjects the good to one's own group. The attitude shown towards offenders often carries a quality of scapegoating as people psychologically distance themselves from someone who, but for the grace of God, could be themselves. Likewise, we are often irrationally prone to reducing our anxiety about becoming a victim ourselves by blaming victims for somehow provoking their misfortune. This tendency often leads to the creation of secondary victimisation (Winkel & Koppelaar, 1988). However, the significant point, here, is that there was a high level of public awareness of the problems of crime and the expectation that they should be addressed.

In this chapter we shall first review the recent developments in the criminal justice agencies. We shall briefly pick out the challenges each posed in the drive to develop accountable and coherent services. We then turn to consider the courts in more depth. The recollection of recent history is always a perilous exercise. What one party considers an advance, another might consider a betrayal of professional integrity. What one sees as a responsible measure to ensure social justice may be seen by another as a travesty of justice or an infringement of human rights. We shall take each of the main public sector criminal justice agencies in turn and focus on the sorts of features that have generated concern to those outside of the particular professions. We shall risk the charge of treachery in the knowledge that there are complementary reactionary tracts defending a golden age of professionalism, when there were no complaints procedures against probation, police or prison officers or court clerks and when local authorities dictated which school and which class your child attended. We shall argue that significant improvements in accountability, reliability, efficiency and effectiveness were needed in each of the criminal justice agencies and that these have, on the whole, been achieved.

2.2   THE CRIMINAL JUSTICE AGENCIES

The following brief, partial and incomplete sketches of the main public sector criminal justice agencies are designed to provide an impression of attitudes and events over the last two decades.

2.2.1   Probation

In the 1970s the probation services were almost independent social work agencies working 'to advise, assist and befriend' (House of Commons 1984a, p. 10) offenders referred to them by the courts. Each service was locally managed by a probation committee even though 80 per cent of the funding was provided by the Home Office. The scale and nature of the services provided varied enormously, depending on local enthusiasms and professional prejudice. Most work was done with offenders who had committed minor crimes or who were petty persistent offenders, alcoholics, in and out of the courts and prisons on a regular basis.

A set of studies published in 1976 (Smith et al, 1976; Celnick, 1976) suggested that when probation officers had low caseloads they would provide a high level of social work assistance to their clients but that this was often ineffective, inappropriate to the client's needs and sometimes counter-productive. The 'Impact Studies', as they became known, had a profound effect on the probation services. In 1978, the head of the Home Office Research Unit wrote an open letter asking the probation services to define what they did since the Impact Studies had indicated what they should not be doing. If they could not say what they were going to do, then someone else would. And, indeed, that is what happened.

The work of the probation services started to diversify away from an exclusive social work practice. In particular, community service and other forms of non-custodial restrictive supervision were introduced. Then, in 1982, the Home Office issued a circular 'A note from the Home Office' setting out four priority objectives for the probation services. The significance lay less in what was said and more in the fact that something was said at all. Suddenly, those who paid the piper were starting to call the tune. There was a debate amongst chief officers as to whether to acknowledge the existence of, and, by implication, the right to issue the note. Having been reassured that the same process would be extended to the police and courts' services (as it was, but much later), and with more than a few misgivings, the new relationship was entered. In 1984 the local probation services agreed a 'Statement of National Objectives and Priorities'. The following year local objectives and priorities were agreed and an annual cycle for setting objectives and monitoring them was instigated. Various attempts at management information schemes were attempted. The Probation Inspectorate was reformed. In addition, the Audit Commission wrote a report comparing costs of different services and asking why the services being provided varied so much in terms of cost and comprehensiveness (Audit Commission, 1989). Later, in 1992, the funding of probation services was transferred from an open to a cash-limited system calculated on a national formula rather than on traditional locally determined expenditure. This greatly changed the central-local balance of power in probation.

In 1989 the Home Office issued a set of 'National Standards for Community Service' which laid down minimum levels of performance and service. This move was extended later to other areas of work. From 1986 onwards, the probation services became involved in preparation for the Criminal Justice Act, 1991. A series of papers were published by the Home Office concerning, among other issues, the provision of punishment in the community as an alternative to incarceration. 'Prison' said the then minister, John Patten, 'is an expensive way to make bad people worse' and so other ways of dealing with offenders were to be sought which might be more successful in diverting them from careers of crime whilst also being punished. The probation services were asked to provide many of these alternatives to custody and to take a larger role in the supervision of those released from prison.

The probation services of 1993 are very different from those of 1978. Probation officers still write reports for sentencers, assisting magistrates and judges with the anxiety that accompanies all grave decision making. However, they now work mainly with perpetrators of much more serious crimes and spend little time with first offenders who had formed the majority of their caseloads in the 1970s. A wide range of facilities designed to confront offending behaviour is provided in probation centres and other projects. Probation services run a network of provisions and contacts to provide accommodation, employment opportunities and debt counselling as well as alcohol education, literacy programmes and critical work with sex-offenders and drug addicts. This is a far cry from the old benign services that advised, assisted and befriended confused and inadequate minor offenders. Probation officers now work to nationally agreed policies, accomplish more within their budgets and are more accountable internally and to government. Indeed, recently the Government has taken steps to introduce a standard performance appraisal system and a performance related pay scheme for all local probation services. These, and many other changes, have met with great resistance and resentment by many of the professional social workers whose activities were being directed (May, 1992). Without doubt, working for a local probation service is much harder, tougher and bleaker than in the past.

2.2.2   *Prosecution*

Prosecution in England & Wales was a police function until the mid 1980s and prosecution rates varied widely as different police forces all exercised discretion in their own way. Further, since the officers who made the arrests also prepared the papers and were involved in the prosecutions, it was often difficult for them to recognise that, whatever their intuitions about defendants, there might be insufficient evidence to satisfy a court. They were also reluctant to prosecute offending police officers. The courts were hearing too many unsubstantiated cases. Further, many courts still seemed to be under the influence of the police and to live up to the old name of 'Police Courts' rather than 'Magistrates' Courts'.

The national Crown Prosecution Service (CPS) was established in 1986 with a brief to conduct prosecutions in the lower courts and to commission and brief barristers to conduct cases in the higher courts. They were to review all cases referred to them by the police and only to proceed with those where it was judged there was sufficient evidence to prosecute unless it was in the public interest not to do so. A national policy for prosecution was established and a curb placed on the idiosyncratic prosecution profiles of each police force. The CPS was established to be independent of the police but, because it was accountable to government, is nonetheless seen as a state service.

Once again, there was much resistance and complaint from the professionals, especially the police, whose discretion had been restricted. For the next few years the Crown Prosecution Service bore the brunt of much criticism and contempt. Magistrates particularly expressed their strong disapproval of young, inexperienced CPS lawyers, unprepared, inarticulate and unknown when compared to the familiar, confident local police inspector. Yet others noted a continuing reluctance to prosecute in cases of police corruption or falsification of evidence. Questions were also raised about the level of discontinuances or prosecutions. Undoubtedly some of the criticism was warranted since, in the early years, the CPS had failed to recruit sufficient high calibre staff, but much of the criticism only reflected the loss of power and ownership of cases passing through the courts experienced by the police.

2.2.3 Police

Crime rates were rising and clear-up rates falling and policing was also open to criticism. More importantly, the police were no longer perceived as providing the sense of security the community required from them. Resources were poured into improving the work of the police and, in parallel, demands were made that they should improve their practices. The Police and Criminal Evidence Act, 1984, required tape recording and greater rigour in interviews. It also created the independent Police Complaints Authority which was an attempt, not yet credible, to make the police more accountable. Provocative police activity such as 'SUS' (stopping under suspicion) was outlawed and, especially after the Scarman Report (Scarman, 1982), attempts were made to move from 'police forces' to 'police services' and to return to what was now known as 'community policing'. This often proved difficult due to the presence of a salt-pan of poor calibre staff recruited in the late 1960s who had, at best, risen to the level of sergeant and stuck there.

In 1990 the Audit Commission presented the first of its reviews of the allocation and management of police resources (Audit Commission, 1990). In 1992 the Home Secretary set up the Sheehy Inquiry to report on police rewards and responsibilities. The subsequent recommendations proposed the abolition of two ranks in the career structure, the introduction of fixed-term contracts and of performance related pay. The report was immediately and bitterly condemned by police officers, particularly for the individualistic and 'results oriented' culture which it appeared to engender. An internal Home Office review was also undertaken in 1992/93 which resulted in proposals for new police authorities involving local business people as well as councillors and magistrates. Proposals were made too for the introduction of cash limiting of the police grant and for simpler procedures governing the amalgamation of local police areas (see Chapter 4).

Involvement in the miners' strike tarnished the image of the police in the mid 1980s and the corrupt practices of a few officers, combined with tardiness in uncovering police falsification of evidence in many of the IRA cases of the 1970s, have, in the 1990s, severely damaged the reputation of the police in the eyes of both the public and the courts.

Nevertheless the police have become more accountable and more conscious of their role in the community over the last fifteen years. Positive steps have been taken to grapple with society's latent racism and sexism where they are manifested in the police services. High calibre staff have been recruited and there has been a heavy investment in training. It is particularly unfortunate, therefore, that the errors of the past are currently affecting the public's perception of the police.

2.2.4   Prisons

If there were criticisms that the other criminal justice agencies were sometimes ineffective, the prisons appeared not to work at all. Reconviction rates for prisoners averaged around the 85 per cent mark and in terms of a crime prevention programme, all prison appeared to do was remove the offender from society. Nor did prison appear to be effective as a deterrent, most prisoners reporting that they had not intended to be caught.

The state of the prisons in the 1990s increasingly became regarded as a national scandal in need of radical reform, but in most respects the Prison Officers' Association was as effective as the Bar in resisting the Government's reform initiatives. Not only were the prisons overcrowded and insanitary but they seldom provided programmes to 'reform' the prisoners in their custody. Repeated complaints and suggestions about the constructive use of the period of imprisonment came to naught. Prison governors (especially the Wakefield cadres) often tried to instigate education, training and therapeutic programmes but to little avail. The Prison Officers' Association, concerned about the safety of its members, insisted on traditional turn-key roles in the overcrowded prisons. It was enough to make grown men cry and many of the best were driven to tears. Indeed, many of the best eventually gave up and left the Prison Service.

The most significant move to increase the effectiveness of prisons would be to reduce the number of people who would be sent there to complete their education in crime. This was attempted through:

1. the twin-track sentencing policy which reserved prison for the perpetrators of serious offences and encouraged the sentencers to use a new range of community sentences; and

2. efforts to reduce the number of remand prisoners by encouraging bail hostels and bail information schemes in which a verification of a place of habitation and other circumstances would be collected by the probation services so that magistrates would have a better basis on which to grant bail.

An internal attempt to raise the effectiveness of the prison system was the 'Fresh Start' initiative by which new employment conditions, enhanced pay and reduced over-time were to be the inducement to relinquish restrictive working practices. At the same time, prison officers were given the opportunity to elect for deployment in different prisons where they could develop skills and practices beyond that of turning keys. The 'Personal Officer Scheme' which linked individual prisoners with individual prison officers, for instance, was found by many to be a more creative and satisfying form of work and one that also contributed to the rehabilitation of the prisoners.

In terms of accountability, British prisons have been more open to public scrutiny than those in many other countries. The independent Inspectorate of Prisons provided annual, often highly critical, reports on the service. In comparison, Radzinowicz was to conclude that:

'To my knowledge, no independent and competent commission has been established in Italy in the past four decades (or even longer) to reveal the real conditions of penal institutions in that country.' (Radzinowicz, 1991, p. 442)

The Woolf Report (Woolf, 1991) on the prison system, following a riot at Strangeways Prison in Manchester, provided a set of standards that all prisons should, in future, achieve whilst balancing the principles of security, control and justice. Although achieving developments in the prisons seemed difficult and confidence in the prison system had sunk very low, the pressure for improvement and accountability had some effect. The Chief Inspector of Prisons, Judge Tumim, who published a set of outspoken critical reports on the Prison Service, was able to say:

'The state of prisons today is more capable of success than at any other time since the war.' (Tumim, 1993)

The Prison Service - a national organisation - was directly managed by the Home Office but in April 1993 it was hived off from direct government control and established as an executive agency with its own management board and a supervisory board. Pilot schemes were also set up to investigate the possibilities of contracting-out the management of prisons. Prisoner escort duties were also put out to contract with private security companies, ending prison officer responsibility in this respect. Two remand prisons and the rebuilt Strangeways prison were chosen for the pilot privatisation schemes.

Once again, the professionals, whose working practices were challenged, felt misunderstood and misrepresented.

2.2.5   Courts

The fundamental contract between ruler and citizen is that, in return for the citizen's consent to be governed and pay taxes, the ruler will provide external security and internal lawful peace and order.   If the overall purpose of the criminal justice process is to maintain the Queen's peace, then it is her Government's responsibility to provide the framework and means by which this can be done. The framework is a criminal justice policy supported by a body of legislation and the means is the funding of a court system, staffed by a judiciary and served by the other criminal justice agencies. All these agencies must work to restrain lawlessness but, whereas the police, prosecution, probation and prison staff may be directed by the executive, control over the judiciary who conduct the trials and pass sentences is, under the doctrine of the separation of powers, only to be mediated through the laws made by the legislature. Under this doctrine, the judiciary is required to be an independent arm of the state. There is, therefore, a profound tension between a government's desire to ensure that the work of the courts contributes to its interpretation of how criminal matters should be handled and the jealously guarded right of an independent judiciary to interpret the law, adjudicate and sentence, in court.

The Government, then, is responsible for ensuring that justice is provided but is not entitled to direct the judiciary on how it should be done. Government may be concerned with the overall effectiveness of the justice process in giving the citizen confidence that lawless behaviour will be restricted, but it is the judiciary which is responsible for adjudicating and for the sentencing of those found guilty. The problem had been that the courts were not proving effective in generating this confidence. But the Government's dissatisfaction with the work of the courts posed a very different challenge to the one of reviewing and guiding the other criminal justice agencies. Concern focused on three areas:

1. the administration of justice which was often costly and slow;
2. sentencing policy which, despite a national penal code, seemed characterised by disparities and disproportion; and
3. judicial composition and recruitment which seemed increasingly out of touch with contemporary Britain.

Before discussing each of these in turn, we should mention that it was not only the Government that was concerned about these issues. Many members of the judiciary were also very aware of shortcomings and the public was also losing confidence in the courts. Here the increasingly widely held perception was that the judiciary and the whole edifice of the courts was becoming more out of tune with modern-day circumstances and values. Images of courts projected in television dramas probably reinforced this perception. There the typical picture was of an austere court-room, of the defendant standing in the dock, of an ageing male judge adorned by wig and gown, of juries of twelve listening intently to the evidence and to the 'cut and thrust' of the cross-examination of witnesses by the prosecution and defence advocates. All of this does, in fact, represent a reasonably accurate picture of justice in the 3 per cent or so of cases tried at the Crown Court! It was hardly relevant that the main bulk of criminal justice process was actually handled under quite different circumstances. The important point was that people had come to believe that the courts, the judiciary and the judicial process were creatures of another era and, as such, potentially unsuited to dispense justice.

Second, there was popular disquiet about the standards of justice actually being dispensed. An out-of-date judicial process was one thing; but one that failed to act fairly or to achieve other expected aims was quite another. Here, recent revelations about a series of miscarriages of justice had a significant effect on public perceptions of criminal justice. But in addition, opinions had already been shaped by the regular stream of accounts of inconsistencies in sentencing, of unduly lenient sentences for some, and of unduly harsh sentences for others. Opinions were also coloured by the apparent ineffectiveness of the courts and their sentencing to deter offenders and to gain control of the tide of crime.

We shall examine each of the three areas mentioned above and explore how they might compound the pressures of increasing workloads and tight resourcing that we have explored in Chapter 1. In so doing, our argument is that growing public disillusionment, with the judiciary and with the courts' failure to live up to the standards expected of them, also played a part in helping to legitimate the spread of the new managerialism within criminal justice. After all, here also the traditional professionalist values had been found wanting, and while the new managerialism would hardly impinge upon the judicial process in a direct sense, its associated preoccupations with scrutiny, reform, value for money, effectiveness, quality and equality meant that there was every chance that the courts would be shaken out of their complacency.

2.3   ADMINISTRATION OF THE COURTS

The organisation of the courts was not at all orderly. Witnesses and victims often had to wait long hours in the same room as those they were testifying against. There were long delays in hearing cases in the Crown Court and conditions in the magistrates' courts were hardly better. The administration of the court-house is an executive matter but the administration of the court-room is a judicial one and as such could not be under the direct control of the executive. It is this contrast that makes the administration of justice so difficult and so interesting. These matters form an important theme of this book and we will return to them again and again.

2.3.1 Sentencing policy

There has been general concern that the sentencing of those convicted is often ineffective, inconsistent and just plain inappropriate. For example, there persists uncertainty and differences of opinion in the minds of government and public alike over what form of penalties are merited for different offences, and about how a balance might best be struck between the three objectives of criminal justice; those of providing, first, deterrence/prevention against offending; second, punishment of offenders; and third, rehabilitation to crime-free ways. Should sentencing be focused on dealing with the offence (proportionality), on dealing with the offender (incorporating strategies for reducing further offending) or on dealing with the interests of the victim (reparation)? For instance, if it is statistically shown that a custodial sentence (a simple punishment) is more likely to be followed by more subsequent offences than a non-custodial sentence which diverts the offender from a subsequent life of crime, which sentence should be given? Principles of justice might argue for proportionality but the pursuit of long-term social policy would argue for a simple punishment. Proponents of 'social justice' might argue that reparation should be included and a balance be sought of all three.

2.3.2 Sentencing disparities

Disparities in sentencing have long been a subject of concern. During the 1970s and 1980s several empirical studies focused on differences, both between magistrates' courts and within the Crown Court, for example, in rates of custodial sentencing, fine penalties and use of probation and other sentencing options (McConville & Baldwin, 1982; McGuire, 1992; Moxon et al, 1985; Moxon, 1988; Tarling, 1979; and Walmsley & White, 1979). A more recent study of sentencing has demonstrated serious disparities in the harsher sentencing of black offenders (Hood, 1992). The significance of such disparities has been disputed by the judiciary, and the counter-argument frequently posed that many of the apparent variations in sentences passed between courts or between Benches are in fact merely reflections of differences in the detailed circumstances of the particular cases. Moreover, even if variations are a reality, it has been countered, the alternative of uniform sentencing would be just as likely to attract criticism - in this instance of amounting to 'slot machine' justice. But the whole issue has been a sensitive one because of the equity considerations. That was evident, for instance, in the halting in 1984, at a preliminary stage, of a major study of disparities in the Crown Court (Ashworth, 1984) as a result of opposition by certain members of the senior judiciary.

In the early 1980s the Magistrates' Association (the representative body for magistrates) spent much time carefully picking its way towards establishing national guidelines on sentencing while also trying not to aggravate the shades of opinion within its membership which were vehemently opposed to any 'fettering of the sentencer's discretion'. The

Association eventually managed to gain broad acceptance to a 'list of suggested penalties for road traffic offences' and to a 'sentencing guide for criminal offences' (other than road traffic). At the same time, the Judicial Studies Board, which had responsibilities in relation to the training of the judiciary, also sought to address the perceived problems of sentencing inconsistencies by encouraging the use by magistrates of more 'structured decision-making'. However, the principle that individual sentencers should be left free to decide the severity of penalties, within the limits provided by the criminal law, remained one which would be vigorously defended by many magistrates.

Sentencing disproportion for fines

Fines form 93 per cent of motoring and 84 per cent of non-motoring sentences in the magistrates' courts and 34 per cent of sentences for indictable offences in both courts (Barclay, 1993). There has been concern about the differential effects of standard fine penalties upon offenders of different means. For instance, could it be just that a fine penalty of £100 for having no test certificate for a vehicle might amount to about 1.3 per cent of the disposable income of a person earning £10,000 per year; 2 per cent of the disposable income of the unemployed person living on social security, but only 0.4 per cent of the income of the person earning £30,000 per year?

An apparently more sophisticated policy response to these problems was to introduce the 'unit fines' scheme under the Criminal Justice Act, 1991. This meant that each offence would be assessed by the court in terms of a number of 'units' of seriousness. These would be based on a set of guidelines but would also take into account the particular circumstances of the case. Only once the sentence had been decided in this way would a conversion be made into a financial penalty, through a 'means test' of the defendant. In this way, fine penalties would be equalised in terms of their real impact rather than just in terms of monetary value. Once again, the 'professionals' were wary about their discretion being eroded and many were opposed to the scheme, especially when a serious offence by a low income defendant attracted a smaller fine than a minor one by a comparatively wealthy defendant. Indeed, some nine months after introducing the scheme, the Government felt obliged by the weight of criticism, particularly from within the judiciary, to scrap it. Instead, it would once again be left to the sentencers to determine the size of monetary penalties within the legal limits.

'Just deserts'

After a few unsuccessful 'get tough' initiatives, the Government settled in the late 1980s upon a criminal justice policy which implied a major shift in sentencing policy away from the largely 'reductivist' strategy of crime control to one based on the principle of 'deserts' (Hart, 1968). Under the 'reductivist' approach, which harked back to the principle of utility expounded by Bentham, sentencing had essentially been based on the view that, as well as the impact on those convicted, there should be benefits for society as a whole through the deterrence effect (Smart & Williams, 1973). In contrast, the new 'deserts' strategy emphasised the moral requirement of maintaining proper proportion between the offence and the punishment (Von Hirsch, 1976, 1986). As Wasik (1992) explains, the prime determinant of sentencing should thus be:

> 'to ensure that the punishment imposed was that which is deserved for the offence, having regard to the seriousness of the harm caused or risked by the offender and the degree of the offender's culpability.' (Wasik, 1992, p. 119)

The new approach, approved by Parliament in the Criminal Justice Act, 1991, required sentencers to focus upon the principles of 'deserved punishment' for the particular offence being considered. Much to the dismay of many magistrates, judges and other legal practitioners, this also reduced the discretion of the judiciary since it implied that the previous criminal records of persistent offenders could now only be a factor in determining sentence in very restricted circumstances. Such was the scale of opposition among the judiciary to this principle that the Government felt obliged to change the law in this respect also, again within just nine months of its implementation.

The Criminal Justice Act, 1991, also made the imposition of custodial sentences more difficult. Here, however, it appeared that the shift in policy owed as much to pragmatic considerations about the costs and benefits of punishment in prison as to any weakening of resolve to be 'tough on crime'. The Woolf Report (Woolf, 1991) provided a severe critique of the whole philosophy of prison sentencing by spelling out the ill effects on inmates, in terms of the opportunities for further exposure to criminality which a period in prison meant for many people, particularly impressionable younger people.

A further attempt to direct sentencing within a criminal justice policy was the introduction of the Youth Court in 1992 for offenders aged between ten and seventeen and where sentences were to be governed by principles of the reduction of further offending.

2.3.3   The judiciary

The Government could address problems in sentencing and the administration of the courts by legislation, standardisation of procedures and executive power. But its opportunity to address shortcomings in the judiciary itself was slight. The Lord Chancellor did not have the same direct influence over judges and magistrates as he had over his department's civil servants or as the Home Secretary could apply to, say, the local probation services. There are, after all, two sides to the independence of the judiciary, one being that it would not be intimidated by government - compare the steadfast behaviour of the judiciary in South Africa or Italy with the less than independent judiciary of the USSR or occupied Europe in 1940-1945. On the other hand, if a judge or magistrate were incompetent, eccentric or seriously out of touch, and the judiciary's self-regulation had turned to self-congratulation or complacency, then the whole edifice of society's justice would be helplessly betrayed. How, then, do the judiciary recruit themselves and ensure that they are in touch with the rest of society? How do they make themselves accountable if not to Parliament? How do they maintain high standards of competence and deal with their mistakes?

Recruitment and composition of the lay magistracy
The task of finding and appointing suitable candidates to join the 29,000 members of the magistracy had long been assigned to a series of semi-secret Local Advisory Committees which in turn would make recommendations to the Lord Chancellor, as head of the judiciary (or to the Chancellor of the Duchy of Lancaster in the counties of Merseyside, Lancashire and Greater Manchester). The basis on which recommendations and appointments were made were imprecise.   As with the professional judiciary, the foremost official criterion for appointment had long been that of 'personal suitability'.

'The first and most important consideration in the selection and appointment of justices is that the candidate should be personally suitable in point of character, integrity and understanding and should be recognised as such by those among whom they live and work.' (Lord Chancellor's Department, 1948)

More recently, the Lord Chancellor's Department has elaborated on this advice as follows:

'Personally suitable for appointment means first that the person is someone of integrity, with good character and repute and with the ability to command the confidence of both public and colleagues. Secondly, he or she must have the capacity or potential to act judicially and thereby make fair and proper decisions. A justice has to be able to recognise personal prejudices and set them aside, to understand and identify what facts and arguments are relevant and to think clearly and logically. Humanity and sensitivity and a capacity for working with colleagues and contributing to effective discussion by expressing views clearly and concisely are also necessary...Some experience, understanding or knowledge of life outside the immediate circle of family and work is highly desirable. An appreciation of the need for the rule of law in society is also required. A person must have the time to carry out the full range of magisterial duties and have a strong commitment to them.' (Lord Chancellor's Department, 1988, The Qualities looked for in a Justice of the Peace, The Magistrate, (1988, p 78.))

Quite so! But would such description of prodigious virtue really be of much help in the process of selecting particular candidates? Or does it all merely serve to explain the tendency for appointments to be made of those who fit in with the existing culture of the Bench? Certainly, the magistracy is subject to continuing criticism that its membership is largely confined to a narrow social group, which is particularly unfortunate since the rationale for a lay system is founded on the principle of participation by ordinary people.

Composition
The membership of local Benches remains dominated by middle/upper class, professional people and their spouses (King & May, 1985; and Raine, 1989b) despite the fact that an aim of the appointment procedure is that the composition of local Benches should be a balanced and representative microcosm of the local community. These days, a balance is largely achieved in age and gender. Membership of most local Benches typically spans from the late 30s to the compulsory retirement age of 70, with a roughly equal split between women and men. Typically too, Benches include members with declared allegiances to the

left, right and centre of the political spectrum, despite the commonly held perception of the magistracy as an extension of the conservative establishment. However, a balance in general election voting intentions scarcely implies a balance in terms of social class and other characteristics (Raine, 1989b). Furthermore, as King & May (1985) have commented, the majority of appointments from black and Asian backgrounds are of professional people who hardly provide representativeness in terms of the overall occupational structure of their ethnic communities.

Effort has also been directed in recent years at widening the social composition of local Benches, particularly by seeking more nominations from the 'shop-floor' and from ethnic minority communities. But efforts in this respect are continually thwarted, partly by a lack of imagination in seeking nominations and partly by the reluctance of many, particularly working class people and those from certain ethnic groups, to have their names put forward for fear of what colleagues and friends might think about them 'joining the establishment'. The problem has also been accentuated by economic recession, rising unemployment and job insecurity in the late 1980s and early 1990s. Here, especially for those on the 'shop-floor', the concern is that time off for Bench duties could jeopardise their employment prospects. Similarly, many of those looking for work, despite having time on their hands, decline the opportunity for appointment to the Bench simply because they fear that the time commitment involved might count against them with prospective employers. And so it might.

Recruitment and composition of the senior judiciary
The appointment system for the senior judiciary (comprising nearly 1,800 judges - 95 High Court judges to deal with the most serious cases, about 470 full-time Circuit judges, about 780 part-time recorders, and about 440 part-time assistant recorders) has been no less secretive. High Court judges reach office by invitation only, and this is only extended to barristers with more than ten years of experience in the High Court and who have been recommended through an entirely closed and obscure system.

The procedure for recruiting other members of the judiciary for the higher courts is different. Any solicitor or barrister who has been qualified for at least ten years has been entitled to seek appointment, initially as a recorder in the Crown Court. The task of considering candidates, interviewing them and making recommendations to the Lord

Chancellor has been undertaken in private by a small team of officials who make up a Judicial Appointments Group within the Lord Chancellor's Department. In addition to responding to self-nominated candidates, individuals identified as potential appointees have been directly approached. Circuit judges have been recruited by the same method from the ranks of recorders.

The precise criteria by which candidates have been chosen have never been very clear. A publication specifically on the subject of professional judicial appointments (Lord Chancellor's Department, 1990) offers a description of the position only in very broad terms:

'The Lord Chancellor appoints to each judicial post the candidate who appears to him to be best qualified to fill it, regardless of sex, ethnic origin, political affiliation or religion. He looks for professional ability, experience, standing, integrity, a sound temperament and the physical ability to carry out the duties of the post. To achieve this, he follows two principles which affect the system of appointment at every stage. The first principle is that no single person's view about any candidate, whether positive or negative, is decisive in itself, however wise or eminent the person. The second principle is that, before being considered for any judicial post, a candidate must have served in that or a similar post in a part-time capacity for long enough to establish his or her competence and suitability. Before and during the course of this part-time service, the Lord Chancellor seeks the independent views of a spread of observers and colleagues in a position to assess the candidate's work and abilities. These views are gathered over a sufficient period of time, and are treated as having great weight, especially if they reveal a consensus or clear predominance of opinion.' (Lord Chancellor's Department, 1990, p. 5)

As implied here, the system has largely hinged on recommendations. So far as the appointments of Circuit judges, recorders and assistant recorders have been concerned, the Judicial Appointments Group would consider the potential candidates each year for each of the six Circuits (Crown Court areas into which England & Wales is divided). Visits would be made to each Circuit and several serving judges, together with senior members of the Bar and Law Society, would be consulted as to the suitability for promotion of the recorders and assistant recorders already working on the Circuit. In addition, the suitability for appointment of members of the Bar acting as advocates on the Circuit would also be discussed. Reactions would then be collated and presented to the Lord Chancellor who would take further opinions from his most senior judicial colleagues before deciding whom to appoint. In 1993, the Lord Chancellor bowed to long-standing criticisms of the secrecy and restrictive nature of the appointment system by announcing his intention to advertise appointments of assistant recorders, recorders and Circuit judges. He also announced his intention to consider the inclusion of lay people on interviewing panels. Although these plans fell short of the scale of reform many regarded as long overdue, a significant step had been taken. More would surely follow.

Composition

Most judges continue to come from middle and upper class backgrounds, having typically received a private school and Oxbridge education followed by life in the relatively small and sheltered world of the Bar. The abiding perception is of the senior judiciary as being heavily dominated by privileged men of mature years and who, as a result, might find it difficult to remain in touch with the values and concerns of the day. Such perceptions are not unrealistic. In 1985, for example, 97 per cent of High Court judges were male, 80 per cent had been to private schools and 82 per cent to Oxford or Cambridge universities, and the average age was 64 years. Similarly, of the Circuit judges, nearly 96 per cent were men (in France, the majority of the judiciary are women), 66 per cent were from private schools and 63 per cent from Oxbridge. The average age was 61 years. Moreover, as Gifford (1986) put it:

> 'If one looks at the figures for recorders and assistant recorders, the younger people who will be the senior judges of the future, one sees that the position is getting no better. The total of 71 women among 1,629 holders of judicial office is a disgrace. The number of black people is, I believe, four.' (Gifford, 1986, p. 25)

Byers (1993) found that of the twelve judicial appointments made to the High Court in 1992, ten had graduated from Oxford or Cambridge, eight had been to a private school and only two were women. Even though judges today live more ordinary lives than their predecessors, the professional judiciary is hardly the microcosm of society that modern principles of equal opportunity and participative democracy might expect it to be. As Pannick (1988) suggests:

'It is not surprising that a Bench composed almost entirely of former barristers should lack the expertise and knowledge of many of the matters which are central to the lives of those people who come to court as litigants and witnesses.' (Pannick, 1988, p. 53)

2.3.4 Public accountability and the judiciary

Another criticism of the judiciary has been that it operates without an appropriate framework of public accountability. Of course judges and magistrates are accountable to the Lord Chancellor as head of the judiciary and, through him to Parliament in the House of Lords. However, judges are very rarely publicly admonished when they make remarks considered derogatory or insensitive in court. Similarly, public disquiet about sentences perceived to be too lenient or too harsh appears to be ignored and it is left to an aggrieved party to pursue justice through a formal appeal, rather than by any automatic review procedure. Once again, while this state of affairs might seem entirely in order to a legally and constitutionally minded minority, it hardly fits with most people's conception of justice and accountability.

Much the same perceptions had long existed in relation to the lay magistracy. Incidents involving public disquiet and local media attention have not been infrequent. For example, there have been many instances of comments from local Benches being interpreted as insensitive, or in some cases, racist; of sentences being announced that were regarded in the community as being wholly inappropriate; and of decisions made by magistrates' courts' committees (composed entirely of magistrates), for instance, to close a local court-house, that have also been perceived as being quite out of tune with local opinion. Yet the opportunities for the public to exercise their desire to hold those responsible to account have remained largely absent.

Competence
A related theme of criticism which was levelled at the judiciary with increasing frequency in the 1980s and early 1990s concerned the perceived competence of judges and magistrates to dispense justice. Here, while the particular issues were rather different between the lay magistracy and the professional judiciary in the higher courts, the general implication was the same. Both magistrates and judges were

failing to win public confidence in their abilities to do the job required of them.

In the magistrates' courts, a question which has increasingly been asked concerned the competence of lay volunteers to administer justice to the high standards expected in the late twentieth century. The official reaction from the Lord Chancellor's Department has been of continuing faith in the lay magistracy's role, which after all, it is frequently pointed out, is dealing without apparent difficulties with some 97 per cent of the total number of criminal cases each year. But there were others who were less sure. During the 1980s, defence and prosecution lawyers could frequently be heard expressing their views that the lay Bench was becoming 'out of its depth' in the complexity of legal process that was increasingly characteristic of the lower courts. Even many magistrates' clerks, traditionally loyal to their volunteer magistrates, began to express doubts about the lay system's capacity to deliver justice in the modern age. Furthermore, the question of competence was aired from time to time in the media, typically following public outcry over an apparent sentencing anomaly or an improper decision in court.

The issue was made more sensitive by the fact that there was much resistance within the lay magistracy to the idea of significantly increasing the training provided. Partly such resistance was because of disquiet at the extra time demands and partly because of fears for the future of a lay system by a process of creeping 'professionalisation'. For many magistrates, the main worry here was of the erosion of those precious qualities of local knowledge and common sense that a group of lay volunteers could be expected to bring to the justice process. What, after all, would be the point of a lay system if magistrates had to be well versed in the law? As it was, many magistrates already felt that the training requirements had become too demanding. Such feelings were particularly amplified in the early 1990s by the extra training requirements that followed enactment of two major pieces of legislation, the Children Act, 1989, and the Criminal Justice Act, 1991. One consequence of all this was that an increasing number of magistrates began to regard their duties on the Bench as being simply too onerous and time-consuming and, reluctantly, concluded that they would have to resign.

These problems of time, commitment and training were hardly, of course, such crucial issues for the professional judiciary in the higher courts. There, concerns about competence reflected much more the disquiet which persisted about the narrow social composition of the judiciary, about its restricted set of values and therefore the capacity to demonstrate the expected judicious qualities of impartiality, tolerance and fair-mindedness. In this respect concerns were amplified by the stream of 'faux pas' from the Bench, notably in rape trials, where the judges' comments were taken to imply that the victims were considered in part to blame for their attacks (for example, as one judge put it, '...because their dress and behaviour might have suggested...they were asking for it.'). The position was aptly summed up by a Member of Parliament (Mowlan, 1993) after learning that a judge had released a young rapist and had awarded £500 compensation to the fifteen-year-old victim 'to have a good holiday'. The judiciary, she concluded, is:

> 'too male, too white and too out of touch. . .the attitude of the judges and therefore the public's perception of the judiciary...is a problem we will have to address.' (Mowlan, 1993, p. 3)

It was indicative of the scale of public concern that Lord Taylor, the Lord Chief Justice, chose to address the subject directly in a televised lecture in 1992, when he commented:

> 'It is suggested that judges are too stuffy and remote; that they are out of touch with society today, with its lifestyle, its standards and its mores; that they are all in the same mould - white, male, public school, Oxbridge and establishment-minded.' (Taylor, 1992, p. 6)

Lord Taylor proceeded to pose some counter-arguments, notably, that women and black judges were now being appointed in greater numbers; that they would in time reach the most senior positions in the judiciary. He added that the judiciary and the courts still continued to provide a vital and valued check on the excesses of government and other public bodies, as well as being entrusted to conduct important inquiries for government. But it is doubtful whether such assertions, however true, would have a significant impact on popular opinion which, if anything, seemed to harden against the courts.

Popular and expert opinion of the judiciary was further damaged by the discovery of what amounted to a string of serious miscarriages of justice. Most notable among the early cases were those of 'the Guildford Four', 'the Maguire Seven', 'the Birmingham Six', 'the Tottenham Three', 'the Cardiff Three' and that of Judith Ward. Most of these were cases which ended in successful appeals only after the accused had spent many years in prison. The 'Guildford Four' spent 14 years in jail, and Judith Ward was imprisoned for 18 years. The whole criminal justice edifice was tainted. The worry was not just that the criminal justice process had failed to establish the truth during the initial trial process, but that it had done so a second time when several of the cases had been re-opened on appeal. The release of 'the Birmingham Six' raised particularly searching questions about the competence of the courts. There had been protests of wrongful convictions from the outset of this case, but their eventual quashing in 1992 was all the more embarrassing since, in dismissing the appeals by 'the Six' four years earlier, the Lord Chief Justice had gone out of his way to express his view about the guilt of the appellants by concluding that:

> 'The longer this hearing has gone on the more convinced this court has become that the verdict of the jury was correct. We have no doubt that these convictions were both safe and satisfactory.' (Lane, 1988)

With such a succession of revelations, and with more to come, according to many of those who had been tirelessly campaigning for the release of other people believed to have been wrongfully convicted, the restoration of public confidence and trust in the criminal justice process promised to be difficult. As one commentator put it:

> 'Many of those in authority could only come to terms with it by telling themselves that just because a person is found not guilty it does not mean that he did not commit the crime of which he is accused. Others were disturbed at the thought that the English legal system - which they had been brought up to believe was the best in the world - was capable of locking up the wrong people for so many years.' (Rozenberg, 1992, p. 94)

Action was obviously also required to ensure that such events would never be repeated. Within an hour of the release of 'the Guildford Four', the Home Secretary announced the establishment of an inquiry into the circumstances surrounding the trials of 'the Guildford Four' and the Maguires under the head of a retired Lord Justice of Appeal, Sir John May. The Director of Public Prosecutions ordered a police inquiry into allegations that Surrey police officers had lied in court during the trial of 'the Guildford Four'. But as more miscarriages of justice emerged, the pressure grew for more fundamental action. Within minutes of 'the Birmingham Six' walking free, the setting up of a Royal Commission on

Criminal Justice under the chairship of Lord Runciman of Doxford was announced by the Home Secretary with the following terms of reference:

'to examine the effectiveness of the criminal justice system of England & Wales in securing the conviction of the guilty and the acquittal of the innocent.' (Runciman, 1993, p. 1)

Two years later, in July 1993, the Commission reported and made over 350 recommendations. Key among these was that a new authority, the Criminal Cases Review Authority, should be established to investigate possible miscarriages of justice. In addition, the Commission made a number of recommendations aimed at reforming the trial process. These included the abolition of the option for defendants in 'either way' cases to elect trial by jury in the Crown Court. This was to avoid possible abuse of jury trial procedure. The Commission proposed instead that magistrates should decide whether a case should be transferred to the Crown Court. Other important recommendations were that the defence should be required to disclose its case in advance of a trial (one member of the Commission submitted a note of dissent on this point); that a formal system of sentencing discounts for guilty pleas should be introduced; that there should be time limits within which lawyers could discuss and prepare cases; and that pre-trial committal hearings should be abolished (unless defendants claimed that there was no case to answer).

First reactions to the report were mixed. While some commentators immediately welcomed the conclusions, others felt that the Commission had emphasised the efficiency of the judicial process at the expense of justice. This was felt particularly to be the case with regard to the proposals to end the ancient right of defendants to choose jury trial and to introduce incentives (sentencing discounts) for defendants submitting pleas of guilt (see Chapter 6).

At the time of writing, the Government's response to the Commission's report is awaited. Meanwhile, public confidence in the criminal justice process remains fragile. But at least many of the problems are being aired and the likelihood of reform is all the greater.

2.4 CONCLUSION

In any event, as this chapter has described, much change has already taken place in criminal justice. In particular, effectiveness, accountability and efficiency have been vigorously addressed in the courts, police, prosecution, prison and probation services. Reputations always lag behind current performance and things often appear to be worse as they start to improve. We shall argue in Chapter 10 that the criminal justice agencies are now almost ready to be trusted to enter a new era of serving justice, crime control, and social justice. But first we must question some assumptions and equip ourselves with some conceptual models of judicial and management matters. Then we shall turn to examine the strategies employed to curb the excesses of professional and organisational autonomy in criminal justice, consider the intended and unforeseen consequences thereof and also examine some of the great balancing acts involved therein.

CHAPTER 3

Management models for criminal justice

'There is nothing so practical as a good theory.'
Albert Einstein, 1935.

3.1 INTRODUCTION

The previous chapters described three sets of pressures besetting the courts: rising work pressure, tight resourcing and changing expectations. The particular experience of England & Wales was taken to illustrate the impact of these pressures which have affected most West European countries, the USA, Canada, Australia and New Zealand. The account also introduced the shift from the previous 'administrative' paradigm in which the official acted as an almost neutral adjudicator co-ordinating the demands of politicians and professional providers of services to the new 'managerial' paradigm in which the official was actively involved in the setting of objectives, targets, monitoring and emphasising efficiency. There appears to be a logic pushing the courts and other agencies in this direction but we must pause and ask whether this is really so. Why, in the 1980s, was the response to these pressures found in the language of 'management'? What lies behind the assumption that the paraphernalia of target setting, measurement and money-management, set in large hierarchical organisations, was the best answer to the circumstances of the time? Do the economies of scale and business approaches have so much to contribute to the provision of justice?

There are, after all, other strategies available to meet these demands. The merits of the steady, reliable and time-honoured administrative methods are substantial. They might seem especially appropriate in dispensing justice between disputing parties, which is an activity that requires both accuracy and methodical attention to detail. Instead of instigating a management approach in which the services were centralised and amalgamated, the merits of the administrative system could have been retained by adopting the alternative strategy of simply increasing the number of local Benches, courts and court-rooms. Alternatively, in the magistrates' court, for example, instead of building large organisations, the duties of the court could have been sub-contracted, leaving the magistrates' clerk at the centre of a network of users. Instead of employing professional managers, more responsibility could have been given to more volunteer lay people to involve them in this service which lies at the heart of civil life. Pause before discounting these alternatives. The invasion of the courts by the dominant model of management was not, and is not, inevitable and it is important to retain the capacity to think beyond it.

It is time, therefore, to step aside from the detail and narrative history of the English & Welsh example. In this chapter we seek to challenge the inevitability of the responses to increased demands upon the courts. We shall analyse the assumptions and the argument that, whatever the question, the answer was 'management'. What made this assumption so fashionable in the 1980s and so attractive to ministers and civil servants?

First we consider assumptions held about the function of the criminal justice process itself, its social function and the characteristics of the court implicit in each assumption. Second we describe the conventional model of the criminal justice system, which was taken from Systems Theory, and provide a critique of it. Third, we develop a description of other models of organisation and the implications that stem from each of them with regard to strategies for implementing social policy. The chapter concludes with a description of the doctrines of the New Public Management and a final meta-model of organisational cultures which sets management, administration and other approaches to the co-ordination of work in a dynamic relationship with the rest of the world.

Let us sharpen our awareness of the underlying assumptions and processes that inform the way law, order and justice are organised and remember that, as every lawyer knows, the way you frame the question shapes the answer.

3.2   PERSPECTIVES ON CRIMINAL JUSTICE

Crime is an integral part of society. The rules and procedures by which crime is regulated and by which redress and justice are provided reflect and express profound and sometimes contradictory sentiments of society. One cannot consider crime or criminal justice in isolation from the political and social context in which they occur. For most people, crime and criminal justice are simultaneously a major source of entertainment to be enjoyed on television, in film, newspapers and novels and a source of anxiety. Marxists and some radical criminologists would argue that crime and its control is a significant vehicle of class and political oppression. Others see crime as a male phenomenon conducted by men against the feminine in society (Jackson, 1992; Coote, 1993). Criminologists focus on one set of issues, sociologists on another and practitioners of jurisprudence take yet another approach to the issues of justice. Meanwhile, the task of administering criminal justice tends to lead to an emphasis on the provision and maintenance of the institutions and mechanisms of the agencies of law and order. There is an inevitable tension between the perspectives of these different disciplines, just as there is at a different level between the actors in the process - the police, the prosecution, the defence, the judiciary and the defendants, victims and witnesses. Indeed, the court is the confluence of many opposing perspectives and its administration is, as a consequence, a highly sensitive and difficult task.

3.2.1 Social function, process and courts

In his important volume *The Framework of Criminal Justice*, Michael King (1981) describes six theoretical approaches and the implications inherent in each (Table 3.1). Six different social functions of justice are identified along with the process models that are implicit in each theoretical approach. King then describes the features of each process model that one would expect to find in the court's operation were the court applying exclusively that particular model. For instance, if one believed that the function of the 'criminal justice process' was to resolve conflicts that arise between individual citizens or citizens and the state, then it would follow that one would see the courts' social function as to provide justice: features of the court that emphasised this function would

Table 3.1 Theoretical models and their features

Social function	Process model	Features of court
1. Justice	*Due Process model*	a Equality between parties b Restraint or arbitrary power c Presumption of innocence
2. Punishment	*Crime Control model*	a Disregard of legal controls b Implicit presumption of guilt c High conviction rate d Support for police
3. Rehabilitation	*Medical model (diagnosis, prediction and treatment selection)*	a Information collection b Individualisation c Treatment presumption d Discretion of decision-makers e Expertise of decision-makers
4. Management of crime and criminals	*Bureaucratic model*	a Independence from politics b Speed and efficiency c Minimisation of expense d Economical division of labour
5. Denunciation and degradation	*Status Passage model*	a Public shaming of defendant b Court values reflecting community values c Agent's control over process
6. Maintenance of class domination	*Power model*	a Reinforcement of class values b Alienation of defendant c Deflection of attention from class conflict d Differences between judges and judged

(Source: King, 1981.)

be equality between parties, restraint of arbitrary power etc. On the other hand, if one saw crime control as paramount, then the social function of the court would be to provide punishment and one would wish to see an effective deterrent provided through a high conviction rate, uncritical support for the police and a willingness to disregard legal controls on utilitarian grounds.

The first three models, for Justice, Punishment and Rehabilitation, are seen as 'participant' models likely to be held by individuals involved in the court process, whether police, defendant, probation or whoever. They express the basic assumptions such individuals might have about the function of justice in general and in a particular case.

The second group, for Management of crime and criminals, Denunciation and degradation and Maintenance of class domination, are presented as theoretical models about the social functions of institutions and are drawn from the work of social theorists,. This group of models:

> 'emphasise the contributions of all the participants towards the fulfilment of some overriding social objective rather than drawing attention to the specific roles of particular groups of participants and the conflict that emerges as each group struggles to attain its particular goals.' (King, 1981, p. 35)

According to the 'social models', therefore, all the court-room regulars, that is to say police, lawyers, clerks, magistrates and probation officers, are engaged in a social process, be it the management of crime, the reduction of social status or the maintenance of power in the hands of a class elite.

These approaches are not exclusive and, despite the tensions between them, the practice in the court is usually a hybrid. For instance, most criminal justice processes contain elements of both the Due Process model (with its emphasis on justice, a presumption of innocence and rules to protect the defendant against error) and the Bureaucratic model (with its social function of the management of crime and criminals and emphasis on smooth, efficient, economic and impartial procedures). Moreover, there are contradictions where there is an attempt to blend the Due Process model and the Medical model in which guilt and blame are subsumed to issues of rehabilitation.

Groups of participants tend to see justice as having particular social functions and to favour different process models and types of court provision: lawyers might tend to favour the Due Process model, probation officers the Medical or Rehabilitation model, while police officers may sometimes be attracted to the Punishment model. Administrators and other members of the executive need to be aware of their own underlying assumptions and the extent to which they have been drawn to subscribe to the Bureaucratic model through continuous concern with management issues in justice. The court administrator needs to be aware of these assumptions and influences in order to balance them in the practice of the justice process. The Home Office and Lord Chancellor's Department administrators are likely to focus on the Bureaucratic, managing crime and criminals model, and see the courts and their sentencing patterns as a contribution to their crime prevention strategy. The tensions between the priorities of the court - due process - and the executive - crime control - is a healthy expression of different but complementary functions and is not, in itself, a problem until the one starts to undermine the other.

3.2.2 *The Systems model of criminal justice*

The most commonly held model of criminal justice is derived from Systems Theory, a method of describing organisations that was very popular in the late 1970s. Systems Theory was developed by physical scientists who had found the 'natural science' approach inadequate to express the complexity of what they were studying. The natural science approach is a reductive process that recognises phenomena through the process of controlled, repeatable empirical experiments to 'refute the null hypothesis'. Whilst science was concerned with basic and simple laws this approach served well, but it is a very cumbersome methodology if one wants to describe the interactions that balance, for example, the ecology of a rain forest.

Systems Theory is an attempt to express the complexity and entertain the multiple levels of analysis and reality. According to Checkland (1981):

'a system is an organised or complex whole: an assemblage or combination of things or parts forming a complex or unitary whole'. (Checkland, 1981, p. 23).

A forest, for example, can be conceptualised as a hierarchy of systems, starting at the level of photosynthesis in a cell and extending to the symbiotic interactions of the thousands of species in the environment. The forest is an 'open' system with inputs - rain, sun, air, genetic information - and outputs - gases, soil, carbon deposits - and the processes of transformation that occur in the flow of life and other events through the system. Each level of the hierarchy can be conceptualised so as to reveal the communication of information that homeostatically balances the system. In addition, at each level of the increasingly complex hierarchy, one can identify the emergent properties created by the bringing of simpler systems into connection with each other - where the whole becomes larger than the sum of the parts.

Systems Theory was adopted by many social scientists as a way out of the limiting and rigid methods that they had adopted in their attempts to emulate the discipline of natural science. Of course, organisations are not quite like mechanical or biological systems since they are contrived and invented by humans: the structure of the system is of events rather than of physical components and these events cannot be separated from the processes of the system. Nevertheless, in adopting this approach, social scientists found a rigorous but flexible method. It facilitated the description of activity and organisation within boundaries in which the domain of organisational activities could be identified and the adaptive and maintenance mechanisms could be registered. The growth and development of a system could be shown through the internal elaboration of its sub-systems and detailed analysis of any part of the system or its sub-systems could easily be linked to the whole.

Management and organisational scientists found Systems thinking useful since the traditional closed mechanical model had encouraged a focus on economic and technical rationality whilst the Systems method encouraged an open socio-technical approach. The flexibility and rigour assisted management scientists to study managers as they coped with uncertainty and ambiguity and as they adapted their organisations to their changing environments and circumstances (Kast & Rosenzweig, 1971). An organisation was construed to be the structuring and integration of human activities around various technologies. The technologies were represented by the sub-systems in which inputs and outputs were linked by the flow of communication and activities through them. The model could therefore describe any organisation as a system in which the technical sub-systems varied according to task requirements and activities, be it a hospital, a garage or a court. It provided a way of describing the flow of communication, work and other interactions between and within the sub-systems involved. The system could be described as being composed of a hierarchy of:

'entities which may be meaningfully regarded as wholes, which are built up of smaller entities which are themselves wholes...and so on.' (Checkland, 1981 p. 23)

In the early eighties, this thinking and approach was enthusiastically adopted in criminal justice in Britain. Here the Home Office conceived 'the criminal justice system' (CJS) as an hierarchical arrangement of five sub-systems as described in Figure 3.1.

'It is often the case that the parts of a system act in ways which can only be understood by considering their nature as a part of a higher-order whole. For example, the courts may change their sentencing practice because a new law has been passed, or because of a new consensus view or a specific judgement by an appeal court. In addition, the existence of higher-order wholes in a hierarchy is signalled by the emergence of properties attributed to them which are not ascribed to their parts. For example, the magistrates' courts sub-system will include future plans for the building of new court-rooms, which cannot be decided on by a single party alone....Dealing with the system in a holistic way, thereby emphasising that the whole is greater than the sum of its parts, includes an important dimension which is otherwise lost. The CJS model embodies this outlook and the flow model plays an important part in lifting the model above a piecemeal approach.' (Pullinger, 1985, pp. 6-9)

The flow model alluded to provided the basis of a computer simulation (Morgan, 1985) which was designed to allow the exploration of the flow of cases and work through the system. The idea was to construct a model that would describe the nodal points where decisions were made that determined subsequent and feedback flows of cases and work. Hypothetical branching ratios could set at the nodal points, and when the model was run, an indication of the likely flows and queues would be estimated. Different branching ratios could then be compared with each other in terms of the queues and work flow generated in the simulation. It was hoped that this would provide the way of creating an overall model by which future case-flows and work could be estimated. It was also hoped that the approach would serve as the basis of a resource and cost management programme. It was therefore a very attractive model to the administrator who had to allocate funds for the running of the justice agencies. Figure 3.2 illustrates the model developed by the Home Office

Figure 3.1 The Home Office model of the 'criminal justice system'
(Pullinger, 1985)

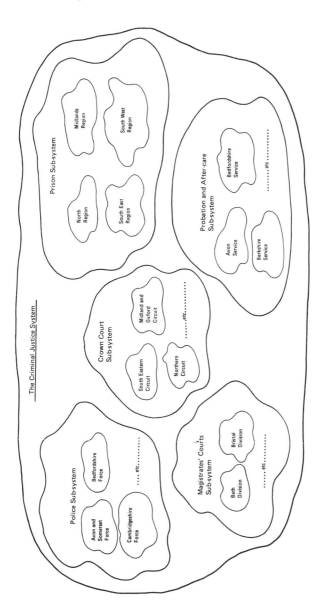

Managing criminal justice

Figure 3.2 The 'Flow model' (Pullinger, 1985)

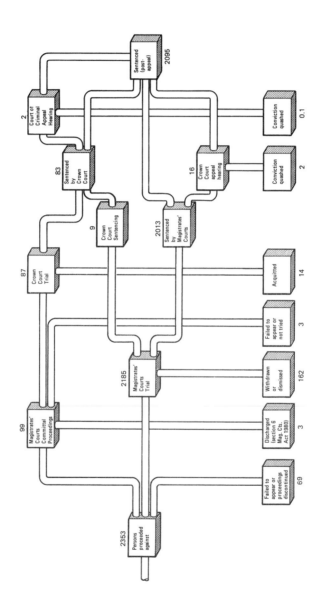

A critique

The Systems model has been a great asset to those charged with the co-ordination of the criminal justice agencies. The most significant contribution was to conceptualise the group of agencies as a system per se. The phrase 'the criminal justice system' now trips off the lips as readily as Fay Weldon's slogan 'go to work on an egg.' And, indeed, that is what they both were, exhortations of government policy, the one for the Egg Marketing Board and the other for the Home Office.

> 'Our principal preoccupation is, and I believe ought to be, the Criminal Justice System which, incidentally, I wish to see treated in all that we do as a system.' (House of Commons, 1984)

The significance of this re-definition of the working environment is hard to appreciate for those who did not know it before, so profound has been its effect.

Systems thinking emphasised the flow between entities and sub-systems and so its adoption made case-flow and delay very much more visible and led to important developments which expedited transactions and communication. Further, once criminal justice was conceptualised as a system, the inter-relationships between the agencies also became visible and were seen as an area of activity which could be managed and for which people could be held responsible. Without a systems approach, it would have been much more difficult to persuade the various parties to negotiate their agencies' inter-dependencies and to forge substantial inter-agency agreements given their differences of interest.

The greatest tribute to an idea is to acknowledge that it has moulded one's thinking and has become the dominant paradigm outside of which it is hard to imagine. This has been the case with the 'criminal justice system'. And, just as with any other model or language where the adoption of the approach sets the agenda for subsequent discussion, it may obscure as it illuminates. For instance, the way the system is drawn determines the way one will subsequently think about it: by drawing the five sub-systems (in Figure 3.1) from a national perspective, the interaction between local police officers, court clerks and prosecutors is given less weight than the interaction between the sections in the Home Office and Lord Chancellor's Department which oversee many of the agencies. In fact, the national picture displaces the local picture which might promote the concept of thousands of small, unique, local networks. The consequence is that it thus becomes more likely that the criminal justice process will be conceived of as a national system in which decisions should be made centrally even when they undermine local agreements. An example of this was the implementation in 1992 of the recommendations on time limits of a Working Group established at national level to address a range of 'pre-trial issues' (see Chapters 4 and 8): this made sense in a single national agency such as the Home Office or the Crown Prosecution Service, but served to undermine agreements made locally between courts, probation and police.

Five additional criticisms of the Systems model in criminal justice should be spelt out in detail since they come from outside the system of Systems thinking and, as such, are more difficult to recognise. First, it focuses attention within the defined boundary of the system. But this act of inclusion excludes others: for instance, defence solicitors, voluntary organisations and local authorities are not included even though their actions are relevant to the working of criminal justice. The exclusion of defence solicitors is a particularly curious anomaly since they play a critical role in the process of case-flow and are mostly publicly funded through legal aid. The exclusion of local authorities hampers direct planning of crime prevention schemes which would normally involve local authority planning, housing and leisure departments. This model of criminal justice also excludes consideration of socio-economic and social policy factors. In itself, this would not be important, but where the Systems model comes to dominate the agenda, those functions it excludes become downgraded. By way of illustration, in Italy the police are not considered part of the criminal justice system.

Second, in focusing on the flow of work between the systems and sub-systems (agencies), and in identifying bottle-necks, queues and ratios at nodal points, Systems thinking excludes the actual activities that must be addressed in order to make the system work. The work is represented, as it were, as a smooth sludge flowing down the pipes whereas it is, in fact, a very lumpy business. As Gottfredson and Gottfredson (1980) have pointed out, people respond to each other in all sorts of different ways and there will be many unique and awkward moments that an aggregated flow model cannot register and therefore will ignore. The approach encourages a focus on process that can be at the expense of problem solving.

The third reservation on the Systems approach is that it directs attention to the effective and efficient flow of cases without inviting commensurate attention to questions of justice (see King, 1981).

Fourth, adoption of this model assumes that the criminal justice system is, indeed, a system. Yet this is open to dispute. There is an argument that if the separation of powers (legislature, executive and judiciary) is designed to ensure that the co-ordinated power of the state cannot be focused upon the individual, then modern attempts to bring justice into a single integrated system that includes the police, prosecution, courts, probation and prison services is inappropriate. A fragmented criminal justice system might, in fact, be a more effective one - again, it depends on which of King's (1981) functions is considered most important. It certainly seems likely that the adoption of systems thinking enhances the possibility of the various professionals - police, prosecution and defence lawyers - colluding to ensure a smooth passage of cases through the system at the expense of attention to individual and unique aspects of due process. Careful attention and rigour are required on the part of the various actors to ensure that the management of the system does not overtake the provision of justice. In the management literature the concept of 'satisficing' is used to describe the tendency of employees to distort the organisation's goals to achieve better their own satisfaction. For example, most company chief executives prefer the extension of market share to increased annual profit, even though the owners or shareholders usually prefer the latter.

Finally, the computer simulation has proved rather ineffective as an aid to management at the local, more complex level.

3.3 OTHER ORGANISATIONAL MODELS

There is an apocryphal story of three blind men who wanted to know the nature of an elephant. They asked the son of one of them to take them to the place where an elephant was to be found and then, in turn, they approached it to discover what it might be. The first reached out and by chance grabbed the tail and declared that the elephant was a piece of rope. The second walked forward and by chance bumped into the elephant's front leg and declared that the elephant was a palm tree. The third chanced upon its trunk and declared that it was a serpent.

There is a similar problem with regard to organisations. You cannot actually see an organisation - you can see a building, some headed note-paper and the patterned behaviour of people 'in' the organisation, but you cannot see it itself. This invisibility makes it difficult to think about organisations and so we create images and metaphors to provide a framework for our thoughts. People often talk about an organisation as if it were alive, had appetites, moods and an existence of its own. Such anthropomorphisation of the arrangements people make to conduct their business in itself makes for further confusion. (Gareth Morgan's (1986) excellent book *Images of Organisation* provides a full and detailed guide to different paradigms used to describe and analyse organisations.)

In another version of the story, there are three old men, each of whom had been a craftsman. Thus it is the chandler who discovers the rope and the carpenter who discovers the tree. Their mistake is both worse and more predictable and it illustrates very well how we are prone to fit the unfamiliar into our set of expectations. For instance, reference to 'court' might concern royalty, romance or tennis since only a minority group, mainly made up of miscreants and lawyers, thinks as you, dear reader, do. The problem, then, when the question begs the answer, is to find a way of stepping back so that we can see both the organisation of the court and the terms of reference by which we see it. In an excellent article on the way one's unquestioned assumptions about organisations can limit one's repertoire of strategic action, Elmore (1977) provides such a route.

3.3.1 Four basic models of organisations

Elmore (1977) suggests that people are prone to select one of four distinct sets of assumptions about the nature of organisations. Each set contains a different set of implications about how one should behave in the organisation and what should be done to implement new policies or improve its performance. The organisation may be the same but, as with the three blind men, our assumptions and expectations make us liable to interpret the phenomena in different ways and then derive different strategies.

The Rational Goal model assumes that organisations and people are rational and that if we arrange a hierarchy of sub-units, each with its objectives and monitored targets for which named people are responsible, then all will be well. To implement a new policy, simply instruct and *manage* properly.

The Internal Process model assumes that the dynamic in an organisation is the link of routine and discretion. It is a complex of interlinked units, each designed to play a part in the operation of the whole. To implement a new policy, simply redesign procedures and *administer* the process.

The Organisational Development model assumes that, since adults can act responsibly in their capacity as citizens, then, if you treat them properly, they will bring that same maturity and discretion to the work of their organisation. Create good, respectful work conditions and all will be well. To implement a new policy, simply *consult* until everyone 'owns' it.

The Conflict model assumes that organisations are the arena of constant differences of opinion and interest and that the best one can do is to negotiate a set of temporary alliances and agreements to get the work done. To implement a new policy, *negotiate* another network of temporary alliances and agreements.

The four different sets of assumptions lead to four different constructions of reality about an organisation. None of them, of course, is a 'true' picture but that is not the point. First we want to understand how we understand 'organisation' and to extend our repertoire of understanding so that we can comprehend aspects that were hitherto invisible. The blind men would have done well to curb their immediate judgement and explore the elephant a bit further!

Second, we seek understanding about how others understand the organisation and how they derive their strategies for working with it. Which set of implications do they appear to be working on - when in difficulty, do they choose to re-design procedures, manage more clearly, consult more thoroughly or negotiate better deals? Only by understanding their conceptual world can we communicate reliably with them.

Third, we require a model of the organisation that will illuminate the dilemmas facing those who work in it and assist them to devise appropriate strategies. However, no model is as comprehensive as reality and it is necessary to be aware that the price paid for illumination in one area is often that another is cast in the shadow. As was shown in the critique of the Systems model, the advantage of the focus on 'flow' was achieved at the expense of other equally significant activities and perspectives in the justice process and of its wider context.

We have argued that a degree of awareness about one's own assumptions and those held by others better equips one to understand the organisation of the public sector in general and the criminal justice process in particular. Nevertheless, there is an argument that even to whisper the phrase 'the management of criminal justice' is to breach the tradition of the court and trespass into territory guarded by the constitutional separation of powers. On the other hand, as the previous section on the Systems model demonstrated, there has been a willingness to grapple with the management of justice by administrative staff. The Home Office and Parliament can develop crime prevention policies and reform legislation and this, according to the administrators at least, need not necessarily undermine the exercise of judicial judgement. The debate has already been joined and, as indicated in the previous chapter, all parties appear to have respectable cases: as authors we have adopted an inquisitorial rather than adversarial approach and still seek understanding before making a judgement. Maybe the tension between justice and management should not be resolved at all but retained and nurtured as an essential dialogue, similar to the dialogue between 'efficiency' and 'effectiveness' in other parts of the public sector (Richards, 1992).

The major shift in the organisation of public sector agencies has been from stable, bureaucratic administration as described by the Internal Process model to a dynamic sort of managerialism that complies with the Rational Goal model. The former stereotypical bureaucracy in which administrators quietly and surely administered, generation after generation, requires little description since it is familiar to all but the young. But the Rational Goal model of the recent managerial decade is less easy to identify since it is a bit too close and, for the courts at least, rather novel. What are the characteristics of this New Public Management? Does its form of management derive from 'manus' - 'can you handle it?' as one might say to a friend - or from its more immediate origin, 'maneggiare', 'to put a horse through its paces'?

3.3.2 The New Public Management

Christopher Hood has analysed the rise and character of the New Public Management (NPM) in a series of publications. He describes NPM as an international trend in public administration that is linked with four other administrative 'mega-trends', namely:

1. attempts to slow down or reverse government growth in terms of overt public spending and staffing (Dunsire & Hood, 1989);

2. the shift toward privatisation and quasi-privatisation and away from core government institutions, with renewed emphasis on 'subsidiarity' in service provision (Hood and Schuppert, 1988; Dunleavy, 1989);

3. the development of automation, particularly in information technology, in the production and distribution of public services; and

4. the development of a more international agenda, increasingly focused on general issues of public management, policy design, decision styles and inter-governmental co-operation, on top of the older tradition of individual country specialisms in public administration.

Hood (1991) suggests that NPM comprises seven doctrines which, in 1990, could be found in some combination in any typical public sector organisation in the UK, Australia, New Zealand and most other OECD countries. The doctrines are summarised in Table 3.2. Each doctrine is described along with an indication of what it is taken to mean in practice and the typical justification offered for its introduction. The list of New Public Management doctrines clearly marks the contrast with those of administration which involve the steady application of rules and precedent.

Hood provides an absorbing and severe critique of the origin and implementation of NPM. This is just as well since the introduction of stereotypical 'private sector' methods - itself one of the doctrines - has mostly been ideologically driven and debate has largely been restricted to the very language of 'efficiency' on which it is predicated.

In this respect, Hood suggests that there are three families of values to be found in the debate about administrative design first recorded by Plato and continued ever since. Although the current fashion is for the family of 'keep it lean and purposeful', there are other values to be considered:

1. The 'sigma family' revolves around economy and parsimony. Classic expressions of this value system are the just-in-time inventory control system and payment by results reward systems.

2. The 'theta family' revolves around fairness and honesty. Checks, balances and independent tribunals that can investigate alleged abuses of political and administrative power will be found where these are in the ascendant.

Table 3.2 Doctrinal components of new public management
(Hood, 1991) reproduced with permission from Blackwell, Oxford.

Doctrine	Meaning	Typical justification
1. Hands-on professional management	*Active, visible, discretionary control of organisations from named persons at the top who are 'free to manage'*	Accountability requires clear assignment of responsibility for action, not diffusion of power
2. Explicit standards and measures of performance	*Definition of goals, targets, indicators of success, preferably expressed in quantitative terms, especially for professional services*	Accountability requires clear statement of goals; efficiency requires 'hard look' at objectives
3. Greater emphasis on output controls	*Resource allocation and rewards linked to measured performance; break-up of centralised bureaucracy-wide personnel management*	Need to stress results rather than procedures
4. Shift to disaggreg-ation of units in the public sector	*Break-up of formally monolithic units, unbund-ling of management systems into corporatised units around products, operating on decentralised 'one-line' budgets and dealing with one another on an 'arm's-length' basis*	Need to create 'manage-able units', separate provision and production interests, gain efficiency advantages by use of contract or franchise arrangements inside as well as outside the public sector
5. Shift to more competition in the public sector	*Move to fixed term contracts and public tendering procedures*	Rivalry as the key to lower costs and better standards

6. Stress on private-sector styles of management practice	*Move away from military-style 'public service ethic'; greater flexibility in hiring and rewards; greater use of PR techniques*	Need to use 'proven' private sector management tools in the public sector
7. Stress on greater discipline and parsimony in resource use	*Cutting direct costs, raising labour discipline, resisting union demands, limiting 'compliance costs' to business*	Need to check resource demands of public sector and 'do more with less'

3. The 'lambda family' revolves around issues of security and resilience. Redundancy (spare capacity) and slack will be high, providing back-up systems for any unlikely event, and the emphasis will be placed on long-term robustness of the operations (Hood, 1991).

Table 3.3 illustrates how each family of values defines success and failure in different terms and also differentiates certain characteristics of organisations. It will be seen that there is a degree of incompatibility between the value systems. The high slack in lambda systems is at odds with the frugality and requirement to cut waste of the sigma value systems. The 'belt and braces' duplication of checks and balances that ensure a high degree of rectitude in the theta value system is probably the same inefficiency the sigma system deems failure. The rectitude demanded in the theta value system may well be incompatible with the resilience required by the lambda value system which might well pro-vide special treatment to certain members in return for their total loyalty or commitment. This is sharply illustrated in the judicial process where there is pressure to accord privileges to judges so that they remain committed to the law. The question posed is how best to balance the opposing tensions of these different value systems. It seems likely that the balance will be different according to the nature of the function of the organisation - does it maintain dangerous or critical plant such as nuclear power stations and water supplies; is it a tax office, a fast food outlet, a hospital or a court?

Table 3.3 Three sets of core values in public management
(Hood, 1991) reproduced with permission from Blackwell, Oxford.

Criteria	Sigma-type values	Theta-type values	Lambda-type values
	Keep it lean and purposeful	*Keep it honest and fair*	*Keep it robust and resilient*
Standard of success	*Frugality* (matching of resources to tasks for given goals)	*Rectitude* (achievement of fairness, mutuality, the proper discharge of duties)	*Resilience* (achievement of reliability, adaptivity, robustness)
Standard of failure	*Waste* (muddle, confusion, inefficiency)	*Malversation* (unfairness, bias, abuse of office)	*Catastrophe* (risk, breakdown, collapse)
Currency of success and failure	*Money and time* (resource costs of producers and consumers)	*Trust and entitlements* (consent, legitimacy, due process, political entitlements)	*Security and survival* (confidence, life and limb)
Control emphasis	*Output*	*Process*	*Input/Process*
Slack	*Low*	*Medium*	*High*
Goals	*Fixed/Single*	*Incompatible 'double bind'*	*Emergent/ Multiple*

What are the values that should be confirmed through the way in which the criminal justice process is organised? Does the 'management of crime and criminals' approach to justice have a different set of values from an approach which emphasises 'due process' (King, 1981)?

What, then, is the impact of managerial doctrines on the agencies of criminal justice? If 'The purpose of the criminal justice system is to sustain the rule of law and to protect the public' (Home Office, 1991c), then the lambda values seem particularly important. On the other hand, the New Public Management seems to emphasise the sigma-type values. How far can one incorporate the management methods without the values that lie behind them also entering the court? What has been the consequence of introducing management approaches to other public sector organisations? The theta-type values of rectitude may have led to a 'belt and braces' approach to administration, but it used to be thought worth the expense to ensure that honesty was the rule:

> '...the change in emphasis, from impersonal bureaucratic control to dynamic control by individual managers, has increased the potential for malversation. The traditional emphasis, which made corruption difficult through elaborate checks and balances, has given way to an emphasis on courageously "cutting waste" - which has often meant removing the duplicated checks and balances which bound public servants to honest conduct. With increased freedom comes room for side-dealing, just as the increase of "up and out" careers for senior civil servants and ministers has increased the potential for dubious deals at a higher level. At present the default position is honesty but by the mid-nineties, the default position will have become that each of us has been compromised too often to protest about quality of service, preference, placemen or sweeteners.' (Willson, 1991, p. 1)

Is the management approach here to stay? Will the balance between sigma, lambda and theta values change again? The final section of the chapter describes a meta-model of organisational cultures and suggests that, as change also changes, the dominance of the New Public Management with its emphasis on change is subject, itself, to change.

3.3.3 Meta-model of organisational cultures

In Britain, as elsewhere, during the mid eighties, the answer to any organisational problem in public services seemed to be 'efficient management'. However, social cultures, and organisations as social phenomena, are subject to fashion. Since fashion is dictated as much by whimsy as by the weather, we in turn might take the opportunity to ask just how warm, dry and respectable - or glamorous - is Justice when, high over the Old Bailey, her lissom form is clothed in management as compared with the traditional Grecian drapes?

Organisational life cycles
Quinn (1988) offers a dynamic meta-model of organisations that focuses upon the relationship between the organisation and the social and information environment in which it operates. The meta-model sets in context the Systems, managerial, administrative and other approaches to co-ordination of work. It is also proposed that there is a cyclic pattern to organisational culture which can be seen in the history of projects, agencies and large organisations and that recognition of the impact of the cycle is an aid to understanding the past and to anticipating the future.

Quinn describes the information environment of the organisation along two orthogonal dimensions - stability/change and long/short time lines. (See Figure 3.3.) Each quadrant presents a different challenge to the person trying to understand what is going on and deciding what to do about it. Each quadrant also represents the territory of a different school or model of management similar to Elmore's approach that was described above. Hence, as a model of models it is called a meta-model.

Internal Process model
Predictable and with long time lines. Understanding is found in searching for accretions of precedent in the accumulated files and procedures of the agency. Key activities are the consolidation and updating of the registry. Reliable and methodical administrators are of great value in this environment.

Rational Goal model
Predictable with short time lines. Understanding is readily available since there is accumulated knowledge which can be drawn upon immediately to meet current demands. Easily accessible knowledge, based upon certainty, permits efficient, goal-directed activities. This is the arena of the 'manager'.

Open Systems model
Changing with short time lines. With no precedent and no time one has to play one's hunch. The individual who travels light, acting as an innovator or entrepreneur, thrives best in this environment.

Human Relations model
Uncertain but with long time lines. There is time to talk and consult about this uncertain or unstable situation with others. The best mode of operation is regular close discussion and comparison of experience and views with a small, coherent team of like-minded committed people. An integrated, committed team thrives best in this environment.

Figure 3.3 Information environment and modes of understanding

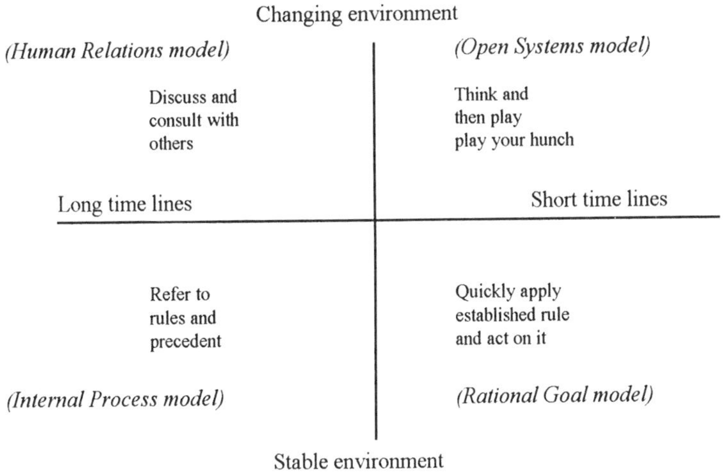

Changing environment

(Human Relations model)	*(Open Systems model)*
Discuss and consult with others	Think and then play play your hunch
Long time lines	Short time lines
Refer to rules and precedent	Quickly apply established rule and act on it
(Internal Process model)	*(Rational Goal model)*

Stable environment

Figure 3.4 illustrates the relationship between the models. This is a fine example of the maxim that one picture is worth a thousand words, and rewards careful study.

Figure 3.4   A meta-model of organisational cultures (Quinn, 1988), reproduced with permission from Jossey-Bass publishers, San Francisco, California.

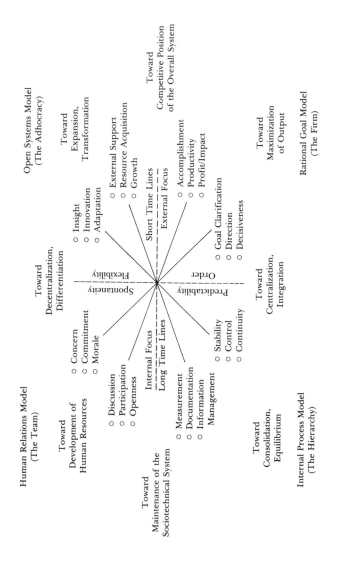

Different activities and values characterise each quadrant as described in Figure 3.4. At any one time an organisation will contain elements of each culture but with a particular emphasis on one of them. As the organisation ages and environmental conditions change, the emphasis also changes. The life cycle of an organisation can be traced anti-clockwise, usually starting in the entrepreneurial Open Systems model (north-east) quadrant. An individual sees an opportunity and 'goes for it', establishing a project and making it grow. If successful, the initiator recruits colleagues and a group or team grows up, usually fired by a shared commitment and enthusiasm, keen to work unfettered by bureaucratic constraint and seeing itself in terms of the Human Relations model (north-west). This episode usually lasts only a couple of years before staff become 'burnt out', when, ideally after a spurt of growth, the agency must move on to consolidate in the quadrant of the Internal Process model (south-west). Here the focus turns to consolidation and institutionalisation. Hierarchies are established and effort is directed to devising and implementing procedures, job specialisms and pension schemes. Then, at last, with procedures and knowledge secure, the agency can move on and pursue production and efficiency in the 'firm', the Rational Goal model of the south-east. So long as the environment remains stable and the certainties are still valid, the organisation can rapidly and efficiently produce what is required. However, the environment changes and technical developments (plastics, computers, nano-engineering) or new political initiatives erode stability so that, if it is to survive, the organisation must embrace uncertainty and some aspects of the north-east entrepreneurial culture again.

The diagonal axis reveals the weak point in each quadrant. The problem for a cosy 'team' in the Human Relations model is its lack of attention to economic objectives and monitoring efficiency: the problem for the 'firm' in the Rational Goal model is the corollary, the need to mitigate the morale-sapping quality of pressured, mechanical work routines with a sense of team and involvement. The problem for the Internal Process model is that the consolidating organisation can become sterile, stale and obsolescent unless conscious support is given to mavericks who challenge and explore new avenues. The problem for the Open Systems market culture is the need to create stability so that people can get on with their work. A frame is required to hold the interwoven web of separate, short-term contracts and projects.

Recent history illustrated by the model

The model is interesting in several ways. It accounts for commonly observed changes that happen to organisations as they grow and it also broadly accounts for the changing fashions in the management of public and private organisations over the last few years. A brief sketch is provided below.

The Internal Process Bureaucratic model in the public sector became outmoded for several reasons, not least being the promise computers brought of real-time accounting and resource management. Cheap and efficient communication within and between organisations allowed them to act faster and to operate on shorter time lines. As the model predicts, there was a move to the managerialism of the 'firm' in the Rational Goal model. Short- and medium-term objectives could be identified, targets set and monitored and many of the administrative and 'custom and practice' procedures became redundant. Organising secretaries became 'managers' and there was a pressure to make organisations 'lean and efficient'. In many countries the public utilities were 'privatised' in order to give free rein to the managerial ethos. The international rise of the New Public Management, described above, dominated most public sector organisations. In Britain, however, the trend towards disaggregation was mitigated by a policy of centralisation and so the institutions remained large or, as in the agencies of criminal justice, were amalgamated and consolidated into bigger organisations.

In the late eighties the British Government attempted a radical change in the institutions of government by requiring them to act in the market culture of short time lines and high uncertainty. Effecting radical change required the break-up of monolithic organisations but the centralising policy required that they be easily controlled, and so policies variously called Partnership Schemes or, in the National Health Service, the Internal Market were introduced. Local authorities and health authorities were required to put many of their functions out to tender. Catering and cleaning, waste disposal, leisure centres and grass cutting, the provision of social housing, prisoner escort duties and the running of remand prisons and many other services hitherto provided by government organisations were now contracted-out. Market mechanisms were to determine the demand-led provision of services to consumers rather than the old supply-led arrangement that was a feature of - and determinant of - the stable environment of the Rational Goal and Internal Process models.

The instability, represented to the north of Quinn's chart, severely challenged organisations and forced all parties to choose between creating a competitive market or collaborative partnerships to co-ordinate their mutual and complementary activities. The model predicts that success will ultimately come to those who find ways of collaboration and developing the security of the 'team' culture. Issues involved in operating in a managed market network of semi-autonomous units are further discussed in Chapter 8.

The strength of any model is that it provides a framework for making patterns from observations and other data so that one can ask and answer further and searching questions about the matter under study. This model invites pattern making about the way patterns are made of organisations and the different ways of co-ordinating business. It generates challenging questions about the way in which we construe the organisation of the justice process. It also sharpens our understanding of what has been happening, of what might yet happen and why.

3.4 CONCLUSION

The purpose of this chapter has been to invite the readers to review the assumptions that underpin their perspective. Emphasis has been put upon the way in which conceptual models both illuminate and obscure and how familiarity with one way of thinking tends to mould the mind so that other perspectives become increasingly incomprehensible.

Which of the social functions of the court described by King (1981) ring true? Which process model seems most familiar? Which are the dominant features of the court (King, 1981)? To what extent has the systems model obscured other components of the work of the criminal justice agencies? Which of Elmore's models of organisations seems most familiar? To what extent have the doctrines of NPM permeated the reader's consciousness? Which family of value systems - sigma, theta or lambda - is emphasised in one's own experience? How does Quinn's description of the way in which fashions change in organisational cultures contribute to the reader's understanding of the environment of the public sector?

Subsequent chapters describe and analyse the work and activities of those involved in the justice process but they do so within a frame of reference.   Awareness of the subjective bias people bring to their interpretation of the criminal justice process illuminates how and why the agencies behave as they do.   The administration and management of the criminal justice process are changing.   Can those responsible meet and manage the tensions and transcend the contradictions?

PART II

Strategies and consequences

The challenge to the courts set out in Chapter 1 was how to deal with an increased workload within a restricted budget. Chapter 2 described the impact of changing policies and expectations on the criminal justice agencies. Chapter 3 set out conceptual models of the social function of justice and models of management and the values that stem from them. Also described was how the Government of the time chose 'management' as the solution to the problems of the public sector. We now turn to consider the main strategies of the campaign to make criminal justice more accountable, more efficient and less idiosyncratic. In so doing, we shall once again touch on the difficulty of reconciling government policy with the values of an independent judiciary. We shall also illustrate the difficulties of importing a management approach into criminal justice and the extent to which the values inherent in sigma-style management conflict with the values of the administration of justice.

The Government's attitude towards the courts was similar to that which it held towards other public services. There was a demand that the efficiency and value for money of the agencies be improved and there was concern to increase the accountability of the administrators. There was now a requirement that court administrators should demonstrate that their organisations were being efficiently and effectively run. A third concern was that performance was often highly idiosyncratic. Above all, the Government decided that the administration of the courts needed review and the employees needed to be controlled or managed better if they were to spend public money wisely, be accountable for providing a reliable and fair service and cease being a law unto themselves.

It was evident even then that government and courts alike faced a severe challenge beset with many difficulties, concerning, for example:

1. *The nature of the judicial process.* Which model of criminal justice might be pursued? Should the Due Process model of justice take precedence over that for the 'management of crime and criminals' (King, 1981)? Should prosecution be mandatory in all cases, even if diversion from prosecution through using, for example, cautioning would be cheaper and more effective in preventing further offences?

2. *The pursuit of efficiency.* Hood (1991) suggests that the challenge facing all public sector organisations is to find and express the optimum balance of the values of efficiency, fairness and robustness and, as was argued in the previous chapter, fairness and robustness are usually curtailed by the pursuit of efficiency. However, fairness and robustness are integral to the very notion of justice and cannot be traded off in the same way as in, for example, health care and education.

3. *The management of professionals.* The prime characteristic of a professional is the special ability to exercise discretion in complex and uncertain circumstances. How might one control professionals without curtailing their ability to act effectively? The professional code and professional opinion of probation officers, solicitors, barristers, police officers, clerks and members of the judiciary are all held sacred by their owners who consider heretical attempts to moderate them.

4. *Organisational size.* Small, simple organisations are qualitatively quite different from sub-units of large organisations and require quite different approaches from those who manage them.

5. *Changes in criminal justice policy.* A major and radical piece of legislation that challenged judicial behaviour, the Criminal Justice Act, 1991, was being developed in parallel with the challenge to the administration of the courts.

Perhaps because challenging the administration of the courts was felt to be such a radical move, two parallel strategies were invoked, one from the Internal Process model and one from the Rational Goal model (Elmore, 1977, and Chapter 3). The first was to curb the autonomy of the individual professionals by standardising their work. The second was to curb the autonomy of the agencies by forming them into amalgamated hierarchies equipped with objectives, targets and performance measures. With hindsight, it would appear that this 'double whammy' was probably unnecessary and energy might have been better directed to other aspects, for example, challenging the hegemony of the Bar. Nevertheless, both strategies were invoked.

Chapter 4 describes the strategy of controlling the professionals' behaviour through the standardisation of procedures and the re-definition of their discretion. This strategy, rooted in the Internal Process or Bureaucracy model, carries the risk of deskilling staff.

Chapter 5 describes the strategies of organisational concentration and performance scrutiny to curb organisational autonomy and gain control. Under this, smaller units are amalgamated and arranged into a hierarchical structure. The previous chief becomes a middle manager who can be set targets and be held accountable for their accomplishment. These strategies, which are rooted in the Rational Goal model, carry the risk of demoralising the organisation.

Chapter 6 describes how the consequence of combining these strategies, together with the drive to increase efficiency, pushed judicial administration towards corner-cutting procedures and towards a change in the nature of the justice being dispensed.

CHAPTER 4

Control through standardisation

'A foolish consistency is the hobgoblin of little minds.'
Ralph Waldo Emerson, 1861.

4.1 INTRODUCTION

The first strategy for reining in the autonomy of the professional is rooted in the assumptions underlying the Internal Process model (Elmore, 1977). Here it is assumed that the dynamic in an organisation is the link of routine and discretion. To implement a new policy, simply redesign procedures and *administer* the process (Elmore, 1977). Thus the idiosyncrasies and inappropriateness of the way in which the professionals were seen to go about their work was addressed by setting down standards which re-defined their discretion and re-designed their routines. This seems an obvious and straightforward thing to do, and so it is when the task is processing applications for driving licences or making up an hotel bill. But when the task is more complex and less certain, it is not so simple. In the administration of justice, as in nursing and surgery, we want experienced and skilled practitioners who can use their discretion to deal with extra-ordinary matters. How do we guide nurses into current approaches to supporting and caring for patients in a highly technical environment without undermining their care and commitment? How do we support surgeons to do the taboo act and cut into the living body and yet also direct them to abandon discredited procedures for better ones? Clumsy interference would destroy both the commitment of the medical staff and the credibility of the manager who tries to influence them.

4.2   MANAGING PROFESSIONALS

What is a 'professional'? In the business and management literature the professional is described as someone who has acquired a body of knowledge and experience that enables the immediate exercise of discretion in complex and uncertain situations (Mintzberg, 1983). The professional mechanic can repair a carburettor whilst all a fitter can do is replace it. The surgeon, the plasterer and the court clerk have all accumulated sufficient informed experience to know how to deal with the unexpected without having to leave either the bleeding body, the setting plaster or the unruly court-room to go and ask a superior's permission to complete the operation. This is the value of the professionals and why we invest in their education and training. The professional will say, 'Tell me what you want doing, tell me how important it is, and when you would like it done by, but please, please, do not tell me how to do it. That I already know.'

And this is what we want to hear from the professional hairdresser, criminal justice worker or dentist. But remember how people are always willing to recommend their own dentist because, one suspects, they cannot bear to think that theirs might not be the best. We know that we want to believe in the professionals, but should we believe them? For the laity it is an act of faith based on the credibility of the 'professional organisation' such as the Institute of Chartered Accountants, the Bar or whatever body represents estate agents and the people who offer to tarmac your drive on Friday afternoons.   For colleagues, it is a calculated gamble that a peer professional who has passed the exams knows how to behave and do the work. We are all concerned that their confidence may be mere arrogance - after all, the tower blocks of the sixties, the nuclear power stations of the seventies and the free market economics of the eighties were all products of professionals exercising their discretion and claiming expertise.

Mintzberg's (1983) synthesis of research into the structuring of organisations provides a useful aid to thinking about the co-ordination of the work of professionals. He takes a number of key dimensions that describe an organisation such as size, control mechanisms and relative power of the different parts of the organisation and finds a clustering of these factors around different structures. Five parts of an organisation are identified, each having different predominance in each structure.

They are:
1. strategic apex (senior management);
2. support (secretarial, canteen and personnel staff etc.);
3. technostructure (management services, standard setters etc.);
4. middle management; and
5. operating core (those who actually do the tasks of the organisation).

Table 4.1 shows how the dominance of each part coincides with the dimensions of size, nature of the task (crucially, whether it requires the exercise of discretion), stability of the environment, and predominant co-ordinating mechanism.

Table 4.1 The structuring of organisations

Structure	Simple	Adhoc-racy	Profess-ional Bureau-cracy	Machine Bureau-cracy	Division-alised Form
Nature of task	Medium complex-ity	Complex	Complex	Simple	Complex: simple in divisions
Stability of envi-ronment	Mostly stable	Dynamic	Stable	Stable	Changing
Type of control	Direct super-vision	Through staff commit-ment	Standard-isation of indoctrin-ation and training	Standard-isation of task	Standard-isation of, or by, output
Dominant part	Strategic apex - usually sole manager	Support (from every-one)	Operating core of working profess-ionals	Techno-structure of standard-setters	Middle managers (who become divisional heads)
Size	Small	Usually small	Small or medium	Large	Large

The Simple Structure is small; staff perform moderately complex tasks. The (usually one-person) strategic apex is predominant and effects control through direct supervision. Being small with little inertia it can cope with a moderate amount of change in the environment. The courts used to be largely autonomous, Simple Structure organisations with the clerk as undisputed strategic apex of its administration.

The Adhocracy is also a moderately small organisation, similar to Quinn's 'team culture' (Quinn, 1988). Staff constantly interact with each other over projects, and control is effected through their commitment to the goals of the organisation with which they identify. Staff undertake complex tasks and cope well with change. However, in the absence of formal structures and lines of accountability, these organisations are vulnerable to idiosyncrasy and a short life. This is not a suitable way in which to order a court!

The Machine Bureaucracy is large; the workers usually perform simple tasks. The technostructure is predominant and effects control through standardising the simplified tasks of those in the operating core. Line managers are supervisors whose main task is to take the flack and frustration of the workers. It copes poorly with a changing environment. A car assembly plant or old-style government bureaucracy provide examples of this structure. It may well be efficient but only after all the uncertainties have been taken out of the work of the operating core. Quinn's Rational Goal model of certainty and immediacy often leads to this sort of organisation. Some of today's larger court organisations risk slipping in this direction.

The Professional Bureaucracy is of a small to medium size. The operating core is predominant and the members have professionalised their work environment, claiming power and discretion as necessary to perform their complex tasks. Middle managers and members of the strategic apex are promoted professionals. Control is effected by only employing professionally trained and indoctrinated staff who can be 'relied upon' (by their colleagues, if not by the laity). It copes poorly with a changing environment since there is little control over staff once they have been appointed and, on their own, they may be reluctant to change the habits of their lifetimes. Law, medical or architectural practices are examples, as are some courts.

The Divisionalised Form may apply to medium-sized or very large organisations like ICI or Unilever. Organisations of this type resemble holding companies with a set of separate but accountable sub-units. The divisional managers are predominant but they are held to account and controlled by the strategic apex through the device of being given objectives and targets that must be achieved: control is effected through standardisation of outputs. Essentially they are told that they can manage their unit however they want so long as they achieve the required output, such as a 10 per cent return on capital, or meet a specified performance indicator on, for example, the delay in cases coming to court, successful prosecutions, community service orders completed or percentage of cases cleared up.

Before we consider how this model assists with the effective control of professional staff, we must acknowledge Mintzberg's warning about the Divisionalised Form. It appears that divisional managers who are set tight objectives and targets are very prone to be anxious to achieve them and will often do so by clamping down on the behaviour of staff in a way that creates the characteristics of the Machine Bureaucracy. In particular, the manager is likely to end up specifying how the work is to be done and effecting control over staff by standardising their tasks into simpler, more predictable units. This, of course, diminishes the capacity of staff to exercise discretion and to be responsive to the unique components of any episode.

Five methods of control are also identified:

1. *Direct supervision.* This requires the almost constant presence of the supervisor and is the administrators' traditional method of controlling the work of their assistants. It does not lend itself to the control of chief administrators unless one provides a super-administrator to each unit.
2. *Through staff commitment.* This requires an active participative team and is essentially a form of self-regulation, that has become increasingly questioned by government and laity alike.
3. *Standardisation of indoctrination and training.* This is the traditional form of self-regulation by professionals that has contributed to some of the idiosyncratic and unaccountable behaviour of the smaller criminal justice agencies.
4. *Standardisation of task.* This is the way in which staff are brought to heel by curbing their autonomy in interpreting the nature of their work. As stated and implied above, the danger of this method is that

it can push the organisation into the Machine Bureaucracy and deskill and demotivate professional staff. This is the subject of this chapter.

5. *Standardisation of or by output.* This is the way that organisations are directed and made accountable. The problem with this method is that it can knock the heart out of an agency and also place irresistible pressure on managers to replicate the environment of the Machine Bureaucracy. It is the subject of the following chapter.

4.3   STANDARDISATION OF TASK

Both standardisation of task and by output require that power is assumed above and beyond the level of the operating core. In order to apply these controls, the status of the organisation must be changed to legitimate this authority. An example of this was cited in Chapter 2 where the Home Office assumed the right to demand that the probation services should abide by a 'Statement of National Objectives and Priorities': the actual priorities were not so important as the relationship invoked by this command - that those who paid the piper now called the tune. In the Crown Court, this relationship was established at the time of its formation in 1972 as a single national organisation. The magistrates' courts were more in the position of the probation services. A series of initiatives including circulars, efficiency reviews, information systems, training programmes and financial formulae, as described elsewhere in this book, served the purpose of invoking a command relationship to hitherto independent magistrates' courts' committees (MCCs).

Three main routes can be identified by which government typically pursues standardisation of task in criminal justice, as in other public policy fields. First is the legislative route, making conformity a legal requirement. Second is the route of standardisation through administrative and technical systems. Third is the route of the promotion of 'good practices'. Let us consider each of these routes in turn with particular reference to the courts.

4.3.1 Standardisation through legislation

Perhaps the least ambiguous method of changing the discretion and procedures of staff is by statute. The major recent example of this is the Criminal Justice Act, 1991, which required the judiciary, the court and other professionals to change the way in which they acted. The Act covered a range of aspects, but five in which standardising principles were directly involved were as follows:

1. *Parole.* Many of the recommendations of the Carlisle Committee, which concluded that a society which incarcerates has a duty to re-settle, were implemented. Discretionary parole was replaced by a programme of unconditional release half way through sentence for those serving sentences of less than twelve months and automatic parole half way through sentence for those serving between one and four years. The probation services were to supervise the parolees.
2. *Pre-sentence reports.* These were to be prepared in all but the most straightforward of cases and followed a standard format in some contrast to the previous social inquiry reports.
3. *Custody sentencing.* Custody was to be imposed only after rigorous examination of the seriousness of the offence and circumstances of the offender. Clear reasons would have to be given in future for custodial sentences.
4. *Just deserts sentencing.* The principle of proportionality or 'just deserts' was introduced in which a sentence was to be made on the basis of the seriousness of the crime and without full recourse to previous convictions (until the Government altered the legislation in response to vehement criticism).
5. *Unit fines.* A scheme was introduced for establishing the level of monetary penalty for those sentenced with a fine (by far the most common form of penalty) on the basis of 'ability to pay'. As we explained in Chapter 2, this scheme, which defined penalties in terms of numbers of 'units' of seriousness and involved a means test to make the conversion into a cash sum, was also scrapped in response to heavy criticism.

The experience of the Criminal Justice Act, 1991, illustrates well the negative side of standardisation of task, in terms both of the inability of centrally defined procedures to achieve their intentions and of the effects upon the professionals whose discretion is curbed. Although the first two of these matters, concerning parole and pre-sentence reports, were generally accepted within criminal justice, the others proved far more contentious. In particular, as we have indicated, the matters of 'proportionality' and unit fines created much disquiet. Despite an extensive and impressive programme of consultation and conferences in preparation for implementing the new sentencing regimes, and despite a series of carefully evaluated pilot studies on unit fines, the immediate aftermath of implementation of the Act was characterised by revelations of a series of apparent anomalies, particularly in relation to unit fines. There was also vehement criticism from the judiciary about the new principles for sentencing because of the restrictions which they imposed on the sentencer. The mood was summed up by the Lord Chief Justice, who warned that:

> 'However forward-thinking the penologists, criminologists and bureaucrats in government departments may be, their views should not be allowed to prevail so as to impose a sentencing regime which is incomprehensible or unacceptable to right-thinking people generally. If that happens, there could be a real risk of aggrieved parties taking the law into their own hands...
>
> I believe the fundamental error underlying the Act is a misconceived notion that sentencing should be programmed so as to restrict the discretion of the sentencing judge...The laudable desire to reduce and confine custodial sentencing to cases where it is really necessary has led to restrictive provisions forcing the judges into an ill-fitting strait-jacket.'
> (Taylor, 1993 - in his address as Lord Chief Justice to the Annual Conference of the Law Society of Scotland).

Lord Taylor further argued that courts should be concerned with deciding what sentence to impose rather than with what penalty they were allowed to impose, and challenged the view, which underpinned sections of the Act, that sentencing practices should be standardised in this way. This seems to demonstrate that control of staff and standard-isation through legislation, which on the face of it seems to make conformity a requirement, can be resented and resisted. This is precisely what one might have expected.

4.3.2 Standardisation through systems

Another powerful but more subtle way of prescribing how people do their work is to set it within a system. This is the tradition of bureaucracy and it has found its place in the administration of courts as it has in most other organisational contexts. Over time, moreover, the systematising of court administrative procedures has been a fairly constant preoccupation of the government departments responsible for the courts. Activity after activity and task after task have been subject to procedural review and specification in regulations. In the Crown Court, as one might expect in a large bureaucratic organisation of the civil service, strong standardisation is a hallmark of the way things are done. The administrative practices associated with, for example, record keeping, listing, information circulation, and accounting are essentially the same at Carmarthen as at Chelmsford, and at Lancaster as at Lewes. Moreover, such procedural standardisation between Crown Court centres is steadily being augmented by computerisation. For instance, the phased introduction of a computerised case management system (the CREST system) will provide a standard data-base for many of the routine functions of staff employed at court centres around the country (Lord Chancellor's Department, 1992a).

In the magistrates' courts, too, the process of increasing standardisation of administrative systems has developed over the past ten or fifteen years. Once it could fairly be said that no two magistrates' clerk's offices conducted their administrative tasks in the same way. This presented problems for staff moving from one court to another who had to learn different procedures. It also created difficulties for management scientists and researchers who sought information in vain from different courts on a consistent basis. However, these are small issues and one wonders whether such procedural differences were especially wicked. Nevertheless, from the early 1980s a succession of administrative systematising initiatives by the Home Office and subsequently by the Lord Chancellor's Department gradually squeezed out most such differences. With accounting procedures, for example, the Home Office, in the early 1980s, required that all magistrates' courts without computerised accounting systems should operate 'standard manual accounting' procedures, for which a contract was negotiated with a single company to supply all the courts with materials and stationery for the new regime.

At the same time, increasingly tight restrictions were imposed as to the purchase of computerised administrative systems. Individual clerks had explored the use of computers to undertake accounting and the processing of court records, preparing court lists, printing the registers of court decisions, monitoring fines and maintenance arrears. However, once the Home Office became similarly interested, an appraisal was quickly carried out of the various software systems available from the computer industry and the choice for the courts was restricted to three or four models. This form of partial standardisation was easily enforced since the Home Office simply exercised its power to sanction all expenditure on new computer equipment for magistrates' courts.

But the Government's desired goal was fuller standardisation by systems. Accordingly, a project was announced by the Home Office in 1988 to develop the next generation of system. This was the Magistrates' Courts Administration Standard System (the MASS project) and all the courts were to be provided with access to it by the mid 1990s. The system was to build upon all the learning derived from the systems already in existence and would provide improved capacity to undertake additional functions, notably electronic communication and data exchange with other criminal justice agencies and court listing management (Dunn, 1993). So far as the standardisation theme was concerned, the title behind the acronym MASS said it all. The system would define the 'one best way' of doing things and, because all procedures would be controlled from within it, there would be no danger of people doing things the wrong way.

To those who had had experience of the difficulties and inefficiencies associated with manual record systems in organisations with the size of workload of most magistrates' courts, the case for computerisation and for the associated degree of standardisation probably seemed compelling. For example, there was the perennial problem of keeping a check on arrears of several thousand separate fine and maintenance accounts, and the inefficiency for the court in having to re-type all of the information provided by the police about each defendant and their offences, first on a court list and then subsequently in a court register.

On the other hand, was it necessary to standardise all courts to exactly the same system and routines? Was there so much interchange of data between courts as to justify this approach? Was not the more important factor compatibility or communication and exchange capacity between the agencies within a particular court area? Moreover, if part of the motivation behind the MASS project was to create more consistency by reducing local variation in procedures, the critical question concerned the opportunity cost. Might there actually be other and better ways in particular courts and might not the opportunity be lost for learning about these if all courts were to do everything in precisely the same way?

The history of computerisation, as everyone knows, is littered with expensive disasters that have acted as a black hole down which money and, more importantly, staff hours and commitment have been sucked. Every month a new horror story is revealed about large and complex computerisation projects. Yet the technologies continue to provide an obsession for many managers to the extent that any questioning and expressions of doubt about the value of computerisation is considered positively Luddite. Interestingly, about the same time as the Stock Exchange TAURUS system had to be abandoned and many millions of pounds of investment written off because the ambition of its designers had exceeded the reality of its execution, the consultants who had been commissioned to undertake an important part of the design work for MASS failed to satisfy the Lord Chancellor's Department on their progress with the contract and so had to be paid off, and the whole project rescheduled.

4.3.3 Standardisation through promoting 'good practice'

The third commonly adopted approach towards curbing the autonomy of professionals is to issue guidelines advocating how they should do their work. The promotion of 'good practice' has been an increasingly familiar strategy of government, particularly in its dealings with services at local level over which it has no direct control. The principal vehicles are the government circular, the advice note, and the 'good practice guidelines', although in recent years additional emphasis has also been given to promotion of standards through training and seminars, and through the issuing of 'consultation documents' (which are often more about advocacy of the ideas than invitations for comment).

The probation services, for example, have received various sets of guidelines defining what officers should do and how they should do it. While there have been no official sanctions for non-compliance, their implementation is certainly backed up by the presence of the Probation Inspectorate. Police, too, receive each year a stream of circulars and guidance notes from the Home Office suggesting what chief constables should 'consider as priorities', 'treat as matters of urgency', 'take into account', 'give thought to' and so on. Often the guidance bears the hallmarks of excessive zeal on the part of the civil servants responsible for their drafting, who spell out every little detail, from the obvious to the unimaginable, and leave little, if anything, to the discretion or common sense of the recipient. To remove any ambiguity, such guidance notes all state that agencies would normally be expected to comply (the word 'normally' is crucial as the traditional qualifier in all civil service communications and as a sop to the independence of locally governed service organisations).

We will mention two illustrations of such promotional strategies from the magistrates' courts. First is the initiative within the Lord Chancellor's Department to identify and propagate 'good practices' in court administration. In fact, those responsible for this particular initiative appeared to have had rather more confidence in their work than is implied in the phrase 'good practice', for the series of reports that were produced were all entitled 'Best Practice Guides'. The initiative was not, however, entirely undertaken within a government department, for it involved the formation of small teams of practitioners, working with and under the invitation of a member of the Lord Chancellor's Department. The task was to compile short reports on what were felt to constitute 'best practices' in relation to specific administrative matters, such as fine enforcement, listing, court user groups and so on. The reports were for the individual courts to use or neglect as they felt appropriate, although accompanying their promotion was the implicit judgement that any court not employing the particular practices would be operating a less than ideal system. Such matters would almost always be the focus of discussion when the Lord Chancellor's Adviser on magistrates' courts undertook field visits to courts. Moreover, with the establishment in 1993 of a Magistrates' Courts' Inspectorate, there was the increased possibility that in future non-compliance with whatever standards had been accorded 'best practice' status might be formally noted in audit reports and perhaps held against the courts concerned.

The second example of the pursuit of standardisation of practices through promotional strategies concerns inter-agency relationships and agreements on time limits for the completion of different tasks associated with the criminal justice process. This is a subject touched on earlier and to which we shall return again, in Chapter 8 in particular. An initiative was commenced in 1989 to develop a set of standards for each of the various pre-trial tasks and stages of criminal trials. An inter-departmental Working Group on 'Pre-Trial Issues' was set up to review the practices in operation and to recommend new standards where appropriate. The group consisted of representatives of the CPS, the Home Office, the Justices' Clerks' Society, the police and the Legal Secretariat to the Law Officers. Specifically, the brief for the group was to examine the quality and timeliness of police files, delays in processing cases in criminal justice, arrangements for 'warning' witnesses (advising them of the requirement to attend court), and the provision of case results and antecedent information.

The report of the group was completed in 1990 and contained one hundred and sixty five recommendations. Among these were a series of recommended time limits for various functions such as the preparation of case files by the police, case preparation work by the prosecution and the defence and drafting of court reports by the probation services. The recommendations made on all such matters were greeted with enthusiasm by those at the centre, notably in the CPS and the Home Office, and they were quickly promoted as standards to be followed at local level.

Unfortunately, some hostile reactions were encountered, particularly from courts which happened to have been operating to time intervals shorter than those specified in the recommendations. The status of the guidelines was hurriedly re-defined in a circular on the subject. The revised message was that the guidelines were to be regarded as maximal standards and were not necessarily to be adhered to rigidly. On the other hand, it was largely inevitable that in many areas the more expeditious standards which had been successfully established before the publication of the report would be undermined - convergence to the published standards being the consequence of almost all initiatives of this kind. It was a classic example of the pursuit of greater consistency across areas being in conflict with local priorities, agreements and working practices. It was also a case of the diversity of practices and performance (some impressive, others less so) being replaced by uniformly mediocre standards. It had to be so, because the standards had to be set at levels attainable by the organisations with least impressive performance.

4.4 THE CONSEQUENCES OF STANDARDISATION STRATEGIES

Standardisation of task is the method of control for the Machine Bureaucracy in which the task is simple, the organisation large, the environment stable and the predominant part of the organisation is the technostructure, the standard-setters. This is obviously at variance with professionalism. The task in court is not simple and it requires persons who can exercise discretion and deal with the unexpected. The flow through the system is not a homogenous fluid, it is composed of individual cases and circumstances in a volatile environment. So, we would argue, standardisation of task can only be a temporary strategy, not a permanent state. And, like a Band-Aid, if left on too long it stops promoting healing and makes the site go soggy. Writing about the probation services, which went through a tougher period of standard-isation and commenting on the effect it had upon morale as well as behaviour, May comments:

> 'In more general terms, the organisation, as represented by the ascending discourse surrounding organisational work and its corresponding production of information, moved from a 'problem-solving' orientation to a 'performance' orientation. As a result, the end, or purpose for work, was lost for the majority of organisational members and the means for transformation (of the organisation) became an end in itself...In the process, past organisational goals were replaced by a new orientation to short-term objectives which also structured rewards for its members on the basis of their adherence to this new mode of operation... Organisational members then felt themselves to be evaluated, not valued and managed to control, not enabled by management.' (May, 1992, pp. 22-3)

But let us add one qualification to our argument. This is that it would be wrong to attribute the responsibility for standardisation wholly to the Government and to its requirements for control. The professions and their representative organisations have also been important forces for standardisation, albeit largely through training and qualification. Indeed, in many instances, it was the standards that the professional bodies had developed for their members that were subsequently taken up by the Government. Two main differences were apparent between the character of standard-setting undertaken by the professions and that undertaken by government. First, whereas the professions were generally most interested in setting 'minimum standards', the Government was generally more interested in pursuing 'prescriptive standards'. Second, while the standards set by the professional bodies tended to be of the status of 'guidelines' for their membership to take into account while exercising their normal discretion, those of the Government were more often accompanied by an expectation that they would be followed to the letter.

Related to this is one of the themes picked up in the next chapter. The Divisionalised Form recruits the professionals who had become managers in the Professional Bureaucracy to be new-style 'real' managers, who visit upon erstwhile colleagues the task standardisation of the Machine Bureaucracy that they would not have accepted from someone totally outside their profession. It is an old colonial strategy and it works very well.

4.5   CONCLUSION

There is a tension, then, between the control of professional staff and ensuring that the conditions exist in which they can act professionally. How can this be addressed? The basic contract of professional staff with the agency might be:

> 'If you will ensure and support my exercise of discretion, then I will undertake to work within the parameters of agency policy and to keep the agency informed of what demands are being made of me and how I am addressing my work'

and, on the other hand, of the agency with the staff:

> 'If you will agree to work within the basic parameters of our policies and will provide systematic information about the work in which you are involved, then we will support the exercise of your discretion.'

However, as we have argued, many professionals in criminal justice seem to prefer the basic contract of the staff member with the Professional Bureaucracy which might be summarised as:

'I have passed my exams and am an upright member of the profession so be assured that I work to the benefit of my clients and our agency.'

In this they risk provoking the contract for the Machine Bureaucracy:

'If you want to keep your job, do these simple tasks as you have been shown.'

But sometimes there is land between the devil and the deep blue sea. And sometimes the Home Office found it and charted a constructive route through this difficult area of bringing the professionals into line without abusing their integrity too much. The guiding principles appear to be:

1. Standards must be developed through consultation.
2. The standards must be sensible and well researched if they are to be seen as a credible contribution to practice. Many of the standards set for the probation services and the magistrates' courts have facilitated practice although others have not. For instance, the Home Office proposed that applications for legal aid should be accompanied by payslips for the previous thirteen weeks, or that probation officers should give their home address to the prisoners whom they were to supervise on release. This demonstrated ignorance on the part of officials and generated contempt among local professional staff.
3. The introduction of external standards to replace internal standards can be problematic in that, whereas the latter are flexible and can accommodate most circumstances, external standards are more rigid and probably will not apply to non-standard circumstances. Therefore, listen, learn and build in discretion.
4. The experience of working to someone else's prescription is seldom as satisfying as working to one's own. The price of calling the tune and making the professionals dance to it is that they usually do so only half-heartedly. So listen and learn and take it step by step.

CHAPTER 5

Towards more accountable organisation

'The business of government is to see that no other organisation is as strong as itself.'
President Woodrow Wilson, 1912.

5.1   INTRODUCTION

A key objective of the Government over the past decade has been to curb the autonomy of public sector organisations and make the professional groups and administrators who dominate them more accountable for their actions.   From 1979 onwards, most organisational reforming initiatives in the public services have been, in part at least, underpinned by this aim.   In this chapter we examine why this particular objective was given priority and, by focusing particularly on the magistrates' courts, we consider some of the strategies that were pursued to this end, and some of the consequences that followed.

What was the motive for wanting to challenge the traditional autonomy of public sector organisations and for wanting to curb the discretion and strengthen the accountability of the professionals and administrators within them? Was it a matter of ensuring propriety in the public services? After all, revelations of serious malversation had occasionally spilled out through the media into the public consciousness and had tended to tarnish the reputation of public provision.   But if the motive of the Government was simply to inject a greater sense of rectitude into public policy making and management, then serious questions would have to be asked about the purpose and impact of other policies pursued at the same time, notably those concerning the deregulation of certain services, the extensive resort to contracting-out of service provision responsibilities, and the introduction of fixed term contracts performance related pay schemes for senior managers across the public sector. These, of course, were the kinds of policies that, in involving 'freeing up' the public sector, removing the 'checks and balances', and replacing bureaucracy with an 'enterprise culture', created the ideal conditions for self-interest to spawn and for the old fashioned ideas of public service to wither (Hood, 1991).

So what other reasons might have underlain the desire to curb the autonomy and strengthen the accountability of public sector organisations? Here, arguably of more profound significance than the matter of propriety, was the Government's perception of shortcomings in the old order under which the professionals and administrators had exercised considerable influence. As we suggested in the previous chapter, in many respects the perception was that these groups had failed to deliver on the promises made, that they had not exercised wisely the responsibilities entrusted in them, and that they had too often put the protection of their own organisational interests above those of the communities to be served. The position, so far as the 'New Right' politicians were concerned, could be summarised as follows:

'Some see the public sector professionals as middle-class parasites living comfortable, salaried lives on the backs of working people; others see them as unproductive and inefficient meddlers compromising the natural market forces of society; and even those in the middle suspect that the bureaucracy places greater emphasis on its own maintenance than on that of the community.' (Willson, 1986, p. 37)

What was needed, it was confidently asserted, was less of the professional and administrative tradition and more of a management culture in the public sector. This was the way to achieve the goals of improved efficiency, sharpened accountability and reduced idiosyncrasy.

But how exactly was a management culture to be injected into traditional public sector bureaucracies? Essentially the process followed the pattern described by Elmore (1977) as the Rational Goal model. This was summarised in Chapter 3, on p. 64, as follows:

'The Rational Goal model assumes that organisations and people are rational and that if we arrange a hierarchy of sub-units, each with its objectives and monitored targets for which named people are responsible, then all will be well. To implement a new policy, simply instruct and *manage* properly.'

The process, which was actually apparent in organisations long before the new managerialism became established in the public sector in the 1980s, involved the creation within each organisational unit of accountable hierarchies and more explicit line management control. To this end, the old order of the Machine Bureaucracies and the Professional Bureaucracies, described in the previous chapter (Mintzberg, 1983), that had been characteristic of many public service organisations in the fairly stable context of the past would have to give way to new Divisionalised Forms of organisation; these being regarded as more suited to the implementation of a radical government agenda.

Under Mintzberg's ideal conception of the Divisionalised Form middle managers would be given objectives and targets to achieve and otherwise left to run their divisions as they felt best - in other words, they were held to account and controlled only in terms of their results or outputs. However, in the public service context of the 1980s, the pattern was a little different. The middle managers as well as the operational staff were subject to controls upon the way in which tasks were to be done.

In criminal justice, as in many other fields of the public service, then, the experience was largely one of increasing central control; with more accountability being sought whilst at the same time imposing checks on professional and administrative discretion. This had a number of manifestations. One, of course, was the standardisation of the tasks and processes that we considered in the preceding chapter. Two others concern, on the one hand, rationalising organisational structures and, on the other, the development of systems and procedures by which government would be better informed about the performance of the organisations, and so be able to guide, intervene, and control. We refer to the first of these two as the process of 'organisational concentration', and to the second as 'performance scrutiny'. Let us consider each in turn and elaborate both some of the main symptoms and their effects within criminal justice and particularly in the magistrates' courts.

5.2   ORGANISATIONAL CONCENTRATION AND CRIMINAL JUSTICE

The process of rationalising organisational structure, of reducing the number of sub-units and linking them in a management hierarchy was one which most of the criminal justice agencies experienced at some stage over the past twenty years. In each case the argument was essentially that control would more easily be effected with fewer sub-units and clearly defined hierarchical relationships. In the magistrates' courts, on which we will shortly focus, the achievement of greatly increased central control owed much to the process of organisational concentration. Before looking at what exactly this entailed, however, it is worth pausing to consider the position in some of the other public sector agencies of criminal justice.

Prosecution
The Crown Prosecution Service (CPS) was established in 1986 as a single national organisation with a territorial sub-structure of 31 areas and about 130 branches. This unitary organisational structure was chosen in preference to the option of completing the network of separate local prosecuting solicitor offices that had been developing steadily in previous years on a county-by-county basis. The main argument made by the Government at the time was that a higher level of consistency would be achieved through a single national organisation than through a series of independent prosecuting organisations. And surely this was true. However, there were other motives behind the decision besides those concerning standards of professional practice. In particular, the decision also reflected the belief that the best way to emphasise accountability and to maximise efficiency was to create a single management hierarchy, with the thirty-one area chiefs being directly accountable to the head of service, the Director of Public Prosecutions (DPP). The importance attached at the time to the achievement of effective control and accountability in this context was illustrated by the fact that, within six years of establishment, the territorial structure was rationalised to just thirteen areas. The main reason, of course, was that this would greatly facilitate the centre's task of controlling the organisation.

Police

The organisational structure and accountabilities of police services, too, came under scrutiny by the Home Office in the early 1990s. Policing had always been a locally organised service, with accountability being to local communities through local police committees composed of councillors and magistrates. But during the 1980s arguments about the economies of scale, about the increasing geographical horizons of criminals and about the constraints which police territorial boundaries imposed on crime-fighting techniques were frequently emphasised. Many senior police officers came to the view that a single national police force would be the better way to organise policing responsibilities, and that view certainly enjoyed some sympathy within quarters of the Home Office. The main obstacle was public opinion which had generally been as opposed to a national police force as it was to the routine arming of police officers. In 1992 the Home Secretary initiated an internal review on the future organisational arrangements for the police, partly prompted by a concurrent review of local government structures. The review produced no specific recommendations for a more rationalised territorial structure for policing. However, the instincts of the Government in this context were evident in the conclusion that procedures for amalgamating areas should be simplified. The review also concluded that new police authorities should be established with greater independence from local authorities and involving local business people as well as councillors and magistrates (House of Commons, 1993).

Probation

Concentration of the territorial organisation of probation services was also given serious consideration in the 1980s. Here too, the Home Office put forward various proposals for reorganising structures, including one to rationalise the number of separate local services and committees from 56 to 30 (Home Office, 1990b). However, discussion of the proposals was later abandoned by the Home Office in the face of much disquiet within the local services and because a higher priority at the time was felt to be the implementation of the new Criminal Justice Act, 1991, for which the full co-operation of the chief probation officers and their subordinates was considered vital.

Prisons

In contrast with probation and policing, the Prison Service had long operated on the basis of a single national organisation, being, in fact, the direct responsibility of a department of the Home Office. Further organisational concentration could not therefore be expected and, indeed, rather the reverse process was witnessed in recent years. However, this was not simply because concentration was now disapproved of or because it was being blamed for ills in the Prison Service. Instead, it was more a reaction to other circumstances specific to the prison context, notably, the difficulties which the Government was encountering in winning co-operation from the influential Prison Officers' Association. Industrial action by the Association, and a series of disagreements with the Home Office over matters of policy, pay and conditions, had the effect of sharpening the Government's resolve to act both to distance itself from the day-to-day problems of running the jails and to break the monopoly position of the Association. So far as the first objective was concerned, the decision was taken in the early 1990s to establish the Prison Service as an executive agency, separate from the Home Office and with its own chief executive. The argument underpinning this move, as with all the executive agencies which were set up in the late 1980s and early 1990s, was that the quasi-contracting relationship which agency status would establish with a government department would sharpen managerial accountability (though weakening political accountability) in a way that had never been achieved under the previous arrangements within departments (Cabinet Office, 1988). As to the second objective, the Government decided to pioneer contracting-out the responsibility for running some of the new prisons to the private sector, and indeed, ultimately, it was planned, some of the older ones too.

Higher courts

The process of organisational concentration affected the higher courts at least a decade before the advent of the new managerialism, when the Crown Court was established in 1972. This followed a Royal Commission, under the chairship of Lord Beeching (who had previously oversaw the rationalisation of the railway network), the main recommendations of which were for the abolition of the county-based Quarter Sessions and Assizes court system and its replacement with a new, unified, national, higher-tier court organisation - the Crown Court for England & Wales. The proposals had been underpinned mainly by the need to 'modernise' the system; after all the Assizes and Quarter Sessions did date back to the thirteenth century and anomalies were now apparent. Some large cities, like Coventry and Hull, for example, had no Assize courts while a number of other much smaller towns (with populations of under 10,000) did.

In consequence, the recommendations were that nineteen Assize towns and sixty-seven towns with Quarter Sessions should lose their criminal courts above the tier of the magistrates' courts (which were excluded from the Commission's terms of reference). Moreover, fourteen former Assize towns were no longer to receive visits by High Court judges and so, as a result, many people involved in cases in the most serious offence categories would have to travel much further than before to a court centre where the High Court judges sat.

Administration of the new Crown Court was established on a strictly civil service hierarchical basis under the Lord Chancellor and his Department. However, as with the organisation of the senior judiciary, a territorial sub-structure of six Circuits (covering England & Wales) was devised, each with a Circuit Administrator, accountable to their senior officer in the Lord Chancellor's Department, and responsible for the work of their subordinates, the chief clerks and court administrators based at each Crown Court centre.

Twenty years later, the Lord Chancellor proposed a further change to the administrative arrangements for the Crown Court. This entailed the establishment of an executive agency similar to that for the Prison Service. The presence of the new Courts Service Agency would reduce the Lord Chancellor's Department's responsibility for running the 80 or so Crown Court centres but, since the Lord Chancellor's Department would retain budgetary control, the Department would inevitably retain the power to prescribe policy and practice.

5.3 MAGISTRATES' COURTS AND ORGANISATIONAL CONCENTRATION

At the same time as the establishment of the new Crown Court was resulting in rationalisation of the network of higher-tier court centres, so too a similar process of rationalisation of court-houses was effected in magistrates' courts, though prompted by different reasons. Here the reorganisation in 1974 of local government (with which magistrates' courts had long been organisationally linked) meant the establishment of nearly ninety new magistrates' courts' committee areas, one for each new county council area, one for each metropolitan district area, one for inner London as a whole, and four covering the outer London area (though in 1986, as part of the new arrangements following the abolition of the Greater London Council - the strategic upper-tier authority for London - new magistrates' courts' committees were established for each outer London Borough area, making a total of 105 committee areas). Many of the new committees began by reviewing their internal organisational structures and, particularly in rural areas, decisions were taken to close a large number of the smallest court-houses and to amalgamate many of the smallest Benches (many of which had been in existence as separate judicial entities for over 100 years). As a result, in 1979 there were under 700 magistrates' court-houses in England & Wales, compared with nearly 800 in 1970.

This, however, was organisational concentration effected on a voluntary basis; it was the local magistrates' courts' committees themselves who were deciding where their sittings should take place in the new structures. As such, it was distinctly different from a second wave of the process that came some fifteen to twenty years later. This second wave was largely as a result of pressures from the Government in its pursuit of stronger accountability, more efficiency and less idiosyncrasy. Let us consider some of the symptoms.

5.3.1   *Guidance on size of Benches*

Of considerable significance in this context, was the production in 1986 by the Home Office of a consultation document on the size of local Benches (Home Office, 1986). Despite the 'consultation status' of the document, the purpose was clear; to press for the abolition by amalgamations of the many very small Benches (those with under 12 magistrates were defined as being too small) and to reduce the number of petty sessional divisions (the territorial units for each of which a local Bench was appointed). The guidelines were especially relevant to Benches in rural areas, where most of the smallest Benches were to be found. The arguments for amalgamations were largely about improving efficiency, and built on the view that, as every magistrates' clerk who had served small Benches knew, the fewer the number of petty sessional divisions, the less time need be spent on administrative functions (for example, organising rotas of magistrates' sittings, attending Bench meetings and arranging training sessions). Moreover, although, not explicitly addressed in the guidance, the number of Benches in an area was a key factor affecting the number of court-houses (since each Bench would normally expect its own accommodation). Reducing the number of separate Benches, therefore, was a key to closing some of the lesser-used courts and thus to saving costs both of premises and of travel for staff having to journey out from their main offices. Concentrating the workload instead at the main court centres would, it was argued, also offer advantages of greater flexibility in the scheduling of cases and, as a result, potentially reduce delays (Raine, 1989a).

The significance of the 'consultation document' to the process of organisational concentration was illustrated by the fact that letters were subsequently dispatched from the Home Office to all those magistrates' courts' committees whose areas included Benches with twelve or fewer magistrates, requesting to be informed of the actions which were intended to be taken locally. Furthermore, in the letter, the committees were reminded that the Home Secretary had powers to conduct his own review of the petty sessional division structure and to decide on amal-gamations if he was not satisfied by the actions of a local committee. A flurry of local reorganisations involving Bench amalgamations took place around the country, and by 1990 the number of Benches had fallen to just over 450, having been nearly 650 just five years earlier.

5.3.2   *Cash limiting and concentration in magistrates' courts*

Another very significant factor in the process of organisational concentration was the introduction in 1992 of a cash-limit on the Government grant paid to magistrates' courts. In preparation for the new discipline many magistrates' courts' committees were forced to decide on further court-house closures, amalgamations of Benches, compulsory redundancies for some of their magistrates' clerks and closure of some of their court administrative centres.

In one shire county, for example, implementation of the new cash limiting formula meant a loss of over 15 per cent of the grant previously received, a challenge lessened only slightly by the fact that the Government had agreed to phase in the new regime over a five year transitional period. Moreover this was a county, like many others, in which the magistrates' courts' committee had only recently completed its own review and rationalisation of organisational structure (closing seven of its least used court-houses, reducing the number of Benches from twenty-two to eleven, and reducing the number of magistrates' clerks from eight to three). In this review court-house closures had been confined to those settlements of under 10,000 population and the decisions had been made on the basis of a careful analysis and debate about relative needs and accessibility. Now, however, the process was much more capricious and driven essentially by the requirement to respond to a cash shortfall.

Two indicators suggested that the scales might have been tipped too far in this instance in favour of parsimony. First, no-one within the particular county spoke in favour of the package of economies that the magistrates' courts' committee had reluctantly voted to accept in December 1992. Second, the local County Council subsequently appealed against the decisions to the Lord Chancellor on the grounds of undue damage to the local community infrastructure, despite a traditional pre-disposition towards economical service provision. Whereas in general it had been magistrates' courts' committees that had proved to be the reluctant bodies when it came to debates about possible closures of courts, and local authorities (as the funding bodies) that had been most willing to countenance closures for the savings in costs which they represented, in this county at least, it now seemed that the tables had turned. The magistrates' courts' committee was now framing the rationalisation plans, albeit under government-imposed financial pressure, and the County Council, the funding body, was (unsuccessfully, as it turned out) opposing them!

At the same time as the Government was indirectly effecting rationalisation in the number of court centres through the impact of cash limiting, it was also applying direct pressure in many instances by making closures of smaller courts a condition of approval of new court projects. This pressure affected court-houses in metropolitan districts as well as in rural county areas, since many of the courts in most urgent need of replacement were in the cities where workloads had generally risen fastest. Thus, court-houses in the suburbs of several metropolitan centres (in many instances, in areas with long histories of civic pride and identity, but which no longer had separate local authority status) were closed to make way for large, new, inner-city complexes.

5.3.3 A new framework for local justice

A further step in the direction of organisational concentration for magistrates' courts was made in 1992 when the Government published a White Paper on the future organisational arrangements for the service *A New Framework for Local Justice* (Lord Chancellor's Department, 1992c). This followed a Scrutiny report prepared some two years earlier which had found much evidence of inefficiency in the local services, and of idiosyncrasy in management style and practices. The report had particularly criticised as weak the framework of accountability for magistrates' courts.

'There is no coherent management structure for the service. At national level, the role of the Home Office is so uncertain and its powers so limited, that it might be truer to say that there are 105 local services, each run by a committee of magistrates. But the local structure is just as confused, with 285 justices' clerks enjoying a semi-autonomous status under committees which are fundamentally ill-suited to the task of management. It is impossible to locate clear management responsibility or accountability anywhere in the structure... It would be difficult to think of any arrangements less likely to deliver value for money than the present ones. The Home Office provides most of the funds but has no say in how resources are allocated or used, or even the total level of spending, other than by detailed approvals which are themselves an obstacle to optimum value for money. The immediate funding body, the local authority, has too little stake in the service to provide effective budgeting discipline, while the magistrates' courts' committees are too dependent on local authorities and their management capacity is too underdeveloped to plan and manage resources effectively. Most justices' clerks have little control over resources and little information about costs. Spending is not properly controlled and the audit arrangements, despite improvements, are still deficient.' (Home Office, 1989a, p. 6)

The authors of the Scrutiny report had recommended nationalisation as the solution and had advocated the creation of an executive agency, akin to the Prison Service, as being the best means to provide the advantages of a unitary hierarchical management structure while protecting judicial independence. However, following elaborate consultations with the magistrates and their clerks and staff at local level, in which the widespread dislike of the ideas became apparent, the Government took the decision to reject the agency model and instead to seek improvements in accountability and efficiency in other ways.

First, it was decided to concentrate all government responsibilities for magistrates' courts in the Lord Chancellor's Department. This decision had a certain logic about it in so far as it meant that administrative responsibility for all courts (magistrates' and the higher courts) was now under one roof. Moreover, it was precisely what most magistrates wanted. Their view, at least, was that the service would be likely to receive much more sympathetic treatment from the Lord Chancellor who, after all, was the head of the judiciary and whose prime interests, they thought, would therefore naturally be those of justice rather than of economy and efficiency.

Second, it was decided to halve the number of magistrates' courts' committee areas from the 105 already in existence. Here too, the aim was to establish a more concentrated organisational framework for the local services, the view being that, with a smaller number of sub-units, the Lord Chancellor's Department would find it easier to control committees and their managers and hold them to account. Of course there were underlying efficiency considerations as well. Here the argument was that, with larger areas at their disposal, each new committee would be able to deploy its resources more efficiently, for example, by transferring cases between court-houses in each area to facilitate reductions in delay, by lending and borrowing staff between court offices to 'smooth out' peaks and troughs in the workload or to provide cover for holiday and sick leave. In keeping with the managerialist values of the time, the aim was to engender a strong 'resource management' approach to court administration, much akin to the approach that was being adopted by the Government in other public service contexts, notably in the health service.

Third, the White Paper included proposals directly to sharpen the framework of accountability within the local services. This involved the abolition of the traditional autonomy of magistrates' clerks. While each clerk would continue to be responsible for the administration of one or more Benches and court-houses, they would in future be placed in a line management structure, being accountable to a new tier of chief justices' clerks each of whom would be the chief executive for their new magistrates' courts' committees. In this way a framework would be established which, while not quite the single agency model that had been proposed in the Scrutiny report two years earlier, offered much of the essence of the hierarchical structure; the key to controlling the local services and to curbing the autonomy of the professionals within them.

5.4   PERFORMANCE SCRUTINY

At this point, let us suspend discussion of the theme of organisational concentration and switch to the other avenue down which the Government chose to curb professional autonomy and to enhance accountability.   This was the avenue of organisational performance measurement, of target setting, monitoring and applying sanctions where under-performance or breaches of rules were revealed.

During the 1980s, all the criminal justice agencies experienced having their performance questioned and placed under scrutiny in response to government concerns with efficiency, accountability and idiosyncrasy.   Reviews were undertaken in turn of the performance of the police, the CPS, the probation services, the prisons and the courts. Some were conducted by government officials, for example, the Scrutiny study of magistrates' courts (Home Office, 1989a), some by quangos with specific remits in this respect, for example, the Audit Commission studies of police and probation management (Audit Commission, 1989) and the National Audit Office study on the CPS (National Audit Office, 1990).   Some were conducted by select committees of the House of Commons, for example, a review of the CPS, and some were conducted by outside consultants, for example, a study of value for money in magistrates' courts (Raine & Henshaw, 1985).

5.4.1 Management information

Let us again focus on the magistrates' courts, to illustrate the nature and implications of this kind of performance scrutiny approach so far as accountability was concerned Let us note how the Government at the same time sought to reinforce the hierarchies of control which it had shaped through the process of organisational concentration.

A significant starting point for magistrates' courts was the preparation of a report in 1982 by a Home Office Working Group on the enforcement of fines and on delays in completing cases (Home Office, 1982). In fact the report went well beyond its terms of reference and provided a much wider analysis of the need for better management within the local services. Indeed, it included the first comprehensive set of statistics on cost efficiency and productivity (costs per case and numbers of cases dealt with per court hour). It was effectively the start of the Government's data-base on efficiency in magistrates' courts and other aspects of their performance.

Shortly afterwards a government circular on efficiency and effectiveness was distributed (Home Office, 1984) emphasising the high priority that would now have to be given to these matters - the other criminal justice agencies each received a similar circular at about the same time - and instituting an annual statistics gathering exercise for all courts. This was to provide the Home Office with the data for a national Management Information System (MIS) for magistrates' courts, to be published each year and providing information on performance in each magistrates' clerk's area in England & Wales.

The magistrates' courts MIS found few friends among its subjects, who claimed the data was both statistically unreliable (and the clerks should have known, since they provided it!) and misleading as to the full picture of performance at local level. But such arguments had little effect in dampening enthusiasm in government for the new tool. Over the succeeding years, the MIS was steadily refined and increasingly became the most important source of information on magistrates' courts available to government policy-makers and resource planners. Spot checks were even introduced to ensure that the data returns from each clerk were to be trusted. The MIS information was now being used by the Home Office in the estimation of requirements for staff, accommodation, equipment and other resources for the courts. Without an adequate justification in the MIS figures, the magistrates' clerk now stood little chance of obtaining an extra slice of the cake!

What information did the MIS system provide? Most important in this context, it provided a measure of the workload of each court. Here, the Home Office statisticians had devised a composite statistic - 'weighted caseload' - which was based on the number of cases completed, but adjusted by a series of weightings to take account of differences in the average disposal time (for example, indictable cases and matrimonial cases generally required more time than summary traffic cases). It was all fairly crude, though an advance on the data vacuum which had existed before. It was symptomatic of the pioneering status of the initiative that both the categories measured and the weightings applied were modified several times in successive years. Nevertheless, the general approach remained the same and was used in the computation of one of four Key Indicators of performance: 'the average cost per weighted case'. League tables were published showing the comparative efficiency of the magistrates' clerkships in this respect, and subsequently the weighted caseload measure became the most important factor in the distributional formula for the cash-limited grant. The other Key Indicators concerned delay (as measured by the proportion of cases dealt with during a sample two month period); fine enforcement (as measured by the proportion of imposed fines in arrears); and quality of service (as measured by a range of indicators of consumer-oriented service). In addition, the statisticians computed a series of Secondary Indicators, each providing a more specific focus on aspects of the Key Indicators. In all, the MIS contained about forty performance indicators.

Over the second half of the 1980s, the Government tried hard to promote the MIS as a management tool for use by local courts. However, it was obvious that the rather generalised nature of the annually produced information would always be of more value to the Government's scrutineering purposes than to the management role of magistrates' clerks, most of whose information requirements related more to present-day problems than to last year's performance. Nevertheless, most courts did their best, and after a few years and a great deal of grumbling, clerks began to take the annual data collection exercise more seriously. A number, indeed, developed their own data collection systems to provide more up-to-date information during, rather than just at the end of, the year. Then the Home Office began to encourage each court to set itself objectives to improve on the previous year's MIS performance. Later the objective-setting idea evolved into target setting, this time with the Home Office civil servants specifying what they thought might be realistic targets for each court, particularly with regard to improvement on the delay indicator. Thereafter, further efforts by the Government to promote the use of MIS by local courts proved unnecessary, for in 1992 the introduction of the cash-limited grant provided all the incentive that was needed. From then on, every court knew only too well that it had to improve its performance on all four Key Indicators, for these were the determinants of grant entitlement through the new distribution formula.

5.4.2 *Inspection and monitoring*

Even then, the search by government for better information on performance and for mechanisms to effect still greater accountability and improvement in performance on the part of local courts did not relent.

The White Paper (Lord Chancellor's Department, 1992c), which had contributed much to the process of organisational concentration, also included two other important proposals, both of direct relevance to the performance scrutiny theme.

First was the proposal to establish a Magistrates' Courts' Inspectorate. This was to be located within the Lord Chancellor's Department - the Chief Inspector being directly answerable to the Lord Chancellor - but at one remove from the section of the Department responsible for overseeing the administration of the courts. In many respects, the new Inspectorate would be akin to others which had existed for many years in probation services and the police, as well as in other public service fields outside the criminal justice area, for example, in fire and social services. As with all these counterparts, the Magistrates' Courts Inspectorate would carry out an annual programme of efficiency and effectiveness inspections, and would also undertake thematic inspections of certain aspects of the work and organisation of the courts. Like the other inspectorates, the aim was that it should play a significant role in the development and propagation of 'good practice' ideas and become the chief authority in the assessment of the performance of the sub-units (in this instance, the courts) and in advising the Lord Chancellor in this respect. A key point was that the role of the Magistrates' Courts Inspectorate would be confined to administrative and managerial matters, and that it would not have any responsibilities in relation to judicial functions of courts. Despite this limitation, the importance of the new body to future performance within the service was indicated by the fact that the Government also planned to provide the Lord Chancellor with statutory powers to intervene in the management of a local courts' committee area if the advice of the Inspectorate was of serious or consistent under-performance.

Second, the White Paper announced the intention to introduce changes in the appointment procedure and conditions of service of magistrates' clerks. These would have the effect of further emphasising performance scrutiny as a vehicle for enhanced accountability and curbed autonomy. In future, the appointment procedure for all magistrates' clerks and all the new chief justices' clerk posts would involve the screening of all candidates by the Lord Chancellor's Department (as was already the practice in the Home Office for chief constable and chief probation officer appointments). At the same time, all magistrates' clerks and the new chief justices' clerks would be placed on fixed term contracts, again with the terms of service to be laid down by the Lord Chancellor, and to include a performance related pay scheme. Thus no longer would local magistrates' courts' committees be able to exercise autonomy in the appointment of clerks and no longer would the clerks enjoy the privilege of being entirely responsible for the administration of their courts. Instead, their appointment would be subject to a process of scrutiny by the Lord Chancellor's Department, the performance of their organisations would be closely monitored by the Inspectorate, and their personal career futures would hinge upon gaining a satisfactory report in this respect.

5.5   IMPLICATIONS

The picture, then, which emerges from all this is of local magistrates' courts' management increasingly coming to operate in a 'command relationship' with the Lord Chancellor's Department. Indeed, seen in conjunction with the changes that had been wrought through the process of organisational concentration, it could be concluded that the structure had become essentially that of the Divisionalised Form (Mintzberg, 1983), although with the added ingredient of increasing standardisation of tasks and methods as well as scrutiny of outputs or performance. In effect, magistrates' courts had been nationalised, even though, formally, that recommendation in the Scrutiny report (Home Office, 1989a) had been rejected by the Government. What else, after all, might one deduce on learning of an absorbing little competition sponsored by the Lord Chancellor's Department in 1992 to devise a corporate identity logo for 'the magistrates' courts service' (MCS, as the winning entry proclaimed)? What else might one deduce from the effort similarly devoted to devising a single 'mission statement' for the service? What else might one deduce from the encouragement given by the Lord Chancellor's Department to all senior managers in magistrates' courts to attend the same management development programme in small groups over a period of several years? What else, indeed, might one deduce from the repeated reference by civil servants to 'the magistrates' courts service', as though it was a single entity, rather than 105, or just half that number of separately constituted magistrates' courts services?

Even if there was no deliberate intention to subvert 'local justice', it was clear that, at the very least, it was gradually being re-defined into something quite different. This would be something much more like the Crown Court (or the CPS, for that matter) which, of course, was already a national organisation, with a clear hierarchical structure connecting the most junior court assistant through a series of accountable (line management) relations with the Lord Chancellor. Indeed, a possible implication was that, in future, the distinction between the tiers of courts could be less obvious. With responsibility for the administration of both tiers now falling under one government department, it also became more likely that the next generation of new courts would be combined Crown Court and magistrates' court complexes. That, of course, would offer advantage in terms of the more efficient use of space. It would also serve to reduce some of the confusion frequently experienced by those having to attend one or other of the courts for the first time and who would be unfamiliar with the system. But it would also serve to weaken differentiation between the tiers of courts, between summary justice and the justice of the higher courts, and between lay justice and the justice dispensed by professionally qualified judges.

For many users of magistrates' courts - the defendants, witnesses, and applicants, as well as the solicitors, police, other professional parties and the magistrates themselves - the immediate and most obvious effect of the changes might simply have been an increased journey length to court where the local court-house had been closed. However, other possible short- and longer-term effects also required consideration. Might, for example, the closure of local courts and the amalgamation of Benches have an effect on criminality? Would the magistrates know the larger territories over which their new jurisdictions now extended sufficiently well to dispense justice as sensitively as before? Indeed, could they be as efficient as before if, for instance, in traffic or public order cases, more questions would have to be asked about the particular road junctions, visibility conditions or public houses and clubs where the alleged offences had taken place? Local knowledge, as every magistrate understood, was often a valuable aid to the work in the court-room; indeed it was arguably the fundamental currency of the local justice process. Without it, was there sufficient justification for sustaining a volunteer-based magistracy? Furthermore, was there any point in having a lower tier of courts at all if, as a result of the rationalisation of court-houses, most cases were now being heard in the same towns and cities where the Crown Court sat? Only time will tell in this period of volatile government policy-making in criminal justice.

CHAPTER 6

Pushing for efficiency

'Philistinism! We have not the expression in English. Perhaps we have not the word because we have so much of the thing.'
Matthew Arnold, 1884.

6.1 INTRODUCTION

In the preceding two chapters we have explored in turn how government strategies aimed at enhancing accountability and reducing idiosyncrasy affected the organisation and administration of justice. In this chapter we take our exploration of the consequences of managerialism a stage further and consider the effects, particularly of the pursuit of greater efficiency, upon the form of justice itself. Efficiency and productivity were clearly objectives right at the centre of the Government's strategy from the early 1980s onwards. However, those objectives were to take criminal justice in directions that were not always fully considered in advance with the result that some of the effects were unanticipated. Accordingly we focus here on changes and trends that were, arguably, more the side-effects and consequences, than the intentions, of government strategy.

In recent years several criminologists and jurists have commented upon the way in which the concern with managerialist values and with the quest for more efficient processes for handling cases has affected justice. In a paper to the British Criminological Society Conference, for example, Jones (1991, p.28) refers to:

... a cutting back of due process rights and a new philistinism in criminal justice, in which the goals of economy, efficiency and effectiveness prevail over substantive justice ends.'

Jones (1993, p. 196) also comments that:

> 'there is now in the ascendant an ideology which wholly legitimates the pursuit of administratively rational ends over substantive justice goals.'

In similar vein Green (1992, p. 19) refers to the effects of a cash-limited grant in magistrates' courts, by stating that:

> 'The product of justice will therefore be increasingly disregarded, and the budgetary rewards will go to courts with the efficiency of the sausage machine.'

The argument that managerialism has affected not only the organisation of courts and their administration but also the nature of the justice dispensed has been developed most cogently by Heydebrand & Seron (1990). They have referred to the 'rationalisation of justice' to describe various changes which they have charted with regard to judicial administration in the USA. The argument has been that changes there have taken the form of increasing reliance on new forms of judicial administration with profound consequences for the process of justice and for the role of the courts. There are clearly many parallels between the 'rationalisation' trends which Heydebrand & Seron have described across the Atlantic and trends now taking place in Britain, even though the jurisdictions of the courts and judicial-organisational structures in the two countries differ significantly.

Accordingly it is instructive to consider in a little more detail exactly what is implied by the notion of the 'rationalisation of justice' (Heydebrand & Seron, 1990). Above all, the trend to which they have referred involves a change to more 'technocratic' methods of case-handling. Particularly significant here has been a decline in the process of formal justice as provided under the adjudicative and adversarial (or inquisitorial) court systems and a corresponding increase in the use of alternative, more informal, ways of dealing with offenders.

Five key characteristics of this technocratic and rationalised form of justice have been identified by Heydebrand & Seron as follows:

1. *Respect for a business orientation*, by which they refer to the adoption of 'scientific management' principles and the introduction of business methods and management into court administration.

2. *Decline in judicial service orientation*, by which they refer to a shift having taken place from a domination of the courts by a professional elite of judges and from an emphasis on 'due process' to a domination by an administrative hierarchy, with a new emphasis on the achievement of results in terms of speedy case completion.
3. *Legitimation of court administration*, by which they refer to the new focus on administrative procedures and on how to simplify them, which has reached the point where they have begun to affect judicial outcomes.
4. *Decline of independence*, by which they refer to the process under which the courts are gradually becoming incorporated into the broader system of public administration.
5. *Decline of autonomy of the judiciary*, by which they refer to the gradual erosion of the separation of powers between the judicial and executive branches of the state.

The main driving force for such changes has been the implementation of managerialist values, particularly the desire to enhance efficiency and to facilitate a more economical use of resources. A prime aim has usually been to achieve increased flexibility within the system, for which technical solutions, such as the employment of computers to speed up information processing and retrieval in court administration, have seemed attractive. At the same time, the search for greater flexibility would lead to much of the traditional formality and rigidity of legal process being seen in rather negative terms. Encouragement would thus be given to their replacement by more informal practices with more loosely defined rules and boundaries. For example, greater flexibility might be sought in the ways in which cases are categorised for jurisdictional purposes because this could increase options with regard to the organisation of hearings. An example of this in England & Wales was the re-definition of certain previously categorised 'indictable' (serious) offences as 'triable either way' following the recommendations of an inter-departmental committee (James Committee, 1975). This meant that they could now be decided by magistrates in the lower courts (where costs of hearings are cheaper) rather than being automatically committed to the higher courts, as in the past, for hearing before a jury and professional judge.

Similarly, increased flexibility might be sought in relation to working agreements between courts and other agencies in criminal justice. Here, for example, encouragement might be given to the practice of having requests for adjournments decided by the magistrates' clerk rather than by a member of the Bench in the court-room, providing that the prosecution and defence are in agreement.

More significantly, increased flexibility might also be sought through a shift of emphasis in the judicial decision-making process from a formal, essentially adjudicative approach, in which 'due process' is the uppermost consideration, to one involving greater reliance on informal approaches such as 'pre-trial' conferences and 'reviews', 'plea bargaining', and 'administrative penalties' as alternatives to formal proceedings in the court-room. This shift of emphasis would, of course, imply some transfer of responsibility for decision making away from the judiciary to other agencies. In so doing, prosecution in the courts would come to be seen as just one option in a wider system for dealing with offenders, and the judiciary as just one part of a larger system of law enforcement (see, for example, our discussion in Chapter 3 about the Systems approach).

That, then, is the essence of the argument about the push for efficiency in criminal justice. But what have been the particular effects and how might these be judged in terms of benefits and disbenefits? In this chapter we will explore some of the consequences of the strategy that are apparent in criminal justice in England & Wales today. In particular we will consider in turn three broad categories of pressure which might be regarded to have contributed to a change in the nature of the justice being dispensed:

1. pressures for alternatives to prosecution;
2. pressures for guilty pleas; and
3. pressures to complete cases more quickly.

So far as the first category is concerned, we will explore the shift which has taken place from adjudicative to administrative justice, illustrated, for example, in the increasing use of cautioning and administrative penalties for minor offences as more economical alternatives to prosecution through the courts. Then turning to the second category, we will consider various court procedures and practices, such as sentencing discounts and plea bargaining. These, it is sometimes argued, have the effect of encouraging more pleas of guilt and therefore reducing the number of resource-intensive trials that have to be held. Finally, we will investigate the effects of cash-limits and particularly the attempts to speed up the throughput of cases, for example, by new, more restrictive, policies in relation to adjournments and time limits for case preparation.

6.2 PRESSURES FOR ALTERNATIVES TO PROSECUTION

6.2.1 Cautioning

In Chapter 1, we touched upon the trend away from formal prosecution in the courts for cases of a comparatively minor nature. This trend has been evident in the increasing use of 'cautioning' by the police. Cautioning has been extensively used in England & Wales in minor cases involving offenders under the age of 17. A landmark in this context was the implementation of the Children & Young Persons Act, 1969. This encouraged cautioning for young offenders and, since implementation of the Act, the cautioning rate for juveniles has risen markedly, to the extent that by 1986 six out of ten of those under the age of 17 who were apprehended received cautions instead of being prosecuted. The policy of cautioning has subsequently been extended to adults, and a Home Office circular on the subject, issued to the police in 1983, precipitated its use for those aged 17 and over. As a result the cautioning rate for adults rose from about 4 per cent in 1983 to 10 per cent in 1986. In the early 1990s, cautioning rates rose again as local police prosecution policies further changed in favour of cautioning, largely because of the perceived time-savings involved.

What of the effects of this trend? Here, as Ashworth (1988) has pointed out:

> 'there is no doubt that this trend reduces the costs of the system as a whole, since it avoids court proceedings; whether it is economical in terms of police expenditure seems less clear, since some decisions to caution have to be referred higher in the police hierarchy than decisions to prosecute.' (Ashworth, 1988, p. 50)

As to the effectiveness of cautioning policy, several studies of juvenile offenders suggest that those cautioned are no more likely to be caught re-offending than those convicted in the courts. However, so far as the adult group is concerned, little research has yet been conducted which compares recidivism rates between those cautioned and those prosecuted. Partly, no doubt, the lack of government-sponsored research in this field reflects the view that the policy was justifiable by its cost savings alone and by the fact that no indication had been given by the police of any widespread loss of crime control. On that basis, cautioning might well be perceived as a sensible alternative to prosecution in the courts and one with the added advantage of providing a speedy response to crime without the potential humiliation and publicity normally associated with a court hearing. On the other hand, there is a potential disbenefit of cautioning in that victims are denied the opportunity to see justice being done (since cautioning normally takes place in the privacy of an interview room at a police station).

6.2.2 Vehicle defect rectification schemes

The shift from prosecution for minor offences to alternative approaches, or from adjudicative to administrative justice, as many authors describe it (Ashworth, 1988; Heydebrand & Seron, 1990), has also been evident in the introduction around the country of 'vehicle defect rectification schemes'. Here, motorists with minor vehicle faults, such as faulty lights or tyres, are offered the opportunity to rectify them and present their vehicles for inspection at police stations within a set number of days, thereby escaping prosecution. In this way the motorist is given the chance to comply with the law, while the police, the Crown Prosecution Service and the courts are saved work. At the same time, with the repairs effected, public safety on the highways is enhanced. There is also the further potential advantage that, without a fine penalty from the courts, many motorists are more likely to be able to afford to have their vehicle defects rectified. Moreover, since the kinds of infringements of the law which are treated in this way involve no third parties, there is no' issue about victims being denied access to the justice process.

6.2.3 Fixed penalty procedures

Then there is the alternative to prosecution of fixed (or administrative) penalties. In October 1986, implementation of Part III of the Transport Act, 1982, brought about a significant extension in the use of such penalties in England & Wales for minor road traffic offences. Before then only a few offences, such as illegal parking, could be dealt with in this way. However, the new legislation allowed for their use in some two hundred other minor traffic offences. Police officers were assigned the responsibility of deciding whether or not to issue a fixed penalty ticket to those whom they believed to have committed one or more of the newly included offences. Where the officers considered a fixed penalty appropriate, the alleged offender would be invited to pay the standard fee (to the court office within a given period of weeks) or request a court hearing to challenge the allegation.

Since the extension of fixed penalty provisions in 1986, many people have elected to pay fixed penalties and, as a result, have saved the magistrates' courts a great deal of time. On the other hand, additional administrative time has been necessary for the police in processing all the tickets and for the magistrates' courts administrative staff, who are charged with collecting the payments and with taking enforcement actions if the fines are unpaid.

The main argument in favour of extending the use of fixed penalties in 1986 was that most of the minor road traffic offences to be made eligible for this approach were not serious enough to warrant the time and resources involved in a court hearing. The argument was also that the fixed penalty could be more appropriate since it would be an immediate sanction rather than one imposed some weeks later when the case finally came to court. At the same time, it was felt that fixed penalties were unlikely to be any less effective in terms of law enforcement. Moreover, some argued, the use of fixed penalties might even improve public respect for the law, if it was seen that disproportionate public financial resources were not being consumed by the prosecution of minor matters (Ashworth, 1988). Ashworth has also suggested that the approach could sensibly be extended to other routine offences, such as minor thefts from shops. While recognising the disadvantage of 'flat rate' penalties in so far as no allowance is made for 'ability to pay', the conclusion reached is that:

'... as a proportionate and economical way of dealing with minor crimes, fixed penalty systems deserve close scrutiny.' (Ashworth, 1988, p. 50)

This view has also been supported by the Director of Public Prosecutions (DPP) who has suggested that common offences such as failing to have a valid vehicle licence, as well as shoplifting, might be treated in this way (Mills, 1992). The DPP has also lent her support to the extended use of cautioning, including the idea of 'Caution Plus', whereby a penalty might be imposed at the same time as the caution. For example, she has suggested that shoplifters might be cautioned and asked to pay a money penalty to the stores from which they had stolen in return for avoiding prosecution and criminal records.

6.2.4 From adjudicative to administrative justice

Undoubtedly the strongest motivation for such fixed penalty procedures, as indeed for cautioning and vehicle defect rectification schemes, has been the economic one, namely that time is saved for the courts, prosecution and police. However, other advantages have also been stressed. For example, for many offenders it has proved a relief to have had done with the matter immediately, to have accepted the punishment and been able to avoid any further inconvenience and humiliation associated with a court appearance or possible exposure in the press. To that extent, fixed penalties, cautioning and so on have represented more humane responses to offending. Moreover, those who have protested their innocence have never been denied their right to plead 'not guilty' and to have the case heard in the magistrates' court.

On the other hand, the counter-argument is that the procedures 'short-circuit' the due process of justice by shifting the decision-making responsibility from the courts to the police or other authorities (unless the alleged offender elects to challenge the accusation in court). The procedures have also been criticised on the grounds that they are likely to encourage pleas of guilt simply because of the attraction of escaping formal prosecution and a court hearing. Whereas traditionally the legal system has been founded on the presumption of innocence until proved guilty, the fixed penalty and cautioning procedures, in effect, provide the converse, namely that alleged offenders are invited to plead guilty (with an implicit presumption being made here by the police) but have the right to prove their innocence (before a court).

Whatever the merits and demerits of such processes from a judicial perspective, their acceptance by Parliament and their increasing adoption within criminal justice reflects a perceived need to reduce some of the pressures on the prosecution and court processes. That was a point we made clearly in Chapter 1, and we emphasise it here as crucial to our argument about some of the consequences of the new focus on managerialist values. Without the pressures of rising workloads and tight resourcing, we assert, such procedures would not have been considered appropriate since they offer little improvement in terms of justice, except perhaps with regard to more convenience and humanity for the accused. But those advantages could have been achieved within a traditional judicial setting had the will been there to institute, for example, appointment systems for hearings and to conduct proceedings in a less formal and less humbling manner. In any case, there has always been a school of opinion that regarded the inconvenience and humiliating experience of a court appearance as an appropriate part of the punishment - the Status Passage model (King, 1981).

With less work to handle as a result of the shift from traditional adjudicative justice to greater reliance on administrative procedures, the court organisations would, of course, be smaller. Their status as administrative units would also be correspondingly less - organisational size is nearly always a relevant factor here. On the other hand they would have benefited, at least in terms of saved time, by the alternative procedures. But it was not at their instigation. Indeed, so far as cautioning was concerned, many magistrates expressed grave reservations about the idea of the police dealing with more offenders in this way rather than bringing them before the courts. There was also concern from the Bench that cautioning would prove ineffective in deterring further offending and that many adolescents were accumulating what were perceived to be quite dreadful records of criminality and yet were escaping the sanctions of the court. The view of many magistrates, at least, was that cautioning was too soft an option and that bringing the offender before a court, even for the first offence, was likely to prove a more effective deterrent to future criminal behaviour.

Despite such views, and emphasising the extent to which the controlling influence of the courts had diminished, repeated cautioning of offenders continued to be practised by the police. It was an example of the 'rationalisation' process to which Heydebrand & Seron (1990) referred. It illustrated how traditional judicial responses to criminality were being encroached upon by the pressures of administrative convenience. Moreover, the favouring of cautioning as a policy by the police, even though there was little evidence to suggest that it was any more effective in reducing recidivism than prosecutions, indicates that the advantages of administrative convenience and efficiency to the agencies involved was the first priority. Whatever their shortcomings from the viewpoint of justice or deterrence, the various alternatives to prosecution fitted well with the new culture of more business-like disposition of cases, increased productivity and smooth-functioning administration. Broadly speaking, the arrangements suited the police and the prosecution authorities, as indeed they suited the administrative departments of the courts. Thus, having moved significantly further in these directions during the 1980s, it would be hard to imagine the clock being turned back, at least so long as the sigma values of efficiency and parsimony held sway (Hood, 1991).

6.3 PRESSURES FOR GUILTY PLEAS

A second symptom of the push for greater efficiency with implications for the nature of justice being dispensed has been the increasing tendency of courts to countenance procedures which, like fixed penalties, could amount to incentives for the accused to plead guilty. Over the years many commentators have remarked upon the pressures on defendants, particularly in the magistrates' courts, to plead guilty (see for example, Carlen, 1976; McBarnet, 1981). Indeed, some have tended to regard the lower courts largely as 'the guilty plea courts', a title which reflects not just the kinds of pressures over plea that we will shortly elaborate upon or the reality that the vast majority of cases heard there do involve a guilty plea, but also the long-standing perception of magistrates as being rather conviction-driven. What is implied here is that many are inclined to believe the police evidence rather than that of the defendant. Accordingly, more cynical observers would argue, there is little point in contesting a case in the lower courts, and if the case is one that can alternatively be heard at the Crown Court (a 'triable either way' case), there would be merit in electing trial before a judge and jury to ensure a better chance of an acquittal. In fact, the statistics hardly support this perception since, on average, magistrates find about half those who contest cases before them not guilty and this is roughly the same as the proportion who are acquitted in the Crown Court (Hedderman & Moxon, 1992).

But our concern in this chapter is less with long-standing perceptions about the justice delivered in the upper and lower courts and more with pressures to plead guilty that might perhaps be linked with the trend towards managerialist values in the way courts operate. Here we particularly focus on three practices: that of accepting the non-appearance of the accused in certain cases where a guilty plea has previously been submitted in writing; that of offering discounts on sentences for those pleading guilty; and that of plea bargaining.

6.3.1 Guilty pleas in writing

In England & Wales, a large category of offences can these days be prosecuted in the courts, without the accused persons (or their solicitor) being present, providing a plea of guilt has been submitted in advance. Under the Magistrates' Courts Act, 1980, a large category of relatively minor offences, again mainly relating to traffic matters, was made subject to this procedure in the magistrates' courts. The cases are scheduled for hearing on particular dates, the prosecution evidence is presented, often by the court clerk, any letter of mitigation from the accused is read, and the magistrates will then decide the size of the penalty, in cases of speeding, usually on a standard basis (of so much per unit in excess of the legal limit).

In comparison with fixed penalty procedures, because such adjudications are conducted in a court-room setting by magistrates, they retain at least the basic elements of traditional judicial decision making. But, of course, there are efficiency advantages in not having the accused present in terms of saving the time otherwise required by ushers to find and escort each party to the particular court-room and dock; of not having to listen to (frequently lengthy) personal accounts of the alleged events and (often extended) attempts at mitigation; of the Bench not having to retire to consider what sentence to impose; and not having to provide a homily and explanation for the decision. Time is also saved in not having to explain the administrative arrangements for paying fines because the procedures can be documented with the court order and dispatched by post to the convicted party.

The advantages in case-flow management terms would be significant. Under the 1980 Magistrates' Courts Act (MCA) procedures, a court might be able to dispose of, perhaps, one hundred cases in an afternoon, compared with, say, only ten in the morning when attendance of the accused parties was required. MCA courts (or 'paper courts' as they are often entitled by magistrates' courts personnel) may be very dull, but they certainly score well from the perspective of productivity! However, the question is whether the invitation to the accused to choose between submitting a plea of guilt with no requirement to attend court, and contesting the case but having to go to court to do so, amounts to an incentive to plead guilty. What is more, another question ought to be asked, namely whether the absence from court (and therefore exemption from the element of punishment by ordeal of attendance) would have been deemed acceptable, but for the priority afforded to speeding up the throughput of cases. If so, why should more serious cases not be dealt with in this way as well? Where is the line to be drawn?

6.3.2 Sentencing discounts for guilty pleas

Concerns have similarly been expressed about the implied incentive to plead guilty associated with another common practice within the courts, namely that of providing discounts on sentences for those submitting guilty pleas. According to Sprack (1992), the expectation of such sentencing discounts provides one reason why so many defendants plead guilty. If so, this practice, too, may well be viewed as a symptom of a 'rationalisation' of justice and as offering advantage to the courts in minimising the number of trials requiring to be arranged and conducted.

Although there has long been a reluctance by the Bench to give official recognition to the principle of sentencing discounts for guilty pleas, the practice, as every legal practitioner and most persistent offenders know, has been widespread. In the Crown Court, a guilty plea typically results in a discount in the length of a custodial sentence, typically of between a fifth and a third. It may, on occasions, even result in a lesser type of sentence. For example, in *R* v *Hollyman* (1979), two out of three co-defendants pleaded guilty and each received suspended sentences of two months; the third defendant, however, pleaded not guilty and received an immediate sentence of three months' imprisonment, even though his case was similar.

In 1992, the Bar Council (the representative body for barristers) proposed that the practice of offering discounts for guilty pleas should be formalised and made explicit. The proposal immediately won the support of the DPP and a year later was endorsed by the Royal Commission on Criminal Justice (Runciman, 1993). A strong argument here was that discounts were justified partly as a reward for saving the court time and money, and partly for sparing the victim from the witness box. A further argument was based on the theory that someone who shows contrition (which the plea of guilt is taken to imply) does not deserve to be punished so much as one who does not.

Such arguments would tend to suggest that the earlier a guilty plea is submitted, the greater should be the level of discount. This is because notification of a guilty plea at the first opportunity would save the court having to reserve time for a trial, and would save the victim the anxiety associated with expecting to give evidence. Arguably it would also follow that a greater degree of contrition would be demonstrated by an early acknowledgement of guilt than were a guilty plea to be submitted at the last minute on the day of a planned trial.

Although such scaled discounts have not been evident in practice to date, the justification for a scheme of this kind might seem strong from a managerialist perspective. Indeed besides being recommended by the Royal Commission on Criminal Justice, the idea formed one of the recommendations of the Scrutiny report of magistrates' courts to which we referred in Chapter 5 (Home Office, 1989a). Here a particular problem which the report's authors were addressing was that created by changes of plea from 'not guilty' to 'guilty' being made after court-room time had been scheduled and after magistrates and staff had been rostered for a trial. In this context, the study concluded that:

> 'It is clearly not practicable to prevent or sanction late pleas nor would one want to insist on a trial if a guilty plea is entered, however late. However, it has long been a practice of the courts to reduce the sentence on a defendant who pleads guilty on the grounds that this reflects remorse, spares witnesses from giving evidence and reduces the burden on the courts. We understand that the Court of Appeal in R v Hollington & Evans explicitly approved a reduction in discount for a late plea. We therefore recommend that courts should make it clear that late pleas will attract a lesser discount.' (Home Office, 1989a, Vol II, para 1.32)

But other views are also to be heard on sentencing discounts. For example, Liberty, the campaigning group for justice, has long regarded them as unjust. In evidence to the Royal Commission on Criminal Justice it was suggested that:

> '... it is wholly improper for defendants to be penalised for exercising their right to put the prosecution to proof.' (Liberty, 1991, p. 46)

Similarly, in a letter to a national newspaper by way of response to the Bar Council's proposals for a formal system of sentencing discounts, the campaigning organisation Justice pointed out that:

> 'In their desire to deal with rising costs, the Bar Council and the DPP appear to have ignored the defendant's right to be presumed innocent. The basis of the proposal is to avoid trials collapsing at the last minute when a defendant pleads guilty, by increasing the pressure on the defendant so that he or she cracks at an earlier stage. It is our view that the proposals will put unacceptable pressure on innocent and vulnerable defendants to plead guilty at an early stage for fear of a longer sentence. . Contrary to widely held belief, innocent defendants do plead guilty. A defendant who is confronted with strong circumstantial evidence, identification evidence, and/or a contested confession, and is then told that testing the evidence may cost him/her an extra year or more in jail may well decide not to take the risk... It is right that a defendant should be properly informed about the likely sentence, and it is right that the defendant's attitude to the crime should be taken into account when the judge considers the sentence, but a thirty per cent reduction in exchange for a guilty plea at committal is not based on these principles - merely on a desire to reduce costs'. (Wadham, 1992)

Whatever the justice arguments about sentencing discounts for guilty pleas, the recommendations of the Royal Commission and of the Scrutiny report sit happily with the new managerialist values. In that respect, as with the alternatives to prosecution, the strongest case for discounts would be the contribution that they might make towards fewer trials and therefore speedier disposition of the cases. But that means that they must be viewed as another symptom of the push for greater efficiency and of the trend under which the administrative advantages of maximising the number of guilty pleas comes to outweigh most doubts about the justness of the practice.

6.3.3 Plea bargaining

It has not, however, only been through such discounts that the pressure to obtain guilty pleas has been applied. In addition there is the more controversial, though related, issue of 'plea bargaining'. This is the process by which deals may be struck between the prosecution and the defence, with or without the involvement or approval of the court.

Typically such a deal would involve the prosecution, on learning that a 'not guilty' plea was to be expected to the initial charge, agreeing to press a less serious one in return for a plea of guilt. The practice clearly involves questionable judiciousness, and for that reason has been the subject of controversy for some time in this country.

There are strong contrasts, in this respect, with the position in the USA (where plea bargaining has long been accepted as an integral part of the criminal justice process). In Britain, unlike in the USA, the convention is that it is not part of the prosecution's role to make suggestions about sentence. Thus there is less opportunity for institut-ionalised plea bargaining. Whereas in the USA the vast majority of guilty pleas follow some negotiation or deal between the prosecution and the defence, and whereas the Supreme Court has endorsed and encouraged the process, on this side of the Atlantic, the attitude, at least among the senior judiciary, has remained rather ambivalent.

> 'Plea bargaining has no place in the English criminal law...In our law the prosecution is not heard on sentence. That is a matter for the court, after considering what has to be said on behalf of an accused person.' (Lord Scarman in *R* v *Atkinson* (1978))

Such sentiments from the judiciary are not entirely surprising. After all, the judge's reputation for impartiality could be seriously brought into question were any indication to be given that the Bench was party to bargains being struck between the prosecution and defence, if only because these could imply that the judge had already presumed the guilt of the defendant. But while the practice of plea bargaining has generally not been condoned by the judiciary - indeed many judges do not even acknowledge that the practice exists - the reality is that bargains of some form or other are routinely struck in the criminal justice process in England & Wales. For example, it is commonplace for the prosecution to 'offer no evidence' on certain disputed counts but to accept a plea of guilt to the lesser of alternative charges, in what amounts to plea bargaining. A key factor here would be the prosecution's desire to obtain a conviction, in pursuit of which the preference may be for a lesser, but safer, charge.

This strategy is also often adopted to increase the chances of a case being decided in the magistrates' courts (assuming the lesser charge is a summary offence or one which is 'triable either way'). As indicated earlier, this saves money, since the cost of completing a case at the magistrates' courts is a fraction of that at the Crown Court (a conviction at the magistrates' courts for criminal damage was assessed in 1988 to cost, on average, £147, while at the Crown Court, the average cost was £414). The prosecution's tactic of waiving charges of, say, causing actual bodily harm (an indictable offence) and accepting instead charges of common assault (a summary offence) in return for a guilty plea is certainly routinely practised. However, it raises questions as to whether defendants' interests are being compromised, particularly if they are being denied the opportunity for trial by jury at the Crown Court.

Plea bargaining, it has been suggested, also takes place at the Crown Court immediately prior to, or during, a trial (White, 1991). This too has proved controversial, and there has been a steady flow of cases over the years in which defendants have appealed against conviction on the grounds that unreasonable pressure had been placed upon them in relation to their plea.

The frequency and nature of plea bargaining was highlighted in research conducted by Baldwin & McConville (1977) who found that 'hinted bargains' or unspoken understandings in this context were more commonplace than had previously been supposed. The research, which was based on over 100 cases listed at Birmingham Crown Court and in which late changes of plea were made, revealed that in less than one third of the cases could it be confidently asserted that there had been no deal or no pressure in that direction. In some 18 per cent of cases the plea appeared to be the direct result of an offer having been made and accepted by the defendant. In a further 13 per cent of cases it was assumed that bargains had been struck (though the assumption was not necessarily correct). Most significant, however, was the fact that in nearly 40 per cent of cases, the defendants indicated that they had changed their pleas because of pressure from their own defence barristers even though no 'offer' of a lesser sentence had been made in return. The other interesting conclusion to be drawn from the research was that a number of the defendants whose cases had featured in the research appeared to have been ill-advised to plead guilty and might well have been acquitted had their cases been heard before a jury, as they might have preferred. This, at least, was the conclusion of independent legal analysts whom the researchers subsequently invited to assess the cases.

While the process of plea bargaining, then, is not as explicit in the English & Welsh context as in the USA, the reality is that deals are regularly reached, albeit usually in covert, 'behind the scenes', fashion.

What is more, the findings from Baldwin & McConville's research suggest that the deals are often struck more for the benefit of the court and the other criminal justice agencies than for the defendant. This is congruent with the Bureaucratic model (King 1981). In this context, plea bargaining serves to ensure a smooth flow of cases in court by reducing the number of trials. Moreover, at least so far as the Crown Court is concerned, a principal motivation for deals to be sought is, as White (1991) suggests, the desire of counsel to avoid gaining the reputation among the judiciary for being 'difficult'. At the end of the day, after all, appointment to the Bench may well depend on showing a co-operative attitude. Similarly, in the lower courts, although the magistrates would rarely be involved in pre-trial reviews or in other settings where plea bargaining might take place, a significant motivation factor would again be the desire of regularly-appearing advocates to maintain the respect of the Bench, the magistrates' clerk and the prosecution, perhaps to enhance their chances of favourable consideration on future occasions.

Managerialist values within the courts' organisation may not, of course, be directly responsible for the existence of plea bargaining. After all, it is more likely to be the prosecution and defence that would actively seek deals. Indirectly, however, the court probably plays a significant part in so far as it usually countenances those prosecution and defence strategies that result in speedier dispositions. Indeed, there seems to be an element of 'returned favours' about plea bargaining. The court welcomes smoother case-flow and speedier dispositions wherever possible. Advocates can help in this respect through the deals which they seek, and are predisposed to do so in order to sustain a favourable reputation with the court. In terms of our analysis of the push for efficiency and its impact on justice, the existence of plea bargaining provides another example of administrative and professional convenience replacing due process.

6.4 PRESSURES TO COMPLETE CASES MORE QUICKLY

Managerialist values also lie at the root of many of the new policies and practices with regard to the scheduling of cases in the courts. Again the aim is increased efficiency and the speeding up of 'throughput'. In this respect, during recent years many courts have sought to rein back on the granting of adjournments or on the time allowed to agencies to complete their various tasks, such as initial file preparation by the police, preparation for trial by the prosecution and defence advocates, and the preparation of pre-sentence reports by the probation officers (we shall return to such policies in Chapters 7 and 8). Ostensibly, the reason given at many courts for adopting a tougher stance in this context has been the moral one of 'justice delayed is justice denied'. But, for the most part, it has been another, more managerially inspired pressure that has provided the real incentive to act. In particular, for many magistrates' courts, it has been the introduction of a cash-limited grant regime that provided the raison d'être for initiatives to speed up the disposition of cases, both through new, more rigorous, policies in relation to adjournment requests, and through other practices in relation to the scheduling of hearings.

6.4.1 Cash-limited grant and policy on adjournments

This assertion is largely endorsed by the fact that, before 1992 and the new cash-limited grant regime, most courts seemed generally resigned to accept the fact that, with apparently increasing frequency, prosecutors and defence solicitors would arrive at court for a hearing only to request a postponement for one, two or more weeks to allow them to complete their preparations. The practice was not welcomed, particularly by many lay magistrates who had become thoroughly frustrated at having so often to spend the better part of a whole day in the court-room without completing many, if any, cases, simply because so much of the business consisted of acceding to requests for adjournments. But it was generally accepted as an inevitable modern-day reality. Due process, after all, demanded that adequate time be allowed for the prosecution and defence to prepare their cases, and it would seem unfair in most instances to deny the lawyers the opportunity to do a thorough job. In any case, it was surely not the prosecutor's fault that the local police service, being hard-pressed with other work, had been slow to prepare the relevant case files. Nor surely was it the defence solicitors' fault that so many defendants were unreliable and slow to seek legal advice, therefore leaving their representatives with little time in which to investigate the allegations thoroughly and conduct their interviews with the accused and with any witnesses. In the interests of justice, requests for adjournments must be granted!

But with a cash-limited grant it all began to be seen rather differently. Suddenly it mattered to the court far more that cases were completed as quickly as possible, because a key factor in the formula by which the total government grant available would be distributed was the number of completed cases (weighted for different types as explained in Chapter 5). That meant that courts now had a direct incentive (the prospect of an additional share of grant) to maximise the number of cases completed, particularly the more serious ones - the ones most likely to be subject to adjournments.

Most magistrates' courts therefore began to rethink their strategies and policies. At Bench meetings up and down the country, the message about the imperative of prompt completions of cases was preached. Monitoring systems were established and some magistrates' clerks began to talk about their workloads more in terms of 'points' (five points for each indictable case completed, two points for a summary case, and so on - these being the MIS weightings) than as human interest stories.

Inevitably there were implications for justice. From now on, with the principle being that budgetary rewards would go to the courts which proved the most efficient in completing their cases, the pressure would be on each magistrates' clerk and each Bench to do better than other courts in reducing costs per case, most obviously by increasing throughput rates. The magistrates' clerks who wished to protect (let alone augment) their resources (such as staff and equipment budgets) would have to consider very carefully, for example,

'... how the pace of the Bench's decision-making with respect to legal aid, adjourning, remanding, venue, verdict, and sentencing might be accelerated.' (Green, 1992, p. 19)

6.4.2 Strategies to speed up case completions

For the tactically minded magistrates' clerk, as Green (1992) suggests, the purpose from now on would be to reduce to a minimum the complexities and time-consuming processes of the court. First and foremost, the aim would be to reduce the number of 'not guilty' pleas and to reduce or simplify mitigation. This, in turn, would recommend the pursuit of strategies such as discouraging applications for legal aid, for example, by insisting on meticulous documentary proof of income and expenditure and extracting maximum contributions; and refusing all applications where the decisions could not be appealed against, thereby reducing the number of trials and adjournments. Then there would be the longer-term strategy of influencing magistrates through training and in other settings to remand wherever possible on unconditional bail (to save the time involved in hearing the prosecutor argue for a remand in custody or the defence for remand on bail). Similarly, influence might be brought to bear to encourage larger discounts for guilty pleas and, in sentencing, to avoid custodial sentences, because of the extra consideration and time involved; to encourage 'tariff sentencing' (sentencing according to pre-determined scales) - which requires little or no thought; and to discourage the Bench from retiring from the court-room whenever possible (thereby almost inevitably reducing the opportunities for the 'winger' magistrates to contribute effectively to the decisions announced by the chairperson). The tactically minded magistrates' clerks would perhaps also be pressing the Bench to sentence with smaller fines, in view of the fact that this would increase the likelihood that they would be paid (another factor affecting the cash-limited grant formula). They might also press for acceptance of the lowest possible weekly instalments of fines on the same principle.

Stand-down adjournments
Would such strategies and tactics find their way into everyday reality in the magistrates' courts? Certainly so far as adjournments were concerned, the signs were there of pressures to save time resulting in corner-cutting practices. Here, for example, one practice adopted at many courts was to reschedule cases for which adjournments were requested for a later hearing on the same day. This practice of 'stand-downs', as they are called, seemed ideal from the courts' viewpoint in so far as the parties gained at least some of the extra time which they had requested, while the court avoided the extra administrative task of re-scheduling cases to different days and obtained the benefits of speedier completions. However, defence solicitors perceived the practice very differently. They regarded it as simply not being in the interests of justice to restrict the defence to a time limit of a couple of hours or so, and to expect the defence case to be prepared at court where there are seldom either adequate facilities or the appropriate ambience in which to take proper instructions from clients. As for the prosecuting solicitors, they too frequently found the practice of 'stand-downs' an unsatisfactory

alternative to their requests for adjournments. But with the meter of cash-limited grant ticking away in the background, such arguments must have seemed fairly incidental when set against the court's own desire to complete the cases quickly. It was another example of managerialist values, particularly the push for efficiency (which underpinned the imposition by government of cash-limited grant), appearing to undermine the due process of justice.

6.5 JUDICIAL INDEPENDENCE AND JUSTICE UNDER THREAT?

In the wake of cash-limiting lay the prospect of government-inspired reforms to the structure and framework of accountabilities of the magistrates' courts (Lord Chancellor's Department, 1992c). Here, as we saw in Chapter 5, one of the Government's intentions was that the accountability of magistrates' clerks should in future be more explicitly linked to the Lord Chancellor's Department through such mechanisms as fixed term contracts, performance related pay and by the increased involvement of the Department in the appointment process. Concern was expressed that such changes would put at risk the independence of the lay judiciary in so far as magistrates' clerks would in future be under greater pressure to act as their 'parent' executive government department might expect than as the local Bench, to which they had traditionally been accountable, might wish.

Conceiving magistrates' clerks of the future under these conditions as but servants of a multi-faceted executive, Green (1992) has speculated about the undermining of justice in the magistrates' courts in the following withering scenario:

'There will be many ways in which justices' clerks can use the influence they have with their magistrates to assist the executive compromise the rights of defendants and members of the public, and render sterile an oath which requires that decisions be made without fear or favour to, inter alia, the executive.

"Speaking as your clerk", they might say, "I would advise you to grant legal aid, were it not that as Lord Chancellor I must think of the cost to the Legal Aid Board. Or to commit the accused for trial or sentence, were

I not aware, as the Chancellor, that the local Crown Court is too busy. Or that you fix a trial for hearing in 21 days, were it not that as Attorney-General I wish the CPS to have 8 weeks for preparation of the case. Or that you fix the hearing for 8 weeks hence, were it not that as Home Secretary I cannot allow the Chief Constable to incur the expense of a police witness on a rest day. Or that you try the accused, were it not that as Attorney-General I recognise a binding over to be the cheaper course. Or that you should order the prosecutor to pay wasted costs, were it not for the embarrassment this would cause me as Court Manager when I next chair the Court User Group. Or that you order a pre-sentence report to be prepared within two weeks were it not that as Home Secretary I require four. Or that you commit the accused to prison, were it not that as Court Manager I could not take the risk, by increasing the court's percentage of custodial sentences, or of disqualifying myself when as Lord Chancellor I consider the renewal of my contract." (Green, 1992, p. 21)

How likely might such a picture become? Could the interests of justice be thus compromised and blurred by the priorities of the executive? The point here, of course, is not so much about whether the intentions of the Government were to create such a threat to the independence of the judiciary as that the Government's proposed accountability reforms created a structure that would be susceptible to the transmission of executive power.

Moreover, as Green (1992) has also pointed out to those who might tend to regard all this as mere conjecture, some of the symptoms of the undermining of justice through the push for greater efficiency are already there to be seen. By analogy to one of America's chemically polluted and sewerage-ridden great lakes where, it is said, a new strange mutant carp lives off the poisons in the water, he suggests that:

'The criminal justice system can be likened to Lake Erie. The idea that it should be dictated by the Government is the poison. Individual members of the judiciary, the police, the prosecution service, and the probation service who can live with that idea, and who propagate others in their own image, are the mutant carp. There are already many who are in the process of adapting. Police officers caution offenders they would prefer to prosecute. Prosecutors discontinue proceedings against defendants they would rather continue to prosecute. Probation officers recommend conditional discharges in circumstances where their predecessors would have suggested, or accepted, the inevitability of prison.' (Green, 1992, p. 27)

Pressures on the defence

Finally, what of the defence in all this? How concerned about the implications for justice were the private solicitors who provided legal advice and representation to defendants in magistrates' courts? Here, of course, as we described in Chapter 3, the Home Office model of 'the criminal justice system' includes 'the big five' - the police, CPS, the courts, probation and the Prison Service but not the defence. At the local level of the magistrates' court the regularly appearing defence solicitors generally operate in fairly close liaison with the court. But at the national level, on the whole, defence solicitors and the Law Society have hardly been outspoken on the implications for justice. This might well be due to the fragmented nature of the solicitors' profession (compared with the Bar), and the fact that criminal defence work typically forms only one component of their professional work. To be sure, there have been complaints from many solicitors about the recommendation of the Royal Commission on Criminal Justice (Runciman, 1993) to abolish the right of defendants to elect trial before jury and judge.

More generally, however, it was largely only when solicitors' interests were directly affected by the efficiency-oriented actions of the Government or the courts that concerted opposition could be expected. This, for example, was the case with regard to remuneration rates for defence work in magistrates' courts. This had become a subject of increasing dissatisfaction among practitioners from the late 1980s onwards as the Government repeatedly refused to sanction the scale of increases in legal aid rates that the Law Society regarded as fair. Many solicitors, in fact, withdrew from undertaking defence work in the courts as a result, regarding the work there to be barely economic. This left many courts and defendants dependent on just a few regularly appearing practitioners.

There was a twist of irony, of course, that it should be the actions of a Conservative government, strongly committed to private sector values and practices, that should threaten the future of the private practitioners' role in criminal justice in the lower courts in this way. But then, as we saw, the commitment to controlling public spending, including the legal aid budget, was just as great a priority for the Government at the time! What of justice? Inevitably it would follow that any withdrawal of solicitors from undertaking defence work for legally-aided clients would mean a reduction in access to legal advice and assistance for defendants in criminal cases. In that sense too, the prospect was again of justice being further undermined.

PART III

Questions of balance

The previous sections described the pressures on the courts to work within the policies of government in a period of rising workload and strict financial control. Now we turn to consider three critical dilemmas in the day-to-day running of the courts.

First, in Chapter 7, we consider some of the detail of the daily task of scheduling cases into the court-room. How do the courts arrange a date for a trial and, more difficult, arrange that everyone involved will arrive on time ready to proceed? Those responsible for managing the courts must balance a set of opposing objectives, namely ensuring efficiency in the use of court resources, the minimisation of delay and the convenience of the different parties involved in a trial. The process is further complicated by the fact that different parties have incompatible requirements of the court administrator.

Second, in Chapter 8, we consider the relations of the criminal courts with the other agencies involved in the criminal justice process. In that they are involved in the same process with the same cases, there is a degree of inter-dependence between the agencies, but at the same time, the special characteristics of the justice process, and the position of the judiciary in particular, require that there be a high degree of independence in these relations. How can the functions of court management balance the need for inter-dependence with the other agencies on the one hand and the requirement for independence of the judiciary on the other?

Third, in Chapter 9, we consider the relations between the paid professional staff and the unpaid laity. How can the professional staff counter the tendency to patronise, ignore or deny the needs and interests of the laity? How can the management of courts achieve balance between the demands and expectations of the professionals and those of the laity?

In order to explore these components of the courts' balancing act, we shall describe in some detail particular operations of the court. In some instances, the description may not exactly fit the local practice with which the reader may be familiar - total standardisation has not yet been achieved! Indeed, this local variation demonstrates the way local balances are found that reflect local circumstances: alternatively, they may reveal the reasons why some courts' performance is so lamentable.

Our purpose is not to instruct but to offer ideas and frameworks and, above all, to assist court practitioners in thinking about the dilemmas and balancing acts that underpin their everyday work.

CHAPTER 7

Organising the workload

'This is the bureaucrat's lot. Those who like to feel conscious of hiding such light as they possess under a bushel get satisfaction from it. On the whole I did so; although on occasion I wished for the immediate applause given to the acrobat, the pop singer, or the tennis star. But perhaps the administrator has a more continuously pleasant sense of not being truly appreciated than any of these.'
Angus Wilson, *The old men at the Zoo*, 1961

7.1   INTRODUCTION

Maybe the harvest of the managerial revolution will indeed be reaped in efficiently administered courts - but what is it that, efficiently or not, court administrators actually do?   Here, to invert the saying, we are concerned with 'doing the thing right' rather than 'doing the right thing'. Given the current structure of criminal justice, how is the workload best organised?

Go down to the law library and you will find shelves of books about the law and how the judiciary enforce it in court but nothing on how court staff administer courts. We know what the police do from films and thrillers as well as from seeing them on the street. We know what prison officers do from the documentaries and sit-coms on television. We have a vague idea about probation officers interviewing clients and supervising them on community service projects.   We know what lawyers, judges and magistrates do from watching court-room dramas. We might just have an idea about the court clerk sitting below the magistrates and judges and sometimes murmuring advice, but the rest of the work of the court administration is invisible. Such is indeed the lot of the administrator.

Behind the police officer, probation officer and the lawyer stands a silent, unsung infrastructure comprising the administrators who make it possible for them to do their work. The clerk in the barrister's chambers never struts before a jury, but nor would the barrister without the clerk. The police officer would not be out on the beat if someone else were not attending to the administrative back-up and ensuring that the salary cheque arrived each month.

Similarly, none of the work of the judges and magistrates would happen if the court administrative staff did not make it happen. So what do they do? What is involved in scheduling the simultaneous appearance of defendant, prosecution and defence lawyers and witnesses, backed up by reports, statements, committal papers and legal aid agreements, all in a warm and dry court-house, staffed by clerk and ushers and equipped with refreshments, waiting rooms and toilets? We can identify five sets of task.

1. The court has to attend to its own infrastructure so that it can then attend to that of the visitors and guests. Essential tasks include:
    the maintenance of the buildings, cleaning, heating, energy management;
    purchasing supplies of paper, files, paper-clips, receipt forms and other office sundries;
    pay-roll management so that everyone is paid, as is their national insurance and tax; and
    arranging rental and service agreements for telephones, fax machines, photo-copiers, computers, printers and typewriters;
2 A second group of activities revolve around the administration of other agencies' business. Amongst these are:
    performing the role of taxing officer in the Crown Court or clerk in the magistrates' court in the allocation of legal aid moneys;
    the collection and recording of fines, this being undertaken for both courts by the staff of the magistrates' court; and
    the checking of papers. The staff of the Crown Court check that the committal papers sent from the magistrates' courts are in order and are complete before creating the judge's file for each case. Similarly, magistrates' court staff check warrants before they are issued and also check the status of defendants' applications for legal aid.

3. A third set of activities concerns liaison with court users so that procedures and understandings can be developed for the benefit of each: this conduct of external affairs is discussed in the next chapter.

4. Fourth is the collection of statistics on the work of the court to contribute to the central administration of the Lord Chancellor's Department. This refers both to those statistics on caseload and performance that contribute to the national picture of the courts' work and also to that data from which targets are set within the broad public finance policies of government departments. Court administrators also collect information that informs their local practice.

5. The fifth administrative task is scheduling cases. In fact, the purpose of the above activities is essentially to support the court in undertaking this prime activity of convening adjudications. Unfortunately, the evidence from both the magistrates' courts and Crown Court suggests that this function is not always done well. Around two thirds of cases do not proceed as planned. Many court-rooms stand empty in the afternoon yet there is usually a waiting list of cases delayed in their progress through the courts. Witnesses are summoned to the court-house but many have to wait several hours before they are called to give evidence and many are not called at all. Since this, the key activity, is an area of concern, we shall take it as the focus of our consideration of the organisation of the workload. But as we do, let us acknowledge that arranging the schedule of a court is more complicated than at first appears and, so as to pre-empt the type of contemptuous advice also received by managers of British Rail, let us agree that it is in a different league from arranging bookings at a clinic or hairdressers.

7.2 SCHEDULING COURT APPEARANCES

Unlike most other appointments, a trial in court involves the presence of several people; up to three magistrates or a judge, a court clerk, one or more prosecutors, the defence advocates, a probation officer, witnesses for the prosecution and defence, one or more defendants, and sometimes a jury. The court administrator must schedule the simultaneous appearance of all these people.

Raine & Willson (1992; 1993) studied the scheduling practices of a sample of magistrates' courts and identified the interaction of three underlying objectives in their scheduling activities. Each court balanced these objectives in a different manner. These objectives were seen to be:

1. *Convenience:* maximisation of convenience to, and interests of, users in the organisation of hearings (e.g. the prosecution, defence, witnesses and, of course, the magistrates or judge).
2. *Delay:* minimisation of delay in completing cases (i.e. the time interval between a case being first 'listed' in court, and its completion).
3. *Efficiency:* maximisation of efficiency with regard to use of court resources (e.g. the time of the judiciary and clerks and the use of court-rooms).

Under the first objective of convenience, the aim of the scheduling function is simply to accommodate those involved: the judges, juries, the magistrates, the CPS, the probation officers, the police, the civilian and expert witnesses, the defendants and the lawyers.

The second objective, minimisation of delay, might be regarded as primarily serving the interests of justice on the basis of the maxim 'justice delayed is justice denied'. Cases should be heard as soon as possible and the court should brook no delay, even if this means that people must work over-time or extra staff be employed to reduce any backlog.

Under the third objective, the aim of scheduling is different again, to maximise the use of resources, for example by concentrating the workload into the minimum number of court-rooms and separate sittings.

Potential conflicts exist between these three objectives. For example, the minimisation of delay in the interests of justice probably implies inconvenience and extra pressure for the defence or prosecution in having to prepare their cases more quickly. Similarly, the minimisation of delay might well clash with the objective of the efficient use of court resources if, in the interests of speed, additional court-rooms are used and extra sittings arranged. Further, the objective of efficiency in the use of court resources might well be at odds with that of suiting the interests of all the parties. This is because an efficiently rationalised sittings schedule might mean a longer wait on the day.

Given the right of the defendant to change plea at any time and the possibility that one of the many people required for a trial might fall sick on the night before, some hearings will always be terminated early or have to be adjourned, leaving the court with unfilled court time. It is in the attempts to minimise these disruptions and deal with their effects that the tension between the three objectives becomes especially apparent. If there was no pressure to manage resources efficiently, then disruptions would scarcely matter and the temporarily idle staff could play cards or take a nap until the next scheduled case was due to start. Nor would anyone be inconvenienced by having to wait since cases could be listed in batches ('block listing' as it is called by the court administrators) or time-tabled just like appointments at a Harley Street clinic. Similarly, if there was no pressure to minimise delay, the police and prosecution would have ample time in which to prepare their cases, witnesses could be contacted ('warned') six months in advance and adjournments would be very rare. And, to continue these absurd illustrations, if the convenience of everyone bar the court was unimportant, then every person required for every case for the week would be summoned to appear at 10 am on the Monday morning, thus ensuring that the court could pick its way through the list and ensure full utilisation of its resources.

7.3 CONSTRAINTS ON GOOD PRACTICE

7.3.1 Constraints on efficiency

A truly efficient court would process cases as soon as they were ready to come to court and would do so with the minimum expenditure of resources. Cases would start and finish on time, as planned and with no unanticipated adjournments. However, it does not work out that way.

Less than a third of the cases that are listed at the Crown Court are heard as planned: some 60 per cent are abandoned when defendants, 'on the day', change their plea to guilty and some 10 per cent are abandoned when the prosecution withdraws its case. Moreover, under an adversarial system in which each party competes to win rather than to discover the truth, it is likely that many cases will only be withdrawn by the prosecution or conceded by the defence when they have assessed the other party's success in getting its witnesses to court.

In the magistrates' court, more trial cases are heard as planned but other preliminary hearings are regularly adjourned because some preparation or briefing expected by the court has not been made. Again and again, the progress of cases is interrupted and court resources made idle.

The scale of the problem is illustrated by the data from a study on trial outcomes over a two month period in eight magistrates' clerkships (Raine & Willson, 1992). The percentage of trials that went ahead as planned varied from only 18 to almost 53 per cent, which is to say that in some clerkships over 80 per cent of trials 'collapsed' because either the prosecution withdrew the case on the day, the defendant pleaded guilty on the day or the case was adjourned. The data is summarised in Figure 7.1.

Figure 7.1 Percentage outcomes of trials in 8 magistrates' clerkships

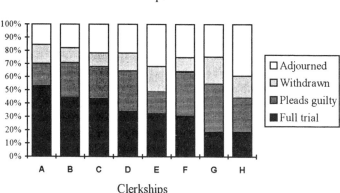

Clerkships

An hotel or holiday tour company (a short trial can cost more than a long holiday) deals with this risk of collapse by charging in advance and specifying a cancellation fee. The courts cannot do this. They are constrained by the special nature of the justice process and the constitutional rules and roles that prescribe the behaviour of those in attendance. These features are described below. The courts have therefore had to evolve their own procedures to minimise the impact of a high variance in demand in an attempt to ensure a steady, if sub-optimal, flow of cases.

First, legal constraints limit the court's scope for improving overall rates of throughput. Especially significant in this context is the principle that, once agreed in the court-room, the date for a hearing cannot subsequently be altered to accommodate an apparently more urgent case. Instead, the principle is that cases are dealt with on a strict 'taxi rank' basis, that is, with no queue-jumping at the initial hearing stage.

Second, unlike most other services where the 'providers' are paid executives, the judiciary cannot be instructed. Magistrates are volunteers and judges do not respond well to being directed and will not always bow to managerial expedient. Most managers operate in an environment providing them with an hierarchical structure of authority and a reward system to ensure that objectives and targets are met efficiently, but this is not the case when managing the judiciary. The volunteer status of the magistracy further constrains scheduling in the magistrates' court. Many magistrates have other demands upon their time which may well require that the clerk shall list less business in the afternoons so that some of them can finish court at lunch time. They also require the clerk to sustain the same pattern of sittings, week in, week out, even when the workload fluctuates, so that their diaries are not disrupted.

Third, some of the parties involved in a case seem little motivated to expedite the progress of their cases. Defendants on bail often arrive late and without the relevant documentation they had been asked to bring. Defendants may also have legitimate reasons to slow proceedings and their solicitor's professional duty may sometimes be to delay by seeking adjournments or by advising their clients initially to plead 'not guilty' in order to secure more time to consider how to respond to the charges.

Fourth, the unpredictable duration of court hearings also makes precise scheduling very difficult. A hearing is composed of a series of contributions made by different people, each of which takes varying amounts of time. The time taken by the prosecution varies, as does the time taken by the defence: time required to accommodate the varying complexity of legal argument varies, as does the time required by magistrates or jury and judge to reach their decisions. It might be more efficient to specify maximum durations for trials but, of course, this is not possible without compromising due process.

7.3.2 Constraints on providing convenience

The objective of convenience itself contains a set of conflicting pressures. The principal parties are magistrates, judges, juries, victims and witnesses, prosecutors, defendants, defence solicitors, police and probation officers, and all have their own requirements that the court staff must balance with those of the other parties as well as the efficiency of the court and the minimisation of delay. The typical wishes of each group are characterised below.

Judges and magistrates generally appreciate short sessions that start and finish on time and do not involve much waiting between cases. They become frustrated by adjournments and, to a lesser extent, by collapses of trials. Most magistrates express a wish to hear a mixed list rather than a series of similar cases since they find this more interesting.

Victims and witnesses generally appreciate the shortest possible delay between the offence and the hearing but at the same time appreciate an ample warning period so that they are not over-inconvenienced by attending court. They wish to be called for a specific time and not to be kept waiting. Adjournments infuriate them, as do the withdrawal of their cases by the prosecution. When they must wait, they like a degree of comfort and privacy and to be free of contact from the defendant and associates who, they fear, might intimidate them.

Prosecutors generally appreciate ample time in which to prepare cases and ample time in which to warn their witnesses of the dates of hearings so that their attendance is more likely. They do not like the last minute re-allocation of cases between court-rooms because they must then present cases that they have not personally prepared. Nor do they like short lists or lists that mix their cases with those that do not involve them, especially if they have had to travel to attend the court and are therefore unable to get on with other work in their offices while waiting for their next case to commence.

Defendants have diverse interests. Some like ample time in which justice is delayed, while others wish to get it over with quickly.

Defence solicitors who regularly appear at the court generally want all their cases in one court-room stacked one behind the other so that they can conduct as much business as possible in one session. They like a weekly time-table that allows them to plan interviews and other work in their office at one time and to attend court at another. They do not like to be kept waiting and appreciate interview rooms for private discussion with clients in the court-house. They generally find block listing and appointment systems reduce their flexibility, particularly when it is one of their cases that has collapsed!

Police generally appreciate ample time in which to prepare the case files and to sort out witness availability. They resent adjourned and collapsed trials for the waste of their time. They do not like to be kept waiting.

Probation generally wish for all their cases to be held in one court-room, in tandem, and like to minimise their travelling to court-houses. Like the prosecutors, they do not like lists that mix cases which involve their officers with those that do not.

As is apparent, these conditions of convenience are often incompatible with each other.

Probation and defence solicitors both (but incompatibly) want their own cases listed in the same court. Meanwhile, magistrates tend to prefer a mixed list which runs contrary to both.

Police, victims and witnesses generally want appointments but defence solicitors and court staff find that this reduces their ability to cope with 'collapses'.

Police, defendants and CPS want ample time in which to prepare their cases but victims and civilian witnesses - and the court team concerned with delay - want this period to be short.

Everyone wants the courts to finish on time, to which end the re-allocation of cases between court-rooms during sittings is often necessary. But the CPS find this inconvenient and consider that it might possibly reduce their capacity to present the prosecution case effectively.

Prosecution and defence solicitors want generous access to adjournments when they consider that they need them: everyone else resents their time being wasted.

It becomes clear that the convenience of one party is often at the expense of another. Further, it seems that there is a price to the strategy of respecting the convenience of those who use the court. It both reduces the court's ability to be efficient in its utilisation of resources, especially when it needs flexibility to respond to 'collapses', and reduces the court's ability to minimise delay because most parties want more time.

7.3.3 Constraints on the minimisation of delay

Both good professional practice and the Lord Chancellor's Department require the courts to minimise the delay between the commencement and completion of cases that come to court. There are two legitimate causes of delay, the first being the backlog of work that may prevent the court offering an appointment as soon as the parties are ready. The second, however, is that time is needed in which to prepare the prosecution and defence cases. Minimising the backlog of hearings can, to an extent, be addressed through efficient procedures but it will always be subject to a fluctuating demand, depending on current levels of offending, police success in identifying offenders, the use of cautioning and other variables. But even if the workload is under control and trial dates can be offered for perhaps four weeks hence, the other parties may not be ready. The preparation of the prosecution case requires time, especially if witnesses must be interviewed and evidence cross-checked by the police. The defence case also requires time. There is a strong argument that the preparation of both cases should not be hurried, even if some of the delay seems wilful on the part of the defendant, because to do so would compromise justice.

What, then, is the definition of 'undue delay'? It appears that the definition is the end result of negotiation. As will be described in the next chapter, local norms are established around the courts as to how long preparation stages should take. For instance, at some magistrates' courts the CPS take four weeks to prepare a case for prosecution and at others they take eight. Similarly, the defence solicitors establish their informal norms with the courts. The constraints on the minimisation of delay seem largely rooted in the local legal culture and the extent to which delay is considered important (Church, 1982).

7.3.4 Balancing the objectives

What emphasis should be placed on each priority? How should the balance be struck between an emphasis by the court on convenience for the various parties, both professional and non-professional, on reducing delay, and on maximising efficiency in the use of resources? All three represent justifiable objectives for court management. The challenge is to pursue all three simultaneously, to minimise delay while avoiding inconvenience to the parties whilst also ensuring that court resources are used as efficiently as possible. In pursuing these three objectives, however, a number of inherent tensions have to be confronted. For example, one possible consequence of a low delay strategy with its associated pressure for early hearing dates is that more trials may 'collapse' on the day, perhaps because of insufficient time for preparation work. This, in turn, is likely to result in inefficiency in the use of court resources. At the same time, to pursue convenience of the parties, particularly the professional users, probably means accepting longer delays. Conversely, attempts to use court resources in the most efficient manner, for example by extending sittings to a full day, may well imply less convenience to those parties, including many magistrates and professional users, who often prefer to complete their work at court by lunch time to enable them to devote their afternoons to other work.

7.4   CASE STUDIES

The rather different methods of scheduling in the magistrates' courts and Crown Court are described below. A typical approach is described for each, as are examples of the activities involved.

7.4.1 *Scheduling practices in the magistrates' courts*

Magistrates' courts schedule a variety of different types of case. In addition to criminal work, they also provide facilities for civil and matrimonial cases and family courts. There are also many non-contested cases which are listed for the day but which require no presence from defence or prosecution. We shall take the scheduling of criminal trials as an example of the way in which the courts go about their most time-consuming work. In the magistrates' courts all the scheduling work is done 'in house', unlike the Crown Court where some of the estimates and decisions are made by lawyers in private practice.

In order to schedule a trial, the magistrates' clerk needs an estimation of the time it will take, an estimation of how long the parties will take to prepare their cases and, of course, a vacant space in the court diary. In order to draw up a list, the clerk also needs an estimate of the probabilities of cases 'collapsing' on the day so that a degree of over-booking can be introduced.

Estimating the time for trials

Raine & Willson (1992) reviewed the estimation of time for trials in magistrates' courts. Data was collected on 527 trials that proceeded on the day and for which 1,499 hours had been allocated. In the event, the total time the trials actually took was 1,253 hours, that is to say that, on average, the time taken was 84 per cent of the time allocated. However, this data was collected from eight different clerkships and their own specific percentages ranged from 63 per cent to 105 per cent, which seems to suggest that, if a standard rule of thumb that was being used in the estimation process (for example, half an hour per witness), it did not always measure up to local conditions.

An analysis was also made of the differences between the time allocated to trials and the time actually taken, i.e. including those which 'collapsed' or were adjourned on the day. Over the two month survey period, the eight clerkships together allocated 3,381 hours for hearing trials of which only 1,596 hours were used: that is to say, only 47 per cent of the allocated time was used as planned. Once again, individual clerkships' percentages varied, this time from 23 to 57 per cent. This gives some idea of the problem in the efficient management of the courts. Even the most accurate estimation left the court with 43 per cent of the time allocated for trials to be used otherwise or wasted.

On the other hand, the collapse of trials is not random. The research data indicated that certain types of case are more likely to collapse than others. In particular, 67 per cent of (359) theft trials and 66 per cent of (168) public order offences trials collapsed but only 58 per cent of (97) criminal damage trials and 57 per cent of (395) motoring trials collapsed. Attention to collapse rates in this fashion provides the administrators with the information and confidence to play the probabilities when over-booking. But the research found that this was generally not the practice.

Once a slot has been identified for a trial and the relevant parties notified, the clerk will usually employ a variety of case status monitoring methods to check whether each case is being prepared on time as planned. Case status monitoring will often extend to checking whether witnesses have been notified to attend (warned) since the absence of a witness is a major reason for adjournment of trials in the magistrates' courts.

The next discretionary exercise happens a week or so before each trial is due. The administrator responsible, who may be a clerk or a designated listing officer, will 'split' the list by allocating hearings to specific court-rooms. This may be done to a variety of formulae. For instance, the rule might be to create a mix of cases; to put all cases of one type, such as motoring, together; to put all custody or remand cases together; to ensure that all of one solicitor's cases are heard in tandem in the same court-room; or by some other or random logic. Court practices also vary over the detail of time-tabling. Some request all parties to attend court at 10 am whilst others hold separate hearings in the morning and afternoon and yet others use the block listing form of time-tabling, scheduling some cases for 10 am, others for 11 am etc. All parties are notified so that they can plan accordingly. The CPS lawyers allocated to each court-room can now prepare the presentation of their cases for each day.

The court team of ushers and clerks have the additional task each morning of re-balancing the list and re-allocating the cases between court-rooms as it becomes clear which hearings will go ahead and which are delayed awaiting a witness or have 'collapsed'. They might also alter the order in which cases are heard when a witness has not yet arrived. Such changes, of course, break up the pattern of the list and can inconvenience solicitors and prosecutors.

By these methods of estimating trial durations, over-booking, case status monitoring, splitting and re-balancing the list, the magistrates' court administration attempts to schedule its trials in a way that best balances the range of competing interests. The clerk's professional concern will be to provide summary justice with minimum delay which nevertheless does not restrict the exercise of due process for either defence or prosecution. The courts' administrative concern is to do this efficiently and to ensure a smooth-running list that will utilise court resources to the full. Convenience to the parties may, at times, be squeezed in the pursuit of these other priorities. After all, the matter of quality of service to users is a less significant factor in the cash-limited grant distribution formula than case completions and delay.

7.4.2 Scheduling practices in the Crown Court

The procedures for scheduling in the Crown Court are somewhat different. The structure of the court reflects a different emphasis placed on each of the three underlying objectives. Certain discretionary activities are performed by people other than the court's administrative staff and usually to the benefit of members of the Bar. From the court administrators' perspective, therefore, it is a more mechanical exercise in which they have less power in balancing either the underlying objectives or the immediate list.

The basic scheduling procedure in the Crown Court is as follows. Cases are referred from the magistrates' court and case or committal papers are carefully checked. Each case is then allocated to one of four categories. High Court judges will hear category 1 and 2 cases, Circuit judges will usually hear category 3 and 4 and recorders will also hear category 4 cases. Decisions about the allocation of borderline cases may be referred to the Resident Judge who may refer them up or down a level. Each case is then listed for plea at a pre-trial review after three or four weeks (less, if the accused is remanded in custody). If a 'guilty' plea is entered, the defendant is listed for sentence or the case adjourned for reports to be obtained.

If a 'not guilty' plea is entered, the case is adjourned for trial at a later date. The prosecution and defence counsel together (rather than the court administrator) make an estimate of the trial duration The court staff collate witness availability data. Most cases are not allocated court time until the week before they are to be heard. Counsel will notify the court that they are ready to proceed (perhaps after the Resident Judge has reminded them that the case is still outstanding). The court listing officer makes up a 'warned list' for the week ahead which sets out the court-rooms and category of judge sitting in each, along with the list of cases to be heard, with the names of counsel and the dates when witnesses are available. The weekly 'warned list' is usually referred up to the Circuit Bar Liaison Clerk who, in conjunction with the barristers' clerks, allocates hearings to slots in the time-table.

Trials are allocated to one of three types of slot:

1. *Fixed list.* These trials are given a specific day and court-room in which they will commence. They are usually distinguished from other trials by requiring expert or child witnesses.

2. *Reserve list.* The majority of cases are put on the Reserve List to be commenced at an unspecified date during the week (although informal representations may well be made to propose preferences for certain days).

3. *Floaters.* These cases, often left over from a previous Reserve List, are specified for a particular day although not to a particular court-room. The court will usually try and match the number of floaters to the number of trials due to start.

A fourth category is the 'Advanced Fixed List' whereon a trial is listed some weeks in advance. This way cases anticipated to take a week or more will be allocated in advance by the Crown Court staff to a date and a court-room with a judge of the appropriate level.

Once a case is allocated to a judge's 'fixed list', any amendment to the date must receive the judge's permission. However, up to that stage, whilst cases are still being prepared, representations may be made by counsel to delay hearings. The listing officers attempt to ensure that cases come to trial with minimum delay and so will try to restrict the granting of such applications. The Resident Judge is the ultimate arbiter. Further, the Resident Judge is responsible for monitoring all work passing through the court and will review outstanding cases, especially those that have lapsed more than twenty weeks since committal.

Thus does the Crown Court build flexibility into the schedule to buffer itself against the variance caused by 'collapsed' (commonly known in the Crown Court as 'cracked') cases. From a management point of view, it is quite different from the approach adopted in the magistrates' court since much of the discretion lies not with the administrators in each court but with the Bar and with the Resident Judge. As we argued in Chapter 4, where the staff do not have discretion, mechanical devices are developed to compensate. Here, the main device is a technology of case categorisation and a bank of cases waiting to fill the gaps left where trials have 'cracked'.

The discretion for Crown Court administrators lies in the use of secondary procedures and interpretation. They keep their ears open for whispers that might indicate that a trial may 'go guilty on the day' but this is a very partial, perhaps improper, way of monitoring case status: in a management context, they would be granted more authority in which to use their much needed experience and discretion. Instead of professional methods, technical approaches have also been used, such as the machinery of 'pre-trial reviews' which are meant to generate useful information about the status and likely duration of each trial but which do not appear to have been significant in reducing the proportion of 'cracked' cases. Another device to improve the situation has been the introduction of a further category of listing, the 'backing trial', where a second trial employing the same defence barristers is listed following the first. Another initiative has been to implement Recommendation 92 of the report of the Working Group on 'Pre-Trial Issues' (Home Office, 1990d & see Chapter 4) by which the magistrates' court allocates a fixed trial date in the Crown Court at the time of committal. This has the effect of reducing one set of uncertainties but at the expense of further curtailing the administrators' opportunity to use their discretion to fill in gaps left by 'cracked trials'.

The interplay of the three objectives of convenience, delay minimisation and efficiency is somewhat muted in the Crown Court. To whom is this system convenient? To what extent does it minimise delay and protect justice? By what criteria is it efficient? And which of these is given primacy?

Convenience for the members of the Bar is very high. It is hard to think of a way of organising the court that would more convenient for them. The principle that the judge shall not be kept waiting is paramount and the barristers' representatives share out and draw up the list to ensure that they will not be kept waiting either. Convenience for everyone else is infamously low. The abject position of victims and civilian witnesses is chronicled in Chapter 9. But scarcely less inconvenienced are the police witnesses whose work programmes are severely disrupted by being summoned to court, waiting for a case to be called - or not - whereon, more often than not, the case 'cracks' and the officers are not needed anyway. The police budget pays for the Bar's convenience. Similarly, the daily extensive escorting of defendants held in custody has been a major strain on the prison system.

Pressure to minimise delay is placed on the Chief Clerk whose court's performance in this respect is monitored by the Lord Chancellor's Department. It is the Resident Judge who has the power to supervise the hastening of cases to court and through court and success is varied. What the administrator can do is to ensure that the witness warning forms are kept up to date so that, when a case does come to court, it will at least not 'crack' because a witness is absent.

Although the assigning of a bank of reserve cases may be efficient for the court it is, of course, wasteful to everyone else, especially the police services which can seldom afford to have officers kicking their heels in court. Neither do barristers nor witnesses like to be placed on stand-by and the Prison Service also resents presenting a defendant remanded in custody to a court at which the case is not heard. Once again, the cost of one agency's efficiency is often paid by another.

In terms of efficiency, the optimal use of the Crown Court's resources might be seen in a high proportion of cases being completed as planned, rather than adjourned, and heard as planned rather than 'cracking'. However, the principal criteria seem to be to keep the judges and court-rooms occupied. If the main resource of the court is the judge who must never be kept waiting then this might be said to be an efficient approach but, in practice, the judge is only one expenditure item among many other larger budget heads. The elaborate set of reserve cases and floaters ready to fill the gaps is efficient for the court but, of course, the cost of the Bar and court's efficiency is paid elsewhere, particularly in the police over-time budget and fees to counsel.

Implicit in these definitions of efficiency is the value given to the resources being used: judges' time, barristers' fees, police time, court overheads, and so on. If one argued that the court's main resource was its credibility with the public, the balance sheet would look different again: but, of course, it is not called the 'Public's Court'. How does this match with the interaction of the objectives of convenience to all users and the minimisation of delay?

7.5   CONCLUSION

Most of the issues raised in the Crown Court are the same as those raised in the magistrates' court even though the way that they are met is different. Balancing the objectives of convenience, delay minimisation and efficiency is a perpetual challenge to which there is no one solution. It might well be that the problem of a high collapse rate which lies at the heart of the courts' difficulties is rooted in the adversarial system of justice adopted in England & Wales. It is possible that the best way of accommodating it has already evolved and is now practised and that all else is merely tinkering. The examination of the conflict within the notion of convenience between the various parties similarly appears irreconcilable - unless there were to be no limit on the criminal justice budget.

We are looking therefore at a task that is characterised by uncertainty, ambiguity and the need for immediate decisions. This is therefore a professional task (Mintzberg, 1983) requiring professional staff empowered to use their high levels of discretion. We would argue that the mechanical solutions of the Machine Bureaucracy are not likely to solve the complex daily activities of scheduling. But the evidence is that the culture of the Professional Bureaucracy, where power is held at the point where it must be exercised, has also failed the court's system.

Examination of these issues continues through the next two chapters, 'Managing independence and inter-dependence' and 'Professionals and the laity'. Maybe, in the end, it all boils down to power.

CHAPTER 8

Managing independence and inter-dependence

'Independence is first in the mind and only then in one's practice.'
Judge Boyadjus, Supreme Court of Cyprus, 1993.

8.1 INTRODUCTION

The doctrine of the separation of powers demands that there should be complete independence of the judiciary from the legislature and the executive. Judicial independence in criminal justice is jealously guarded by judges and magistrates and attempts by government to influence judicial decision making and conduct are critically received. However, at the level of arranging schedules and processing papers, the court is a participant in a network of inter-dependent relationships with agencies that are directly linked to the executive. The court team, therefore, operates in a buffer zone between the judiciary and the executive. This difficult balancing act has to be performed.

This chapter examines issues of inter-dependence and inter-organisational relations. How can the courts exercise a degree of control over the behaviour of the organisations with which they have to work - the police forces, the Crown Prosecution Service, the Law Society, the Bar, the probation services and various voluntary organisations involved in criminal justice matters? How might employees in each organisation work with their counterparts on specific items and issues? What are the organisational, managerial and judicial consequences of any increase in the power exercised centrally from outside the local network?

From the amoeba to the suburban middle class, inter-dependence is a characteristic of all levels of life. Without the capability to make successful transactions of energy and resources between itself and its environment, the organism (or organisation) dies. All organisations are constantly negotiating with their immediate environment of stakeholders - such as customers, suppliers, landlords, employees and competitors - in order to maintain and develop satisfactory business relations with them. As circumstances change, so different arrangements are made and broken as all parties move in and out of each other's environment. Thus employees come and go; different premises are rented from competing landlords; suppliers and customers change with the market and, indeed, an organisation can change its business.

However, some inter-organisational relationships have an additional, externally imposed, formal dimension where there is an expectation that they will work in tandem, each taking a part in a sequence of activities, or alternatively in a network where the work of one is intimately linked with the work of another. The Crown Prosecution Service cannot boycott a particular magistrates' court, nor can a court choose a different probation service to prepare reports on offenders. The agencies are obliged to work together.

It would be very convenient to turn now to consider the mechanisms by which the court can find an efficient equilibrium in its relations with the agencies amongst which it works and to take as read subjects such as the independence of the judiciary and the separation of powers which are so comprehensively considered by constitutionalists and jurists. After all, this is a book on management, focusing on the day-to-day operation of the court and on the strategies for organising it efficiently . Must we really go over these constitutional issues again - can't we just get on with the business?

8.2   THE INDEPENDENCE OF THE JUDICIARY

The complex status of the independence of the judiciary in England & Wales is expressed through the role of the Lord Chancellor: although an independent judicial appointment by the Monarch, the Lord Chancellor is, in fact, a member of the Government who also heads the courts' executive. There are many other instances where the separation of powers is not as clear in practice as it is in theory or as it might be if written in a constitution: some of these have been described in Chapters 6 and 7.

Out of court, the judiciary undertake functions that might just as well be undertaken within the executive. Presiding judges have administrative powers when working with the Circuit administrators; resident judges oversee the work of 'their' courts and chair various consultative committees and advisory panels; the most senior judges contribute to the legislative process by sitting in the Second Chamber of Parliament and are frequently invited to head inquiries for the Government. Certain magistrates are elected by their peers to be members of their local magistrates' courts' committees, the functions of which are entirely administrative and include budget management and the employment of the executive staff of the court. Magistrates are also members of police committees and probation committees.

There are other ambiguities and dilemmas. For instance, some would maintain that the magistrates' clerk must be independent of the executive if the advice given to the magistrates is to be protected from the expedient concerns of the executive (see Chapter 6; and Green, 1992). Meanwhile, the clerk is charged with both the managerial responsibility of ensuring a brisk throughput of cases and providing ample time for the business of the court. Similarly, magistrates on the magistrates' court's committee find themselves dealing with the financial management of the court in a cash-limited environment one day and then must be vigilant that in court the next day they do not compromise or foreclose on due process when hearing elaborate or very petty cases. It will be seen that the highest professional and ethical standards are necessary if corners are not to be cut. How does a manager ensure the application of the very highest professional standards when matters of principle contradict the imperatives of the manager's priorities?

At the more general level, the cultural independence of the judiciary is also rather frail. In some states, for instance Switzerland, judges are elected to the post for a fixed term. usually through membership of a political party. In the USA, Supreme Court judges are appointed by the President for life. In most European countries, the position of judge is a career post occupied by lawyers of all ages who are keenly allied to their profession and mindful of their career progression. Meanwhile, in England & Wales, judges are appointed by the Lord Chancellor from the ranks of senior lawyers, mostly barristers, by a largely secret process of preference. This process has been much criticised, and whether or not more black and women barristers are appointed, judges will continue to be recruited from the dominant social coalition in society and will be more similar to each other than to the populace. One might say that the independence of the judiciary resembles that of the domestic cat which, unlike a dog, may be resistant to overt orders but otherwise fits in with the routines of its owner, recognises mealtimes and is usually to be found enjoying the privilege of the best seat by the fire where it will purr when stroked. The court staff are perhaps more like the householder whose time is spent earning money, buying and preparing food and clearing up afterwards. Their independence is in a different coin.

The presence of these inconsistencies and ambiguities complicates the work of the administrative staff in their attempt to co-ordinate the behaviour of the judiciary. It is a delicate relationship. The court official must ensure that not only are the defendants, witnesses and lawyers present in the prepared court, but that the judge or magistrates also turn up as planned. How does the official manage the judge or magistrate? The relationship is often marked by great deference - or semblance thereof - shown by the administrators to the judge or magistrate. Sometimes one is reminded of the days when the old kings held court to which supplicants would bring matters for adjudication: at other times the court maybe resembles the inside of a hive where the workers rush around serving, but ultimately driving, the Queen. The report of a Scrutiny of magistrates' courts (Home Office, 1989a) describes the role of the magistrates' clerk as 'a combination of butler and family solicitor' which, on reflection, seems very fitting. Required to direct and otherwise influence independent volunteer magistrates of high social status, prone to think more of themselves than they should, the 'butler' role permits the clerk deferentially to challenge the magistrates' wishes without challenging their authority. Similarly, the family solicitor is traditionally permitted to enter delicate areas of family strife and intervene, citing precedent, rules and regulations, without challenging the status of the patron. Now it may well be that the strategy of disingenuous obsequiousness is out of kilter with the expectations of modern judges and magistrates, but a better way of maintaining a happy, committed and amenable Bench seems hard to find.

There is an ambiguity, then, in the relationship between the judiciary and the court staff. On the one hand, the court staff are the servants of the court presided over by members of the judiciary sitting on the Bench. They maintain the physical environment in which the judges and magistrates adjudicate and they do this by scheduling appearances, administering fines and orders and arranging for the building to be clean and warm. On the other hand, court staff must arrange that the judge or magistrates actually do the work presented to them. Further, in the magistrates' court, the clerk is also responsible for providing training and legal advice that should be untainted by contact with such executive functions. Paradoxically, the additional managerial authority the Government has wanted to assign to the clerks may reduce their overall authority with magistrates who could come to see the clerk as only a manager. Directions predicated on an interpretation of the law have greater credibility and correctness than do instructions to comply with efficient resource management.

8.3 INTER-AGENCY RELATIONSHIPS

Whereas at the constitutional level the issue is one of independence as described above, at the technical level of arranging schedules and processing papers, the court team is a participant in a network of inter-dependent relationships. Both the Crown Court team and the magistrates' court team operate at the centre of the criminal justice process in networks with the police, prosecution, defence, prison and probation agencies. The networks are replete with tensions arising from each agency's different interests and priorities such as clearing up crime, managing crime, reducing offending and doing justice. They are complicated since they are not coterminous and they operate at different levels. Here we see the loose, local and idiosyncratic networks in which the work actually takes place and they are messier than the criminal justice 'system' described in Chapter 3.

The web of networks is complicated by the fact that some agencies are formally constituted at an area and national level, while others are not. From the magistrates' clerk's point of view, a network surrounds each court-room. Another network, of which the former would be considered sub-systems, operates at each petty sessional division. On the other hand, from the perspective of the Crown Prosecution Service, their administrative area office is the system and the various courts within the area are regarded as sub-systems. The police will have another perspective again, depending on their size of their service, organisational structure and the geography of their area. At the same time, firms of defence solicitors are likely to experience themselves in a network that is very local but also extends beyond their criminal work to other areas of the law.

What does this mean for negotiations which are conducted at the supra-system level as far as one party is concerned but at the system level as far as the other party is concerned?   The operation of the network has an additional twist since, as already described, there are tensions between the professional allegiances of staff in different agencies: on the whole, the lawyers have one reference group, the police another and the senior civil servants who staff the Home Office and Lord Chancellor's Department have a different professional reference group again.

How do they deal with the potential conflicts of interest over resources?   For instance, although the court is not charged for the preparation of reports by the probation services, they are not free. Each local probation service will have finite resources. The individual judge or magistrate will ask for a report when it seems necessary for the execution of justice.   The clerk and probation service, however, are aware that reports, or requests for them, have to be rationed. On the other hand, if magistrates could be persuaded that they did not need reports before sentencing, there would be fewer adjournments and the flow of work through the court would be that much faster.   But, one might reply, the likelihood of both justice and social justice being done would be reduced and the sentencing patterns might provoke more crime through, for instance, undue use of custody. This in turn has an effect on prison budgeting.   There is an almost infinite set of links and priorities to be balanced.

Faced with this Byzantine soap opera of organisational complexity and politics, one response of those with a deep concern for professional integrity is to turn away and attend to the professional side of the work and hope that these dilemmas will go away. However, this is no longer a viable option in the public sector environment and professionals and professional managers alike have to find ways of operating in the 'small p' political organisational world whilst also maintaining their professional integrity (Baddeley, 1990).

8.4 MODELS OF NETWORKS

How can we make sense of these complicated networks so that we learn how to understand what is happening, anticipate what will happen next and plan how to meet it? Below are described two complementary conceptual models of such networks which, when put to work, help a great deal in making sense of such inter-organisational relations.

8.4.1 The inter-organisational network as a political economy

Benson's analysis of network relations between human service agencies illuminates the issues and strategies involved (Benson, 1975). He takes as his level of analysis the processes of the network as a whole and suggests that there are discernible patterns and consistencies in the behaviour of the member agencies. Each agency is described as being involved in securing its position in a 'political economy'. This demands that each attends to two basic resources, money and authority. The patten of acquisition of these resources then determines the shape of the power dependencies the agencies create with each other, as it also determines the types of strategy open to each in their interactions.

The process of financial resource acquisition for the justice agencies mostly involves negotiating for grants from national and local government. The advent of tight resourcing and various cash limiting formulae has amplified the process because the introduction of methods described in earlier chapters emphasised financial management, performance indicators and the attainment of targets. But, as we have argued, the requirement to meet such targets creates tensions with other agencies since one agency's efficiency or saving is often gained at the expense of another. Consider, for instance, the dilemmas which face the CPS, police and magistrates' courts. The CPS needs to maintain a high conviction rate: the police require a high clear-up rate: the courts require a low level of delay and collapse rate. CPS discontinuances raise their success rate but waste police time. A court's low delay policy (willingness to dismiss cases if the prosecution is not ready and insisting police witnesses attend even at the cost of incurring over-time payments) is at the expense of CPS and police resources. In order to be sure of a conviction CPS may require extra police work in the form of additional identification parades (at twenty police hours per parade) or that all, rather than two, police officers should attend as witnesses. Another tension stems from the financial resource acquisition of defence solicitors who depend on their recruitment of clients to whom they hope the court will grant legal aid - an arrangement in which the balance of power can vary widely. A third example is that of the voluntary organisation which runs a bail hostel and is 'grant-aided' from a probation service budget on condition that certain criteria are met over a specified time. But money is not the only resource that brings power.

Authority is a more subtle and less visible resource. It has a particular complexity in the criminal justice process where the demands of efficiency, social utility and justice are often incompatible. In Benson's model, it is defined as follows:

> 'Authority refers to the legitimation of activities, the right and responsibility to carry out programs of a certain kind, dealing with broad problem areas or focus. Legitimated claims of this kind are termed domains. The possession of a domain permits the organisation to operate in a certain sphere, claim support for its activities and define proper practices within its realm.' (Benson, 1975, p. 232)

The struggle to retain (or gain) authority and status leads the manager of an agency to organise activities in such a way as to enhance its claim on financial resources by staking out its territory and, sometimes, making claims on others. Essentially, oblique negotiations go on in which each agency tries to get the others to agree to its 'authority' over a particular 'domain' or territory until an equilibrium is (temporarily) achieved. Such an equilibrium, according to Benson, will reflect the differential authority and financial strength of the agencies and will usually involve:

1. *Domain Consensus*: agreement among participants in organisations regarding the appropriate role and scope of an agency, e.g.
   What cases will be sent by magistrates to the Crown Court?
   Will fine enforcement warrants be served by the police?
2. *Ideological Consensus*: agreement among participants in organisations regarding the nature of the tasks confronted by the organisations and the appropriate approaches to those tasks, e.g.
   Who arranges the reserve and floating list in the Crown Court?
   Should the probation services provide rehabilitation, supervision of punishment and reports?
3. *Positive Evaluation*: the judgement by workers in one organisation of the value of the work of another organisation, e.g.
   What level of respect do magistrates hold for the police or for the pre-sentence reports of the probation services?
   How do Crown Court judges regard local lay magistrates?
   How do the police regard CPS discontinuances?

4. *Work Co-ordination*: patterns of collaboration and co-operation between organisations, e.g.

Should the police perform the initial listing of cases into the magistrates' court?

Who 'splits' the list in the magistrates' court?

Benson suggests that, in their attempt to achieve a beneficial equilibrium, managers will direct activity in certain ways, including:

'A.   *The fulfilment of program requirements.*   The organisation is oriented to the maintenance of order and effectiveness in its established programs. The organisation's claim to a supply of resources (money and authority) will typically be based upon the adequacy and effectiveness of its established programs. Thus, agency officials are reluctant to undertake tasks or to tolerate practices of other agencies which interfere with the fulfilment of present programs. And they will exert pressures upon other agencies to cease practices disruptive of program requirements.

B.   *The maintenance of a clear domain of high social importance.* The administrators are oriented to the maintenance of a clear-cut, uncluttered claim that includes a set of important activities. Such a domain is characterised by *one or more* of the following attributes: 1) exclusiveness - a claim untrammelled, unchallenged by other organisations; 2) autonomy - a claim permitting the performance of activities independently, without supervision, direction, or shared authority by another agency; 3) dominance - a claim permitting authoritative direction of other agencies operating in a specified sphere. Allocation of funds and authority are based on the domain held by an agency. The greater the domain approximates the criteria above, the greater the hold over funds and authority assigned to the sphere of activities in question.

C.   *The maintenance of orderly, reliable patterns of resource flow.* The organisations are oriented to see that the support network operates in a predictable, dependable way that permits the agency to anticipate an adequate and certain flow of resources.

D.   *The extended application and defence of the agency's paradigm.* The organisation participants are committed to their agency's way of doing things - to its own definitions of problems and tasks and its own techniques of intervention. This might be called a technological-ideological commitment. Organisations which use or espouse other approaches are seen as irresponsible or immoral. And, efforts are made to see that the 'proper' definitions and techniques are adopted.' (Benson, 1975, pp. 232-233)

This list of strategies describes rather well characteristics of organisational behaviour in the criminal justice network. The Home Office, Lord Chancellors' Department, the judiciary, magistrates' clerks, police services, the Crown Prosecution Service, defence solicitors, the Bar, Prison Service, voluntary organisations and probation services all seem to behave in ways that only make sense when seen as conforming to their need to secure their positions in a 'political economy'. This is rather reassuring since it suggests that this strife is endemic to networks and is not just a pathology of these particular organisations and their members.

Situations change and so networks are constantly subject to re-negotiation. In negotiation, it is useful to note whence the power is drawn. Some power will be located in the internal structure of the network and more available to those in the centre where the flow of information may be controlled, (e.g. the court) than to those at the periphery (e.g. the local probation services). Another source of power is derived from external linkages to interest groups - or politicians - who lend allegiance, or exert pressure, to obtain their objectives. Such pressure can be exerted both formally and informally. An instance of both is the pressure on the judiciary to send fewer people to prison.

8.4.2 The organisation-set

The second model examines inter-organisational relations from the perspective of the communications between a particular organisation and others with which it interacts in the 'organisation-set'. This contrasts with and complements Benson's more anthropological description of a society of organisations. Evan (1972) suggests the use of a set of questions to build up a picture about inter-organisational communications.

Four sets of issues are raised about an organisation and its position in a network:

1. *What is the status of the focal organisation?* Is it is a sub-system of a larger organisation, a system in its own right or a supra-system of largely autonomous entities? Less power is derived from sub-system

status, most from the level at which the system exists in its own right and least from supra-system status. For instance, the CPS is a system at national level where the magistrate's clerks are supra-system, and a sub-system at area office level where the clerks are at their MCC area system level.

2. *What is the classification of the focal organisation on the three dimensions of*

   size;

   the diversity of its input and output process; and

   the configuration of its communication networks (do they form a tight vertical pattern; resemble the spokes of a wheel; or perhaps appear as a loose interconnected web)?

These three dimensions comprehensively differentiate organisations: for instance a partnership of solicitors is small, not very diverse in its processes and has a loose and flat communication network; on the other hand, a police service is the opposite on each dimension as is reflected in its internal organisational culture.

3. *Analyse the role-sets of the boundary personnel who make the actual contacts with members of other agencies.* Personnel are categorised as being at one of three grades, Technical, Managerial or Institutional (i.e. executive level).

4. *Consider the links and matches between the boundary-spanning personnel. What is:*

   the ratio of different grades of 'boundary-spanning' staff involved in each agency;

   the quality of their match as judged by the similarity of degree of formal education;

   the position in the hierarchy and degree of authority each has with regard to negotiations with the other agencies; and

   the normative referent group chosen by staff - do they refer to their profession, their level, class, or their employing agency?

We now have an inventory of issues to consider about inter-organisational communication:

1. Check whether the agency is acting as a system in its own right or just a sub-system.

2. Consider the mismatch of the organisations, especially on the dimensions of size, complexity of processes and communication configuration.

3. Note the match or mismatch of the hierarchy of roles in which boundary-spanning interaction is performed: do the personnel involved belong to the institutional, the managerial or the technical level?
4. Consider their boundary-spanning role partners and ask how they match on the four structural dimensions (ratio of staff, match of education/ qualifications, degree of authority and normative referent group).

The method may be mechanical but the answers provide a comprehensive map of the terrain. Consider the relationship between the police and the CPS, as described above, which has been uneasy ever since the CPS took over the prosecution function from the police. The following quotation, taken from an article in the magazine *Police* expresses one side of their power struggle over authority (domain and ideological consensus) and money:

'Far from releasing large numbers of police officers for operational duties, it appears that the service is now devoting more resources, and particularly man hours, to work in connection with the preparation of cases and liaison with the CPS... The CPS is largely responsible for this additional demand on police time, because the procedures it requires the police to comply with appear to be designed for the convenience of the CPS rather than the efficient administration of the criminal justice system. A case in point is the increasing requirement for full transcripts of tape recorded interviews with suspects, - a time consuming and often totally unnecessary task which adds to delays in dealing with cases. If the CPS staff had the task of transcribing the tapes (and surely this should be a CPS responsibility) we doubt if the practice would survive for long... But perhaps the most important impact of the CPS on the police service has been on police morale. The knowledge that the criminal justice system appears to have deteriorated rather than improved since the advent of the CPS has had a bad effect on police confidence in that system... It cannot be stressed too strongly that public confidence in the criminal justice system is of the utmost importance... In many cases, the police have the unenviable task of explaining to shocked or bewildered ordinary citizens why there has been no prosecution against the persons who have harmed them in a criminal way. It is difficult for them to understand that, having lodged a complaint with the police, the decision not to prosecute has been taken by another body altogether.' (Police, 1990, Editorial, p. 5)

Benson's account of the political economy of networks reassures us that this episode in the negotiation over authority is a normal phenomenon. Benson would focus on the network as a whole and see the agencies as involved in the protection of their authority and financial resources through the defence of their domain. The mode of negotiation will depend on the relative power of each agency and this in turn will stem from its internal position in the network and its external links to other powerful groups. One way or another, the two agencies can be seen to be locked into a struggle to create a new equilibrium of domain and ideological consensus and the supporting battle to increase:

1. the fulfilment of their program requirements;
2. the maintenance of a clear domain of high social importance;
3. the maintenance of orderly, reliable patterns of resource flow; and
4. the application and defence of the agency's paradigm.

Evan's approach offers a way of planning a repair to the relationship. The questions form the basis of a diagnosis:

1. The local CPS at branch level is a sub-system whilst the police service is a system in its own right.
2. The police organisation is large, hierarchic and has a complexity of processes whilst the CPS is relatively small, has a flat local hierarchy and deals with a simple and single input-output process.
3. Police constables operate on the technical level as, on the whole, do CPS solicitors: but the interaction is complicated by;
4. The ratio of staff, match of education/qualifications, degree of authority and normative referent group. This is ill matched between solicitor and police constable. Hence the development of the Administrative Support Units which provide a more permanent police presence and can act as a buffer between police officers and CPS solicitors.

A second illustration is the implementation of the set of proposals on time-limits established by the Working Group on 'Pre-Trial Issues' (Home Office, 1990d), discussed in Chapters 4 and 7. Evan invites us to consider the implications of this in terms of the various systems and sub-systems. From the point of view of the magistrates' clerks, the Working Group operated at the national, supra-system level whilst for the CPS it was at the apex of their actual system. How were the boundary-spanning personnel matched? If the CPS put forward their institutional level staff the educational match would be equivalent. However, whilst CPS staff would have had full negotiating rights, the magistrates' clerks, being a constellation of smaller local agencies, would not have had equivalent representation. As a result one would expect that the degree of authority wielded by the CPS would be greater than that of the clerks. Of course, this same analysis suggests that at the local MCC and petty session division levels, the corollary would be true and the power of the clerk would be potentially greater than that of the CPS and, possibly, the police.

The two models supplied by Benson and Evan provide a way of analysing the structural components of inter-organisational networks. From such an analysis of the network viable strategies can be devised.

8.5 COLLABORATIVE ADVANTAGE

Implicit in both the models described above is that where there are differences of interest there will be conflict and competition. These are taken as fact and the task then becomes to work to find a resolution or equilibrium. But this is not the only way. Huxham (1992), writing about inter-agency working, introduces the useful concept of 'collaborative advantage' which occurs when a:

> '... synergistic or unusual creativity is produced - perhaps an objective is met - that no organisation could have produced on its own AND when each organisation, through the collaboration, is able to achieve its objectives better than it could on its own.' (Huxham, 1992, p. 4)

The familiar competitive advantage is assumed to exist as the natural state of affairs whilst the fertile asset of collaborative advantage is not assumed to exist and must be discovered, if not created. Huxham's research suggests that the collaborative capacity of an organisation is limited not just by its environment but by the necessity of placing staff of high individual maturity at critical posts. Roberts & Bradley (1991) also argue that the more complex the issue over which collaboration must occur, the greater the need for self-reflection by the collaborators on their performance and attitudes to the collaborative process.

So, what if, instead of working at conflict resolution, we question the assumption of endemic conflict and work at developing collaborative capacity and creating collaborative advantage? Here, it is instructive to note that, contrary to the popular image, customers and suppliers in industry are usually in collaborative relationships. In the modern motor manufacturing trade, between 60 per cent and 80 per cent of the final product is bought in from outside suppliers. Great attention is therefore given to the conduct of inter-organisational relationships. Customer and provider meet together to forge long-term, robust, collaborative relations. The approach is known as 'simultaneous engineering' in which the customer is at pains to provide the suppliers with the knowledge and competence to perform their part of the process. Both parties, together and in parallel, develop their joint capacity to build the final product. Both parties work to create a framework in which the partners can develop their competence and skills to help the other. The alternative competitive strategy of working may provide short-term advantages to one or the other party but is not very productive.

Support for this view comes from a report prepared for the National Council for Voluntary Organisations on how to approach the new organisation of 'Care in the Community'. Gutch (1992) examined joint purchasing schemes of the pubic welfare sector in the USA to see what lessons could be learnt from them. He noted that the contracting process had become dominated by audit concerns of cost and by those occasions when a contractor 'fails to deliver' and that there was little opportunity to praise or show respect for the other agency's staff.

'Providers are subject to onerous reporting requirements... None of this annual paper blizzard addresses the question of outcome of service delivery. The system, in focusing on the paper chase, has lost focus on the client.' (Gutch, 1992, p. 14)

Spencer and Kunz (1992), also writing about effective inter-organisational arrangements in the voluntary sector, find them in partnerships which they describe as:

'... an agreement between two or more partners to work together to achieve common aims... It is a dynamic process rather than a static state of affairs... It will work best if there is an equal balance between the partners, mutual respect and understanding, and a recognition that each has a legitimate and valuable role to play... from a secure structural foundation providing flexibility and clear expectations and communication.' (Spencer and Kunz, 1992, p.3)

The message is clear: collaborate for greater effectiveness and efficiency. Joint purchasing agreements between health and social service agencies will greatly benefit from careful preparation and attention to collaborative advantage. Similarly, in negotiations with suppliers of office equipment and the maintenance of photo-copier and computer systems, a collaborative relationship is more likely to ensure a robust and reliable service. It is often less expensive, over the long period, than 'playing the market' for cheap offers and then paying again for rescue operations.

There are certain unambiguous areas where simple collaboration between the court and another agency can be made. For instance, in the Crown Court, some senior resident judges have come to agreement with local chief probation officers on 'Statements of Preferred Practice'. The probation service agrees to offer a fast track report service, perhaps quick, one-day assessments on 'stand-down' and possibly another service of reports within four or five days. But, if the probation officer decides that more time is needed in a particular case, the judge will honour and respect the decision. This way, because an agreement containing contingencies protects the probation service, a more flexible response can be made to specific requests for reports. Because the judiciary have agreed to honour the decision of the probation officer that a particular report may not be suitable for the fast track, they have access to fast reports on the great majority of cases. This is a particularly interesting agreement since it has to be based on mutual respect, agreed adult to adult, and speaks of a new relationship between the judiciary and professionals. This is an instance of the mature approach to managing criminal justice to which we will refer again in Chapter 10 and can only be developed when the parties have already proved themselves accountable, reliable and efficient.

But collaboration is not so straightforward at the core of the courts' inter-agency activities. As was argued in Chapter 7, there are special conditions in the court setting where the output is an intangible: it is a 'just process'. There is a serious and possibly insurmountable tension between the maintenance of a convenient, collaborative network of professional users and the dispensation of justice, with minimal delay, to victims, witnesses and defendants.

8.6   CASE STUDY

The challenges and consequences of inter-dependent organisational relations have been described in the study of scheduling in the magistrates' courts in Chapter 7(Raine & Willson, 1992; 1993). Eight clerkships were studied and it was found that different courts displayed different patterns of equilibrium in their inter-organisational relations. Significant cultural differences were found between the clerkships in the way they addressed the inter-agency aspects of this complex task.

Interviews and observations in the research led to the identification of two critical dimensions of culture. The first was the extent to which the courts took the lead and controlled the work. In some areas the power had been claimed to make the other court users accountable to the courts and, through them, to the communities they served. In other areas it seemed that the courts considered themselves more as one of the set of actors in the system, while in others again the feeling was that the courts had very little control over the other agencies and what they did. Those courts which placed great emphasis on holding users to account in addition tended also to employ a system of clear management accountability internally.

The second dimension was the extent to which the courts actively invested in strategy, both externally and internally. Externally some courts placed great emphasis on creating strategic relationships with the professional users - the police, CPS and defence solicitors. Discussion and negotiation were conducted, often in court user groups, to arrange how best to meet the needs of all parties. The magistrates' clerks also conducted high level discussions with the chief executives of other agencies to achieve long-term agreements. At the other end of the scale, the research identified some magistrates' clerks who invested less in strategic arrangements and long-term working relationships with practitioners. Similarly, while some courts had developed information and monitoring strategies as an aid to planning, others worked more on a day-to-day basis.

Control and strategy
These two dimensions of culture were conceived to interact as shown below:

1. higher control/ higher investment in strategy;
2. lower control/ higher investment in strategy;
3. lower control/ lower investment in strategy;
4. higher control/ lower investment in strategy.

Figure 8.1 plots the eight clerkships as they appeared to fit on the two dimensions. Descriptive titles have been attached to the four quadrants of the framework and the clerkships have been labelled A to H (as in Figure 7.1) on a descending scale reflecting the percentage of cases listed for trial that went ahead as planned.

Figure 8.1 Clerkship cultures - control and strategy

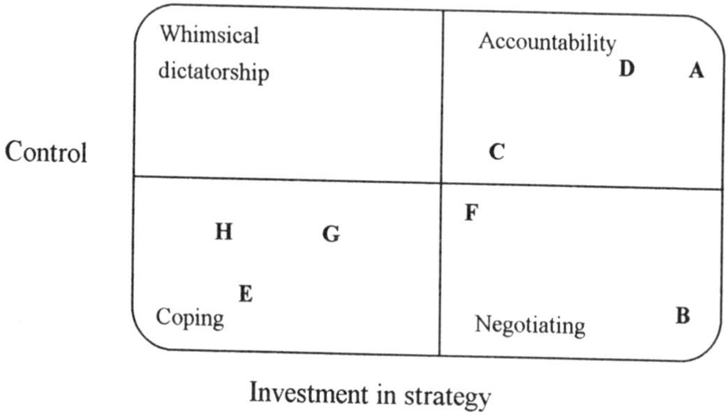

Control

Investment in strategy

Data was also collected on the percentage of trials that were completed on the day, regardless of whether they 'collapsed' or not, and also the 1990/91 average Key Indicator No. 2 (KI2) of the MIS system (see Chapter 5), which is a measure of the amount of delay in cases coming though the court. These are plotted on Figure 8.2 and show a considerable resemblance to the previous figure, showing the relationship of culture to consequence.

Both clerkships A and D had had a difficult transition to their current culture in which they held the other professionals accountable to the court and, through it, to the community. They lacked the close and informal relations found in the courts where less emphasis was placed on

Figure 8.2 Clerkship culture, delay and percentage disposed of on the day

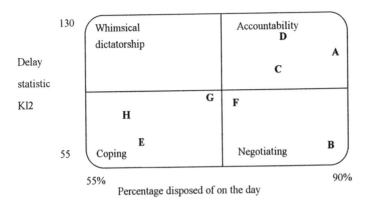

'control'. Might this be the crucial characteristic? On the other hand, clerkship B was very much concerned with negotiating with its user group but did not hold the agencies accountable to the court and did not press them on minimising delay. This is reflected in its position to the bottom right-hand corner in both figures.

Clerkship F appeared to balance the tensions with an economy of effort. Clerkships E and H did not see themselves as being able to negotiate strategically either procedures or expectations with other agencies. Nor did they see themselves as having the power or right to do so, as is reflected in their position in both figures. Clerkship C had a higher level of investment in strategy but only a moderate level of control and yet performed well on both the KI2 measure and the outcomes criteria. The distinguishing characteristic here might be the existence of a long-term local legal professional community and/or a special service from the police who happened to provide fast full-file preparation.

The study demonstrates the impact of relations with other agencies on the work of the magistrates' courts. The issue is the extent to which a court should hold the other professional users accountable or whether it is just one entity in the criminal justice process operating in that locality. This is turn revolves around decisions made not just about the role of the court but also about the manner in which inter-agency relations are planned and inter-dependencies negotiated.

'The court which assumes a high degree of control, while undoubtedly in the best position in principle to minimise delays, may risk paying a price in terms of less co-operative relationships with professional users, perhaps in terms of more 'collapsed' trials, more requests for adjournments, and more unused court resources as a result, because the parties are more often unready to proceed. Similarly, the clerkship which emphasises the convenience of its professional users through active partnership and co-operation over policies and practices, although better able to operate more predictable, resource efficient scheduling, may well pay - or require the non-professional users to pay - a price in terms of longer delays in completing cases.' (aine & Willson, 1992, p. 60)

8.7 CONCLUSION

Normal rivalries for professional and personal preference characterise most inter-personal and inter-organisational relations but these issues have a particular quality to them in the field of criminal justice. But there seems a reluctance to examine these issues in detail, perhaps because of awkward contradictions such as how independence is meant to be paramount even though, managerially, all are held to be bound in one 'system'. It is said that paralysis is the price paid by the millipede who becomes aware of how it walks so perhaps the complexity of inter-dependence in the courts should be appreciated but not examined. The argument of this chapter is the contrary: because this area is ambiguous and contradictory it is particularly necessary that practitioners should gain a clear view of the issues and their options for dealing with them. Strategy can be developed through an analysis of network inter-dependencies and inter-agency linkages. Informed decisions can be made about internal and external organisation. The tension can be held between efficiency and due process, as it can between judicial independence and public service and between the various demands of the court users, the executive, the Government and the vulnerable victim. But in order to do this, one must plot and plan.

CHAPTER 9

Professionals and the laity

'All professions are conspiracies against the laity.'
George Bernard Shaw, *The Doctor's Dilemma*, 1906.

9.1 INTRODUCTION

To a considerable extent the character of the courts' process is governed
by the values of the professionals, for example, the judges, counsel, the
CPS lawyers, the defence solicitors, the magistrates' clerks, the
probation officers and the police. But it is, of course, an environment
for lay people as well. On the one hand, there are the defendants, the
victims and the witnesses in each case. On the other, there are lay
people involved in the judicial process, as members of juries and as
magistrates. In addition, other lay groups provide supporting services at
court. For example, volunteers from the Women's Royal Volunteer
Service (WRVS) frequently operate refreshment counter services for the
public in court foyers, and Victim Support volunteers provide advice and
information to victims attending court. Members of the press also attend
court on a daily basis.

How do these various groups of lay people function alongside the
professionals? What is the relationship between the laity and the
professionals, or more particularly, how do the professionals regard and
respond to their lay compatriots? In this chapter we consider both the
roles and treatment of lay groups within the otherwise professional world
of courts. We do so by focusing especially on two groups of the laity;
essentially as two case studies of volunteers in criminal justice. The two
groups which we have chosen are, on the one hand, lay magistrates and,
on the other, victims and witnesses, particularly those for the
prosecution. The two groups are selected not only because they happen
to illustrate issues of considerable significance concerning the treatment

of the laity within the professional world of the court, but also because they provide clear contrasts with one another in terms of status and role played within the judicial process. We preface these case studies, however, by doing two things. First we ponder upon the difficult issue of what exactly is meant by the term 'professional' in this context, our aim being to draw attention to the pitfalls that so easily arise as a result of our prejudices and preconceptions in this respect. Second, we explore some of the features of commonality and of difference between various sub-groups of the laity, and reflect upon the implications these might have for the way professionals approach their interactions with lay colleagues.

9.2 WHO ARE THE PROFESSIONALS?

There are two types of people in the world: those who divide the world into two types and those who do not. For instance, we hear of:

the professional and the amateur;
the professional classes and the working classes;
the professional and the unqualified staff;
the professional and the conscript;
the professional lady and the wife;
the professional and the volunteers;
the professional and the laity.

These are deeply ingrained distinctions and in all but one case, the appellation 'professional' carries the implication of 'superior'. Even the image of 'the Great British Amateur' does not seriously challenge the understanding that the professionals know best.

It is inevitable, then, that the relationships between the professional and the laity in criminal justice are affected by the assumption that the professional comes first. Let us, therefore, consider what is meant and implied by these terms since it is likely that our thinking and practice are unconsciously coloured by assumptions drawn from elsewhere.

The first real distinction is one of payment. Professional means getting paid. It may also be thought to mean knowing more and having greater experience, but this is not necessarily true. Certainly the lay magistrate knows more about being a lay magistrate than does a stipendiary and the victim and witness know more about their recollection of the particular crime than do the advocates. What they do not know so much about is a different matter, namely, the procedures of the court.

The second distinction is about business. The professionals pursue their business in the courts and, as in any work place, will try and make it as congenial as possible and design it to meet not just the goals of the organisation but their own needs also. This is known as satisficing. The laity, on the other hand, comes to court rarely. A victim, witness and member of a jury may come only once and so they have little opportunity to have a planned and concerted impact on its organisation. Magistrates attend regularly and those who attend most frequently tend to have more impact on the way the court behaves, but again, as volunteers, they are visitors rather than residents.

It is inevitable, therefore, that the court will become organised around the needs and priorities of the professionals and that the role of the laity is relegated and regulated to fit in with them. And this is the challenge for the professionals, to agree not to collude, but to use their influence to welcome and support the laity. Instead of equating the 'laity' with amateur, conscript and labouring classes, the professionals must grant them the respect of colleagues, customers or, best of all, equals. Similarly, instead being equated with prostitute, patron and hired killer, the professionals must make sure that they will be seen by the laity as enablers, resources and equals.

Before proceeding further, however, let us pose a further complication. This is that the typical managerial definition of the 'professional' is of someone able to exercise discretion at the point where uncertainty and complexity occur (see Chapter 4). In many instances that tends to accord with the social status definition expounded and criticised above. But it need not necessarily be the case. In this chapter, for example, which discusses lay magistrates among others, we certainly need to draw a distinction between the two definitions and recognise that although members of the laity, magistrates are also professionals. Thus, for 'professional' read 'paid' and for 'laity' read 'unpaid'. This may seem very clumsy but as Humpty Dumpty said, 'When *I* use a word it means just what I choose it to mean, neither more nor less.' And who could argue with that?

9.3 THE LAITY AT COURT

Having opened Pandora's Box on professionals, let us now focus on the laity and summarise some of the differences and similarities in the status and role of the different groups at court in this respect. First are some differences.

Magistrates will know fairly well the rules, procedures and practices by which their court operates, since most will be working there at regular intervals (typically for half a day each week or fortnight). They will also all have had the benefit of training and experience gained over the duration of their service.

Jury members, in contrast, are mostly 'first timers', and do not receive training. All they get is a rudimentary guide to the court process and to their role within the trial process immediately before they are required to take their places in the court-room jury box.

Victims will mostly be at court for the first time in their lives. Many have to testify as key witnesses for the prosecution, and will therefore be anxious about giving evidence and also at the prospect of seeing the defendant and at having to relive painful memories. Many victims also attend court to observe the judicial process. They feel the need to see justice being done, as do 'third party' victims, such as the relatives of people who have been murdered or maimed.

Witnesses for the prosecution and defence will also mostly be at court for the first time, and accordingly many will naturally be somewhat apprehensive about giving evidence, though probably not to the extent of victims, simply because they are usually neither so personally involved in the cases nor so concerned about the outcomes.

Defendants form a rather mixed group in terms of experience of the courts. Some are 'regulars' (as the professionals amiably refer to them), and have gained at least a basic understanding of 'the system' and of what to expect. Others, however, will be attending court for the first time, apprehensive and uncertain about the process and, of course, about the outcomes of their cases.

Besides such differences in the roles and the amount of prior experience of the different lay groups who attend courts, there are also some important similarities.

First, all the lay groups share the characteristic of a relatively 'low dependency' on the criminal justice process. What we mean here is that they do not receive pay or other rewards as a result of their contributions in the way that the professionals do. Even magistrates, who devote many hours to their work on the Bench, are entitled only to claim travel expenses and financial loss allowance. Victims may be awarded compensation either from the state's national scheme for Criminal Injuries Compensation, or as a result of a compensation order against the convicted offender. They may also claim expenses incurred in attending court if they are required to give evidence, as with all witnesses. The same is true of those doing jury service. But beyond such reimbursement of costs incurred, members of the laity can hardly be considered to gain by their involvement in the justice process. The professionals, on the other hand, always benefit.

Second, and in direct contrast, the criminal justice process does depend heavily on the laity. In the case of magistrates, for instance, the state relies on them to deal with some 97 per cent of all criminal cases. Similarly the criminal justice process depends vitally upon the willingness of victims and witnesses to come forward to report the crimes and to give account of what they experienced, saw and heard. Without the co-operation of lay witnesses, it would be very difficult for the justice process to operate effectively in contested cases. This, for example, was emphasised in a project in Tunisia conducted in the 1970s to improve public relations between the courts and the community which resulted in far more people coming forward to report crime and give evidence in this respect (UNICRI, 1971). Also to be considered here is the high value placed on a participative laity from the viewpoint of democracy, this also being the underpinning of the jury system (which like the lay magistracy, although having often been much maligned on account of its lack of professionalism, has never been seriously threatened).

Third, members of the laity generally lack knowledge of legal detail and process and, as a result, often lack the confidence to conduct themselves in quite the way that professionals can.

Fourth, while the professionals expect to manage themselves (because they know the important rules and expectations and think they should be trusted to get on with their jobs), the laity, to professional eyes, has to be organised. Moreover, the laity must be organised with care and sensitivity, and with the minimum of coercion as befits their situation as being, like us, just 'ordinary people'.

Let us briefly consider a little further what good organisation might mean with regard to each of the key lay groups in turn.

9.4 ORGANISING THE LAITY

So far as lay magistrates are concerned, good organisation means, first and foremost, recognising their status and position as members of the judiciary. Respect is certainly called for, but also they must be nurtured not a little because they are lay volunteers in an increasingly professionalised environment. Accordingly, a great deal of the time and effort has traditionally been devoted by magistrates' clerks to making members of local Benches feel respected, appreciated and comfortable - the 'butler role', as it was described in the Scrutiny report, (Home Office, 1989a) and remarked upon in Chapter 8.

Turning to jury members, good organisation here too, requires that they should be carefully looked after, partly because they will be unfamiliar with the criminal justice process and partly because it is important that their impartiality is protected in the interests of justice. They must arrive at court through entrances which are separate from those used by other members of the public and the professionals. Inside too they must be kept apart from other parties, for which purposes complex circulation zones are designed in Crown Court buildings to channel juries to each court-room without allowing 'contamination' with other groups.

Much the same applies in the case of the good organisation of witnesses on whom the system of criminal justice also greatly depends. Here it has to be remembered that the more calm the witnesses are, the more likely they are to be able to assist the court in the pursuit of justice. It will also be important to keep witnesses segregated from one another and from other parties if their evidence is to be believed as being 'uncontaminated'. To this end, all witnesses in a case must also be barred from the court-room until it is their turn to go into the witness box.

In some respects the position with regard to defendants is a little different. Here in particular, a degree more coercion may seem legitimate in the context of those alleged to have offended. Some, of course, will have to be forcibly remanded in custody on that basis. But even then, there are limits to the use of coercive power, simply because the law presumes a person innocent until proved guilty by the court. Ushers and other court staff may need to be firm in maintaining orderly behaviour in the court precincts and in ensuring that all defendants are ready to go into court when their turn is called. But they must also demonstrate impartiality by treating each defendant with respect and civility, whatever the charges against them.

In summary then, there may be some detailed differences as to what good organisational practice means for each of the different lay groups involved in the criminal justice process. But at the same time there are also some important similarities. All must attend, but, unlike the professional groups, without the lure of payment or other rewards. All will require some form of special treatment, whether deferential or coercive; they cannot be left to themselves. Most are likely to have only limited knowledge and experience of the legal world in which they are involved, when compared with their professional counterparts; they must therefore be assisted, advised, guided or directed. All are required by the judicial process to perform important functions but cannot necessarily be relied upon to behave quite as expected or to understand in quite the way that is supposed of professionals. Many defendants, for instance, do wilfully misbehave in court foyers, and, indeed, sometimes in court-rooms as well, as if to test the limits of the officials. Victims and witnesses too may disrupt proceedings from time to time by breaking down in tears under the pressure of cross-examination. Juries sometimes fail to understand what is expected of them and have to be dismissed and replaced by new groups, and the trials re-started. Even magistrates, with the benefits both of training programmes and of regular experience in sittings, may sometimes make mistakes, and in so doing, serve to undermine the judicial process and their own authority. Often this can happen through an 'innocent' remark by presiding magistrates in the little homilies that often accompany the announcement of sentences.

There is always, then, the chance with the laity that the normally calm ambience of the court-house becomes disrupted by the unpredictable actions of those without the experience and confidence that we all tend to associate with 'true professionalism'. There is, of course, also every chance that efficiency in the conduct of court business suffers as a result of this potential for disorder and as a result of the inexperience or innocence of the laity. But no doubt that is a price worth paying in return for the services of those, as we have said, on whom the courts greatly depend.

Having thus set the scene, let us now turn to our two case studies, to consider in more detail how the tasks of supporting and organising the laity are undertaken in practice. The two case studies, of lay magistrates on the one hand, and of victims and witnesses on the other, provide interesting contrasts with one another, not just in the obvious senses of role and status in the court process, but also in terms of change over time in the nature and extent of support provided. In this respect, lay magistrates have traditionally been treated to a relatively high degree of respect, endearment and support by those responsible for organising them at court, the magistrates' clerks. Victims and witnesses, on the other hand, have long been a relatively neglected group in the criminal justice process. However, rather curiously, at about the time that the new managerialism arrived in the 1980s, the position seemed to change. From the mid 1980s onwards, magistrates generally began to feel more neglected and taken for granted, while the interests of victims and witnesses moved rapidly up the list of priorities in the new, more 'customer-conscious' context of public service.

9.5 ORGANISING AND SUPPORTING MAGISTRATES

As we have said already, magistrates must be regarded as professionals (according to the definition based on the exercising of discretion) even though they are members of the laity in criminal justice. As they often remind each other, they are certainly not to be thought of as amateurs. They are also the real volunteers in the courts' process. Defendants are summoned to attend court, as are witnesses (at least those who admit to being witnesses to a crime). Members of juries also undertake their tasks under conditions of some compulsion (all citizens who are entitled to vote in governmental elections are expected to be available for jury service). Magistrates, on the other hand, perform their duties as a result of assenting to serve on the Bench. Throughout the period of office, they are under no obligation to continue Bench service and may resign at any time.

Magistrates are also, of course, the most institutionalised and powerful of the lay groups. As members of the Benches which they join, they enjoy special status and authority. That status is, in part, a legacy of the history of the magistracy, and harks back to times when the Bench was entirely composed of the local aristocracy who were the feudal landowners who dispensed justice, with the permission of the Crown, upon their serfs, servants and tenants. Moreover, while today the local Bench is supposed to be comprised of 'peers' of the community, magisterial status and power are reinforced by the fact that the appointment system still recruits a predominance of people from the relatively privileged middle classes. Even those most contemptuous of the magistracy, critical of its narrow social class base, of its role as part of the 'establishment', and who question its competence and right to adjudicate know the power granted to lay magistrates in court and that any actions or statements in court which are perceived to challenge the authority of the Bench are likely to be regarded as being 'in contempt'.

But at the same time, being lay magistrates tends to give rise to some feelings of vulnerability in the court-room. Though magistrates may have 'legitimate power', that is power derived from their position on the Bench (French & Raven, 1960), they have little 'expert power'. Accordingly, magistrates' clerks, who are all qualified lawyers, provide the all important professional counter-balance to the lay status of the magistrates. The clerks guide them in the law both in and outside the court-room; they train them, and in so doing, one aim is to minimise the possibility of illegal, unacceptable, or inconsistent decisions, or indeed of 'faux pas'. A key objective here is to protect the authority of the Bench.

Some clerks are able to achieve this objective better than others. Much depends on their ability to establish and sustain control over the Benches for which they are responsible. Sometimes differences in this regard reflect differences in the strength of personality of the clerks, and sometimes they simply relate to different traditions between Benches in terms of the dominance or compliance of their chairpersons. But whatever the traditions or natural assertive qualities of the lay adjudicators and their professional advisers in the lower courts, magistrates' clerks do what they can to serve and meet the needs of the lay Bench, or 'their magistrates' (to use the language of most clerks).

The role of the magistrates' clerk towards the lay Bench can be seen to have two sides to it. The first is to protect its legal authority and the second is to maintain and support. Let us examine these two sides in turn.

9.5.1 Protecting the legal authority of the lay Bench

What approaches might the clerks adopt to this end? We would identify six as follows:

Training
First, magistrates' clerks are responsible for the basic training of all members of their Benches and therefore have the opportunity to implant ideas, to suggest practices and advocate policies which they themselves would wish to be adopted. Sentencing policy, for example, although officially a matter for the magistrates of each Bench to decide, is in practice usually heavily shaped at local level by the magistrates' clerks and promoted through sentencing training sessions.

Consultation before decision
The clerks may also help to protect and enhance the legal authority of lay magistrates by encouraging them to consult before deciding contentious or complex matters in court. To this end, many clerks repeatedly emphasise the importance of the magistrates inviting their clerk to join them in the retiring room in any difficult cases (following them out after an appropriate interval, of course, so as not to give the impression of the clerk being an unofficial partner on the Bench). Here, in privacy, the clerk will explain the legal issues involved in the case, to outline the options for the Bench and, no doubt, to offer guidance on the possible sentence, all of which is much more difficult in public view in the court-room.

Rehearsed verbal contributions
Another approach towards protecting the lay Bench, again largely achieved through training, has been to minimise the verbal contribution of magistrates in the court-room. Only the chairpersons should speak (despite the tradition that lay magistrates should sit in panels of three), and even then, the clerks believe, they should stick, whenever possible, to the prepared lines, as rehearsed in training sessions with the clerk (and often reproduced on cards as 'aide memoires' for the chairperson). Moreover, only those who have received special training are allowed to take the chair in court. Indeed, to minimise still further the risk of mistakes or regrettable behaviour from the Bench, a nation-wide system of appraisal for chairpersons has recently been introduced by the Lord Chancellor's Department, with generally enthusiastic support from magistrates' clerks at local level.

Court-room layout
Protection of the lay Bench by the clerks has also been pursued in some instances through the seating arrangements in the court-room.

Traditionally the clerks have sat directly in front of the Bench at the same level as the solicitors and other professional parties. Most still do, for they are then in a good position to conduct the legal and administrative processes with their professional colleagues, and are able to guard against any direct interaction between those on the floor of the court and the magistrates (it is thus the clerks who personally hand any papers from the solicitors to the Bench chairperson). At the same time, the clerk can easily intervene to preserve the Bench from becoming involved in issues that might be beyond its legal competence. But some magistrates' clerks have preferred to relocate their desks to the side of the court-room, next to the Bench in order to offer support and protection to the magistrates as well as control over the other practitioners. In this position they can maintain eye contact with magistrates as well as with the professionals. They can manage both groups and, as a result, manage the conduct of proceedings better as a whole.

Presence

The desire to protect also underlies the apparent willingness of many magistrates' clerks to accede to requests from the Bench that they themselves should be in the court-room as much as possible, rather than delegating the legal advisory role to their assistants - the court clerks. Compared with other public services, it is unusual that the most senior officers (for that is what the magistrates' clerks are) should undertake routinely the mostly humdrum duties of 'clerking' in the court-room (how often, for example, would a chief constable be seen on the beat, or a chief probation officer be seen interviewing a client?). But the point is that their presence is precisely what the Bench most appreciates. From the lay magistrates' viewpoint, support in court by their most senior clerk is good for confidence, because it can safely be presumed that the best legal advice is to hand (and we would all want that, would we not?).

Amalgamations of Benches

One further approach which the magistrates' clerks may pursue in protecting the legal authority of the lay magistrates would concern the organisation of the local Bench. Many clerks tend to support the idea of amalgamating the smaller Benches in their territories since these are often perceived as the source of the greater risk to their reputations. It is the 'strength in numbers' argument. A Bench of medium or large size is generally perceived to be more confident in itself and to command more respect from the legal practitioner community. The small Benches, on the other hand, particularly those in rural areas, often carry with them the reputation (by no means necessarily deserved) of displaying maverick tendencies and of being pre-disposed towards the justice of an earlier age. Throughout the 1980s, therefore, and riding on the back of the Government's campaign for rationalisation in the organisational structure of the local service which we chronicled in Chapter 5, many magistrates' clerks were actively plotting, and often succeeding, to effect amalgamations of their small lay Benches.

Summary

These, then are some of the ways in which the magistrates' clerks have sought to protect the lay magistracy and sustain its authority, particularly in the eyes of other professionals. No doubt some of these strategies could also serve to benefit the status of the clerks themselves. But, more important, they helped to insure against bad decision making by the lay magistrates; to sustain the credibility of the volunteers, and to ensure that the decisions eventually announced in court would be as close as possible to those which they themselves, as qualified lawyers, would have felt appropriate (Darbyshire, 1984).

9.5.2 *Supporting the lay Bench*

What of the other side to the work of magistrates' clerks in relation to the lay Bench?. This has involved making the membership feel appreciated, valued and content in their public service work at court.   Being volunteers, the willingness of magistrates to give time to the court quite naturally depends on such feelings and much of the work, though interesting in the sense of fulfilling curiosity, is hardly pleasant. They must listen, for example, to accounts of petty crime often committed by the more feckless and less fortunate in society; absorb the harrowing details of more serious crimes; appraise violent and pornographic material; and every now and then they must deprive someone of their liberty by sentencing them to prison. These are hardly tasks for which most of us would volunteer, so the duties should be tempered by an ambience of care and support.

To this end, a host of rather pleasant little rituals and practices have been developed and have been diligently attended to by magistrates' clerks around the country for many a year.   The start of each magistrate's Bench career is marked by a carefully organised 'swearing in' ceremony and their retirement is an occasion for a special gathering, formal presentation and for expressions of appreciation. If a magistrate falls ill an arrangement of flowers may be dispatched and perhaps a visit will be arranged. Social events are organised, including an annual dinner, at which the clerks express their gratitude for the hard work undertaken over the year past. Annual Reports are lovingly compiled, more than anything, to reinforce in print such gratitude. In all respects, the social cohesion of the Bench is taken seriously. The clerks, after all, know just how much most magistrates value the friendship and camaraderie that is derived from involvement on the Bench. The clerks also take care to emphasise the respect owed to the magistrates. They know that that, too, is a quality which most members of the Bench appreciate. There is, for example, the little ritual of their entry to, and exit from, the court-room, which the clerks anticipate by firm command to the assembled company to 'stand please!' (Burney, 1979).

Communications are given high priority. Bench newsletters are prepared to keep magistrates informed about new members, new staff, new legislation and other newsworthy aspects. Moreover, magistrates' clerks take every opportunity to keep in personal touch with members of the Bench. Reliance on memos and circulars will not do. Regular face-to-face contact is preferred, so clerks are in the habit at least of putting their heads around the assembly room doors each morning before sittings commence, and of making sure that they can personally attend all Bench meetings, training sessions and magistrates' courts' committee meetings. As in all lines of voluntary work, unless the co-ordinators and organisers are visibly present, it will be difficult indeed for the volunteers to believe that their efforts are really appreciated.

Respecting the volunteer status of magistrates and the limits on their availability and time is considered important too. Thus great care is also taken to try and accommodate the different expectations and preferences of different members of the Bench, again to heighten their sense of being cared for and respected. The magistrates' rota is painstakingly arranged to accommodate each individual's personal preferences as to sitting times and sitting colleagues. Magistrates' clerks know that it is best not to seek to change the basis on which the rota is organised, even if the particular choice of the magistrates in this respect is regarded as the cause of much inefficiency in the scheduling of cases and of extra work for staff. 'Environmental' factors are similarly taken seriously. Convenient, free and secure car-parking arrangements are made, often with great difficulty in city centre areas; coffee is available in the retiring rooms; snack lunches may be laid on too.

On the other hand, it has to be asked how vital are such practices and rituals to upholding the process of criminal justice in the lower courts? Is the pampering of magistrates to this extent really necessary, and can the time spent by magistrates' clerks in so doing be justified against a background of rising workload, tight public money, and other pressures associated with their other roles in managing busy courts and staff? After all, whatever the past history of the servitude of magistrates' clerks in relation to the magistrates who appointed them, today their salaries are more those of top managers than of butlers (Home Office, 1989a)!

9.5.3   Increasing magisterial disaffection

Over the course of the 1980s, these questions were much discussed and many differing views were expressed. The more managerialist of the clerks seemed only too glad to be able to cite pressures of other work as their excuse for rarely appearing in the court-room, or for delegating more of the magistrates' business to their assistants. Being a manager, many confidently asserted, called for a focus on strategic issues, not aspects such as the resolution of car-parking and coffee-making problems! In any case, the argument proceeded, one could surely provide a better legal advisory service to all the court-rooms by remaining in one's office and available on the end of a telephone line rather than by being caught up in the cases in one particular court-room.

Others, however, were less sure. They could see the effect on morale among magistrates of the steady dilution of the traditional magistrate-clerk relationship; of the push for efficiency and the implications in terms of increased parsimony, possible court-house closures and Bench amalgamations, and the weakening of the links between court and community which mattered greatly to most magistrates.

They could also see that other factors were playing a part in lowering esprit de corps on the Bench, notably the increasing amount of time that magistrates were now expected to devote to training, the increasing appointment of full-time stipendiary magistrates, the introduction of appraisal for chairpersons, and the fact that the magisterial recruitment net was being spread ever wider with the result that the Bench had become more socially mixed, and less cohesive.

There was little outright resistance. 'Most magistrates understood and acknowledged the case for and potential benefits of such changes. The Bench did need to move with the times; it was too elitist; more training would make for better justice, and so on. But all that, of course, did not mean that they were happy with the new circumstances. In fact the number of premature resignations from the Bench grew markedly in the 1980s and early 1990s. The reasons given were usually those of other work pressures and competing demands for limited spare time. But probably it was also partly a case of diminishing satisfaction being gained from service on the Bench as a result of all the change.

To be sure, premature resignations formed but a small proportion of the 29,000 or so band of lay magistrates in England & Wales in 1993. Moreover, in most areas of the country enough replacements were to be found without too much difficulty. But might there be a hidden price to be paid for having a less socially bonded, and more disaffected, lay magistracy? Might the consequence of neglecting to sustain attractive terms and conditions for the volunteers be a diminution in their commitment and confidence, and therefore ultimately in the good reputation of the lay Bench? Indeed, might this not, in turn, bring further into question the future of the lay magistracy? Could this, perhaps, be another effect of the new managerialism?

9.6 ORGANISING LAY WITNESSES AND VICTIMS

Having posed these questions, let us leave the magistrates for the moment and turn to the other case study, that of victims and lay witnesses. Ironically, at about the same time that magistrates seemed to be receiving less care and support from their hard-pressed clerks, victims and witnesses were becoming much more the centre of attention within criminal justice. These contrasting trends were mainly coincidental and there was no consciously planned strategic shift in priorities from the Bench to the witness box and public galleries. But as the new preoccupation with 'customer service' (one facet of the new managerialism) began to settle upon the courts in the late 1980s it was inevitable that the interests of victims and witnesses would be taken more seriously, along with those of other 'users' of the courts, such as jury members, defendants, advocates, and probation and police officers. Perhaps then, with so much attention now being focused on the 'users' of the court, it was hardly surprising that the interests of the magistrates - the 'providers' in the lower courts - should be neglected.

Underlying the new concern with victims and witnesses was a general awakening to the plight of those caught up in crime through no fault of their own. In this respect there was growing sympathy particularly with the position and status of victims within the criminal justice process. In earlier times, victims of crime had faced the additional ordeal of having to pursue justice themselves. At least today there was comfort in the fact that the state now accepted the responsibility for prosecuting alleged offenders. But at the same time the price of this progress was that victims often came to feel rather isolated and neglected in the criminal justice process, having had 'their' offences effectively hijacked by the state and pursued through the actions of the official prosecuting authorities. The victim now had no more status in the process than that of any other witness for the prosecution. Perhaps they should not therefore expect any different treatment. After all, it was imperative that the court remained impartial, and to this end, the provision of special treatment for just one party - in this instance victims - might well seem inappropriate.

9.6.1 Victims' and witnesses' experience of the criminal justice process

How are victims and witnesses treated in the criminal justice process? What are the experiences of those who, being on the receiving end or observers of crime, have found themselves involved first with the police, then with the prosecuting authorities and finally with the courts? During the 1980s and early 1990s a number of research studies provided insights in this respect (see, for example, Shapland et al, 1985). The general picture painted was of victims' feelings of distress and hurt at the offences being compounded by feelings of isolation and neglect by the professional agencies. Consider the sense of helplessness underlying the letter written by 70-year-old Edna Phillips to her MP after she had been burgled and six weeks before she was murdered:

> 'I had a robbery weeks ago but the police didn't even take finger prints. When I went to the police station, a woman working there said perhaps they didn't think it warranted taking finger prints, I had everything that

could be carried away taken. What makes it worse, one of my neighbours across the road heard my two windows being smashed, and she phoned the police, but they said they couldn't see anything wrong. That was at nine o'clock, but when I went home from my friend at quarter to eleven everything had been stolen, and the first thing I saw was the window smashed, so why didn't they see it? And I was supposed to have a victim support officer to call but no one came here. I have been ill since it happened.' (Independent Newspaper, 10th March, 1993)

Here the principal failures seemed to lie in the domain of the police. But there were as many instances of blame lying with the other agencies. So far as the courts were concerned, the accounts from several research studies told of a basic lack of care and attention to victims and witnesses; of apparent disregard for the anxieties that they had to endure from the moment when they were instructed to attend.

Ask any court usher! They would know better than most researchers what victims and witnesses experience once inside the precincts of their building. They would certify how routinely witnesses break down in tears in the witness box and have to 'stand down' for a few minutes before being able to resume the ordeal of the cross-examination (Walklate, 1988). They would confirm just how often the calm and order in the public waiting areas is disrupted by the anguished cries and anger of victims on learning that the defendants had been acquitted or that the sentences were unduly lenient. They would also be able to verify the increasing frequency of intimidation of witnesses in the court precincts by friends and associates of defendants, and the awful fear that many victims bear of being cornered by those who had assaulted them, invaded their homes or committed worse offences. Indeed, ushers would endorse the view that courts are places of misery and anger for victims where their personal tragedies are often amplified. They would also confirm that the tolerance of many witnesses who, with appropriate public spiritedness, had previously offered their assistance to the criminal justice process is routinely stretched too far. They would report that many leave the court building shouting their complaints and declaring this to be the last time they will come forward as a witness.

9.6.2   *Victims and witnesses at court*

Perhaps this is all inevitable. Perhaps disquiet and distress on the part of victims and witnesses at court go hand in hand with the dramatic and highly charged circumstances that tend to surround criminal trials. Some might argue that it could not be otherwise. Emotionality, as Rock (1991) points out, is built into the very construction of witnesses. Indeed, it is demanded by the professionals who have dealings with them. To persuade the jury or magistrates to believe their evidence, it is necessary that witnesses appear to be reasonable people:

> 'reasonable people *should* display anger, grief, frustration, and astonishment when their reputation and liberty are in jeopardy. Credibility will depend, in turn, on lay witnesses making the appropriately emotional response at the appropriate time and juries will be invited to scrutinise just how they conduct themselves under examination.' (ock, 1991, p. 268)

On the other hand, there are aspects about the experiences of victims and witnesses at court which suggest that their anxiety and distress are needlessly enhanced by inept and insensitive treatment. Consider, for example, some of the main findings of a study conducted for the charitable organisation Victim Support (Raine & Smith, 1991), based on interviews with nearly 500 victims and witnesses attending the Crown Court at seven different locations in England.

For many witnesses interviewed, the court system was felt to be falling short of expectations even before their arrival. Many reported feeling extremely anxious and confused when they received their Witness Orders (the formal notification of the requirement to attend court to give evidence). The problem was that the Orders gave no indication of the date for the hearing and yet tersely pointed out that:

> 'failure to comply with this Order may render you liable to imprisonment for three months or a fine.'

Not unnaturally, many witnesses were fearful that they might already have missed the date, and that a warrant might have been issued for their arrest. In fact the usual procedure is that dates are decided at a later stage, but this was not made clear on the Witness Orders. Moreover, few witnesses received any supporting information in advance of going to court, explaining, for example, how to get there, what to do on arrival, or what was expected of them in the witness box. Although an official leaflet, 'The Witness in Court', had been produced for this purpose by the Home Office, less than 30 per cent of those interviewed had received a copy.

Many witnesses also found the date selected for their hearing to be inconvenient, but were given neither the opportunity to say so nor to suggest alternatives. Lay witnesses, it appeared, were the last to be consulted over trial dates, the availability of the Bar and police witnesses being the greater considerations. More than half of those interviewed, in fact, felt aggrieved about the date-fixing process and about the lack of consultation with them on the matter. Furthermore, in many instances little advance notice was given, adding to the inconvenience problem. Here, in some 26 per cent of cases, the witnesses were given less than a week's notice, and in 11 per cent of cases notification of the trial date was provided on the preceding day.

With such cursory treatment, perhaps it was no surprise that seven out of ten of the respondents in the study reported that they arrived at court in a state of some anxiety and uncertainty. Even then, the paucity of information provided meant that many remained in a quandary about what to do. Nearly 60 per cent were given no information about what was expected of them in the witness box; 74 per cent were not advised as to the roles of the different officials in the court-room. Over 40 per cent were not even told which court-room their case was listed in (and had to find out for themselves from the court lists of defendants' names, or by waiting until their names were called over the tannoy system). Furthermore, it turned out that one in three had had a wasted journey and had been put through unnecessary anxiety, for on arrival at court they learned that their cases would not after all proceed as planned. In some cases this was because of unanticipated delays in preceding cases, but in others it was because the defendant had changed the plea to 'guilty' and therefore no trial was necessary. Many such witnesses were sure that the information on the change of status of their case would have been known to the court and prosecution at least on the preceding day, and that a phone call could have been made to save them the inconvenience of a trip to court.

For the other two thirds, the next source of frustration and worry was having to wait some considerable time before being called into the court-room. Here again information provision was scant. Indeed, over half the respondents reported that they were not given any indication by the ushers or other court staff of the time their case might be expected to commence. In fact, four out of five had to wait for more than an hour, and nearly half had to wait more than four hours. Worse, many witnesses had been under the impression that the time they had been told to attend (10.00 am in most cases) was a firm appointment and that they had expected to be giving evidence more or less immediately. Accordingly many had made no special arrangements, for instance, for the collection of their children from school, or to be away from work for a full day. Hurried phone calls from the court were therefore necessary to make such arrangements.

The study also confirmed the potential for problems of intimidation of victims and witnesses while waiting at court. Six out of ten of the respondents reported that they had had to share the same waiting area as the defendants in their cases. For almost all this was a source of considerable anxiety. But it was particularly so for the victims, many of whom had been fearful enough of having to face the defendants across the court-room floor, quite apart from having to do so in the precincts of the building where security was less intensive.

The study also strongly endorsed the view that, for most victims and witnesses, the process of giving evidence in court and of undergoing cross-examination was difficult, and for many deeply distressing and humiliating. Failure, on the part both of the court and of the prosecution, to outline the procedures in the court-room amplified such feelings for many people. The study revealed that almost two thirds of the witnesses felt reasonably prepared about what they were going to say in the witness box, most having been given the opportunity by the CPS to re-read their statements beforehand to refresh their memories. However, only 38 per cent indicated that they felt they knew sufficiently well the procedures within the court-room and what to expect there. Many were particularly surprised at the duration of their ordeal in the witness box. Over half had anticipated that they would merely have to tell their account of events and answer a few questions. In reality, however, nearly one in four were in the witness box for over an hour, and only 16 per cent were there for less than ten minutes. Feelings reported of the experience were almost without exception negative; 47 per cent felt nervous, intimidated, worried or upset, and 46 per cent regarded the experience as having been worse than expected (34 per cent a lot worse). While more than half the respondents felt that the judge and counsel for the prosecution had shown sensitivity, concern and patience towards them, a very similar proportion felt negatively about the attitudes displayed by the defence in these respects.

Finally, and again confirming the findings of other studies (see, for example, Newburn & Merry, 1990), many victims and witnesses were not automatically informed of the outcomes of their cases. While some 40 per cent of respondents did receive notification from the police or from the CPS, 19 per cent either had to read about it in the newspaper, heard about it from a friend, or never learned of the outcome at all. Again, such apparent discourtesy was the source of much surprise and disquiet on the part of people who had freely given up time and suffered inconvenience and, in some instances, abuse and defamation. How could such shoddy treatment of witnesses be justified in return for being public spirited and offering to assist the courts in the pursuit of justice? Could such callous and insensitive treatment of those already offended against - the victims - be excused on the basis that the court had to sustain a position of impartiality and could therefore offer special attentions to no-one? Most of the victims and witnesses interviewed in the study were in no doubt as to their position on such questions.

9.6.3 Campaigning on behalf of victims

Such was the position in 1991. But from about then on there were signs of change. As indicated, a key factor for change was the advent of the new, more 'customer conscious' public sector. Another, however, was the pioneering work of the voluntary organisation Victim Support which took up the cause of victims at court in the early 1990s. This organisation had already done much to ensure better treatment for victims of crime in the community. It had quickly established the respect of the professional agencies of criminal justice for the work that its volunteers routinely undertook at grass-roots level through the nation-wide network of local support schemes. The establishment of a working party on 'the victim in court', followed by a series of demonstration projects in which emotional support and advice services were organised at several courts for those having to attend as witnesses, proved to be a turning point (NAVSS, 1988; Raine & Smith, 1991).

The Government was immediately enthusiastic perhaps particularly about the idea of a voluntary organisation championing the cause and challenging the lackadaisical attitudes of the bigger public sector bureaucracies. Accordingly the Home Office provided grants to support the projects at courts in addition to the funding of victim support schemes in the community and the work of the National Association (Victim Support, 1992). By 1993 about one in three Crown Courts had a court-based victim/witness-support scheme in operation and with strong backing from the resident judges, the Bar, the probation services and the court administrations. At many of these courts reception desks were set up in the court foyers, staffed by volunteers who had been specially trained to provide advice and support to those arriving at court. Special rooms, comfortably furnished and equipped with magazines, coffee facilities and toy boxes for children, were made available by the courts to the schemes. These would provide the sanctuaries where victims and witnesses could wait in the company of the volunteers and where the court procedures could be explained and any questions answered. At about the same time, following recommendations of a report on the confidentiality and privacy of witnesses, the Government legislated to allow, at the judge's discretion, the use of closed circuit television by some witnesses (for example, children, rape victims and others for whom anonymity was considered crucial). The practice of giving evidence from behind screens was also given greater encouragement (Home Office, 1989b).

A little earlier, the Government had also published a Victim's Charter (Home Office, 1990c). Although this document contained little new policy, it certainly provided clear governmental endorsement of many of the aims of the victim support and other campaigners and represented a new benchmark against which police, prosecutors, courts and other agencies would increasingly be expected to perform so far as their involvement with victims of crime was concerned. Moreover, the theme was reinforced two years later under the Citizen's Charter initiative (Cabinet Office, 1991) under which a series of standard-setting publications were produced by, among other organisations, the police, probation and courts at national and local levels alike. The CPS undertook a review of its policies and practices in relation to the treatment of its witnesses. Police forces too began to examine critically their practices, particularly in relation to keeping victims and witnesses informed as to the progress of their cases. So far as the courts were concerned, the lessons of the victim support court-based projects were noted around the country, and at many courts, both at the Crown Court and at the magistrates' courts level, greater efforts were devoted to providing segregated and safer waiting rooms and more comfortable facilities for witnesses. Such efforts were reinforced and extended in a Courts' Charter published subsequently (Lord Chancellor's Department, 1992b), which included the following statements:

> 'If you are a witness in a criminal case, we will send you a leaflet, "The Witness in Court", which explains court procedure...
>
> If you are a defence witness your expenses will be paid within five working days...
>
> If you are a prosecution witness your expenses claim will be paid within five to ten working days of receiving your completed claim form...
>
> In the majority of cases, as a prosecution witness you should not be required to wait for more than two hours before being called to give evidence.' (Lord Chancellor's Department, 1992b, p. 8)

How far might victims' interests be pursued?
Certainly change seemed to be on the way. But, of course, neither governmental commitments of this nature, the associated rhetoric of concern, nor the impressive efforts of some organisations, including Victim Support, could realistically be expected to change over-night the lot of all victims caught up in the criminal justice process. It would be a long reform process. Attitudes would have to be changed, traditional perspectives challenged, and the new, more victim-oriented, values and practices would have to be continuously promulgated through all the layers of police, courts and other organisations.

Moreover there were questions about just how far the Government and other criminal justice policy-makers were prepared to go in reforming the process so far as victims and witnesses were concerned. Was the intention simply to treat this group of the laity rather better, to keep them better informed about their cases, to explain procedures to them and to present a more caring face? That, of course, was typical of much of the preoccupation with 'customer service' in the public sector in the late 1980s and early 1990s. Or was more fundamental restructuring of the status of victims and witnesses in criminal justice also envisaged? In this respect there was certainly little in the charters and policy reviews to indicate the prospect of significant change in the role and status of victims in the criminal justice process. For example, there was no mention of the possibility of victims in Britain being given the opportunity to contribute to the court their perspective on the offence (victim impact statements) or on the possible sentence, as is the case in the criminal justice processes of several other countries.

Why not? Why are victims here denied a voice or even represent-ation in court proceedings (rights which are, after all, enjoyed by the defence)? Why are they denied the automatic right to compensation (compensation arrangements being of the form of discretionary ex gratia payments)? What does the trend towards more cautioning of offenders rather than formal prosecution tell us about the level of commitment towards the interests of the victims of crime? Moreover, welcome though all the talk of improvements in the care of victims and witnesses at court has been in one sense, is there not a smack of paternalism about much of it? Is it not a case of the courts and other agencies being more willing than in the past to provide care and support through a difficult experience in preference to addressing and changing some of the fundamental conditions and circumstances about the trial process and judicial decision making that give rise to much of the anxiety and distress in the first place?

9.7 THE LAITY AND PROFESSIONALS

The search for reasons why paternalism should be preferred to fundamental re-design, and why many of the expectations (rights, many would say) of victims and witnesses continue to be unfulfilled and denied, inevitably takes us back to our starting point about the relationship between professionals and the laity at court. Remember what we said. Professionals in their work place (for that is how many regard the court) will naturally try to make it as congenial a place as possible and design it not just to meet the objectives of the organisation - in this case, the dispensing of justice - but to meet their own needs as well. Members of the laity, on the other hand, whether magistrate, jury member, victim, witness, or defendant, come to the work place less frequently; they are the visitors.

It is inevitable that the court becomes organised mainly around the needs and priorities of the professionals, and that the laity is often left to fit in around them. That is why magistrates today have come to feel more neglected than in the past; the clerks, who used to have time to undertake a 'butler's role', have become more professional and are more busy with 'professional' matters to bother quite so much about the coffee and car-parking. Running a professional and efficient court is given a higher priority. That, too, is why victims and witnesses, conversely, are promised better care and support in the future; after all, no host would want the guests upset in the front room. But it is also why it is likely that the implementation of more far-reaching ideas, such as victim impact statements, will continue to be resisted; for these could interfere with the roles of the professionals (in this instance those responsible for the prosecution) and would add complications and inefficiencies to the already difficult task of running a smooth court. Much the same reasoning underlies the treatment of the other lay groups at court - the defendants and jury members. Could it be otherwise?

PART IV

Consolidation

It may have taken you several hours to get to this point but be assured it took your authors much, much longer. What shall we do now? Some of you, no doubt, will want a brief 'executive summary' and 'bullet list' of the key learning points. Some of you will want resolution of at least a few of the many questions raised in the previous chapters. Those of you who came straight to the last chapter without serving your time in the body of the text probably want the readers' digest. But your authors rather fancy emulating the utopian writers such as Thomas More, William Morris and Samuel Butler. However, this book being about balance, we shall do all four without compromise.

We will commence with a review and then, drawing on the lessons of the past few years, we will look ahead to consider what might constitute good management in criminal justice and what, therefore, might be the goals and priorities for the courts from now on.

CHAPTER 10

The future management of criminal justice

'Let bygones be bygones.'
Station Master Perks in *The Railway Children* by E. Nesbit, 1906.

10.1 TAKING STOCK

We began, it may be recalled, by charting the key aspects of the changing context within which criminal justice has been operating this past ten to fifteen years. First there has been the double pressure of rising workload and tight resourcing, to which the Government's response was to goad the criminal justice agencies towards management. Second, there have been shifts in government policies and in public expectations about criminal justice which also challenged the old order of doing things.

Next we examined the various strategies which the Government adopted and considered some of the main consequences of these. The key aims were identified as those of enhancing accountability, reducing idiosyncrasy, and increasing efficiency. The Government decided that those responsible for the administration of the courts should be made more accountable for providing reliable and fair services and that they should be prevented from being a law unto themselves. We described two parallel strategies which were invoked. The first involved curbing the autonomy of the professionals by standardising procedures in judicial administration and was derived from the Internal Process model (Quinn, 1988). The other involved curbing the autonomy of the agencies by forming them into amalgamated hierarchies, complete with systems of objectives and targets, to provide the basis for clearer accountability.

This was derived from the Rational Goal model (Quinn, 1988). We argued that, with hindsight, this 'double whammy' was probably unnecessary, if not counter-productive. One consequence of combining these strategies with the drive for greater efficiency was that criminal justice was increasingly pushed in the direction of corner-cutting and towards procedures that had the potential to compromise justice.

We then turned to other issues raised by the new managerialism for the courts. In particular, we drew attention to some of the difficult balancing acts associated with management of the courts. First we examined the balance between three conflicting objectives in scheduling the workload. Second, we examined the balance of inter-dependence and independence in the court's relationships with other criminal justice agencies. Third, we examined the balance between the roles of the professionals and the laity.

10.2 THE LEGACY OF MANAGERIALISM

After more than a decade in which managerialism has been promoted, the administration of the courts and of criminal justice has been transformed. Many of the tasks, processes and systems have been reformed. Moreover, further changes can be expected, particularly in response to the report of the Royal Commission on Criminal Justice (Runciman, 1993). The changes managerialism brought about have proved a challenge for those who learned their craft and honed their skills before the late 1970s. Whether making the changes or adapting to them, many have found it a struggle. Of course, those who were recruited during the 1980s have adopted the managerial codes and values with less difficulty. They have known little else, and probably cannot see what their senior colleagues' fuss is all about.

Consider the courts' legacy of the managerialist 1980s and reflect upon which of the various changes might be regarded as positive and which as negative. Some of the main points are as follows.

10.2.1 More efficiency

Rationalisation in the number of court centres: resulting in less accessible justice but greater cost-efficiency in so far as each building is now more fully used.

Fewer and larger administrative centres: again resulting in less accessibility but avoidance of costly duplication of functions and providing greater potential for specialisation in administrative services and for the economies of scale.

Streamlined court procedures: resulting in less delay in the commencement and completion of cases but having the potential to undermine due process.

Alternatives to prosecution: resulting in less pressure on the courts and more time for the important cases, but it also means transferring responsibility for some of the decision making from the independent judiciary to officers of the executive.

10.2.2 More accountability

Cash-limited funding: resulting in tighter control over the public money consumed by the courts but imposing rigidities and economic incentives which may be inconsistent with due process.

Hierarchical structures: resulting in clearer lines of responsibility downwards and sharper accountability upwards but also reducing the scope for organisational autonomy, discretion and diversity.

Performance scrutiny: resulting in courts, as public organisations, being held to account but also increasing pressures to attend only to those aspects which happen to be subject to performance measurement.

Fixed term contracts and performance pay for senior staff: resulting in additional incentives towards high performance and achievement but also undermining stability and perhaps serving to weaken the independence of the judiciary.

10.2.3 Less idiosyncrasy

Standardisation of justice: resulting in more consistency in sentencing but also reducing judicial discretion and responsiveness, including the opportunity for deterrent sentencing.

Standardisation of administrative processes: resulting in less scope for variance, error or malpractice but again reducing discretion and responsiveness.

Shared information systems: resulting in greater efficiency and effectiveness in communications between courts and other agencies but also serving to reduce the status of the court to that of being just one of a network of inter-dependent organisational units.

Standardisation of procedures and practices: resulting in greater control over, and consistency in, the quality of services provided but also undermining the discretion of professionals and, with it, their morale and motivation.

10.2.4 Changing values

The legacy of managerialism, then, may be viewed in different lights depending on one's value base. And in this respect it is useful to remind ourselves of Hood's distinction between three sets of values that have underpinned public administration over the course of history (see Chapter 3; and Hood, 1991). Hood, it will be recalled, distinguished between sigma values of efficiency and parsimony; theta values of honesty and fairness; and lambda values of security and robustness. Clearly, the dominant values of the new managerialism of the 1980s in criminal justice, as elsewhere, have been those of efficiency and parsimony. These led decision-makers in directions that were often in direct conflict with justice and due process. Maybe there was inefficiency within the administration of justice. Maybe it was fitting to proceed along the path of decriminalisation and administrative penalties in place of adjudicative justice for more minor offences. Maybe it was appropriate to hear more cases in the magistrates' courts and restrict access to the Crown Court to the most deserving cases only, in the manner proposed by the Royal Commission on Criminal Justice (Runciman, 1993). Maybe it was reasonable to institute a system of discounts for guilty pleas and to countenance plea bargaining as in the USA. Maybe it was appropriate to cash-limit the grant to courts since, after all, it was public money that was being spent. But maybe it wasn't. It would all depend on how one weighed up the values of efficiency and of justice.

10.2.5 Restoring the balance in values

Whatever view is taken of the past preoccupation with efficiency values, however, our argument is that, for the future, the priority is to ensure that the other two sets of values enjoy equivalent consideration. The values of honesty and fairness obviously lie at the heart of justice and, happily, seem not to have diminished in importance within the decision-making process in the court-room. But there is plenty of scope for greater emphasis on fairness, for example, concerning equal treatment of all under the law, concerning equal opportunities on the Bench and in the professional and administrative ranks of the courts' organisation, concerning equal access to justice and legal aid and concerning the rights and expectations of victims.

Similarly, there is scope for placing greater emphasis upon the values of security and robustness. Here it seems particularly important that the courts, as institutions at the heart of the state, should not be perceived as organisations of fad and fashion. Communities expect courts to be anchor points of stability and reliability, a source of security in an otherwise changing environment. Without that sense of permanence and durability, the authority of the court and its independence is weakened. This is not, of course, an argument for inertia and stagnation. The courts must adapt with the times so that they are able to reflect and respond to present realities. Our point is simply that, in doing so, courts must not lose sight of the important and valued practices and the features that give them the character of robustness and stability which have much to do with upholding public confidence in the justice process.

Besides the need for balance specifically between the values of efficiency, fairness and robustness, we would argue more generally that the notion of balance is a crucial feature of good management in criminal justice. At various points we have emphasised this. For instance, in Chapter 7, we discussed the practical matter of finding an appropriate balance between different objectives in organising court hearings. There we described the challenge to balance the aims of conveniencing the parties (itself a balancing act between different interests), minimising delay, and using court resources efficiently. Similarly, we emphasised in Chapter 8 the importance of finding an appropriate balance between an independent judiciary, and all that this implies in terms of separateness for the courts, and the requirement for the different agencies involved in criminal justice to work together. Balance was also a key notion underlying our comments in Chapter 9 about the roles of the laity and of professionals. For example, a balance here is required between supporting and not patronising the laity, between the state undertaking certain roles - for instance, responsibility for prosecutions and making provision for legal representation - and not excluding or neglecting the parties at the centre of criminal justice, the victims, witnesses and the defendants.

10.3 WHAT NEXT?

For those who worked within the agencies of criminal justice before the 1980s, the imposition of the new managerialism must have felt a little like being given school detention. In their own classrooms, and under the personal and critical-eyed supervision of the head-teacher, they were taught how to behave and to do as they were told. To sustain the metaphor a little, there was a certain amount of shouting from the head, and quite a few threats were issued as well. The class was made to recite out loud 'I must give priority to economy, efficiency and effectiveness', 'I must believe in and practice customer-care', 'I must be accountable for my actions', 'I must be more strategic in my approach', and 'I must do as the head-teacher tells me.' Those caught shirking faced stiffer punishment.

Whether it was the punishment, reformation or deterrent, the old order, with its potential for complacency, delay, inefficiency, inequality, arrogance and poor service, seems to us to have given way to a new order which promises more care, greater celerity, greater efficiency, greater concern for equality, more humility and better service. The period of detention is now up. Reformed and rehabilitated, the professionals must now be resettled and supported so that we can benefit from their capacity to exercise discretion in complex and uncertain circumstances. This is what the work demands and we are fortunate that we have agencies and staff capable of providing it. Let discretion be handed back, both to the organisations and to the individuals who work within them. There are other, more productive, ways in which those at the centre can apply their reforming energies and controlling instincts. Indeed, there is plenty of other reforming work to be attended to within criminal justice (for example, what about the hegemony of the Bar?).

Handing back earned and justified discretion represents one aspect of a more mature form of management of criminal justice. But this must not simply mean turning the clocks back. The enhanced accountability which has been demonstrated through the new managerialism must not be allowed to wither. Indeed, new accountabilities must be established with the local communities which criminal justice serves. Just as the 1980s was the decade in which accountability to central government was emphasised, so the 1990s must be the decade in which accountability to the public is developed.

The public may not be at the centre of the criminal justice process but that process is ultimately conducted for their benefit. Their confidence in the process and their enjoyment of the Queen's peace is crucial to the maintenance of a lawful and secure society. How is this confidence to be fostered, especially in a context in which lurid tales of crime sell newspapers and in which fear of crime is a serious concern? It is so convenient for the public to wash their hands of delinquency in society, as sometimes they do for the care of the elderly, and assume that by paying their taxes they make someone else responsible for it. More is likely to be achieved in deterring crime and in keeping the Queen's peace if the criminal justice process is more strongly oriented towards the communities which it serves. Where the court is perceived as listening and responding to local viewpoints, the community is more likely to have confidence in the process. Of course, the participation of lay magistrates and jury members is one way in which the public are involved but for most people the court is a distant and undependable institution.

If only about 3 per cent of all crimes end up in court (Home Office, 1991a), then each case that does so will have to generate thirty times more than its share of public confidence in the criminal justice process. The ratio for the police is about one to two since only about 40 per cent of crime is reported to them. There is a strong argument in favour of managing the courts in such a way that the press and the public witness an exemplary dispensation of justice in court in which contempt for the offence (but not the offender) is expressed and an accountability to the local community is actively demonstrated. There is a long way to go. Maybe after the Crown Court, the Police Court and the Magistrates'

Court, we might move to a sense of the Community's Court or the Public's Court. This would enhance this prime output of the justice process, public confidence. But it takes time to establish new frameworks of accountability. As Radzinowicz points out:

> 'A good system of criminal justice cannot be brought into existence by a statute or a Commission, nor can it be brought into existence by a feverish endeavour extending over a few months or even a few years. It requires a systematic and gradual approach'. (adzinowicz, 1991, p. 431)

10.4 A NEW PARADIGM

The dominant paradigm of the 1980s, upon which much of the managerialism was based, was the Systems approach. This brought many benefits. It encouraged emphasis on process and flow between agencies. It supported a managerialist, Rational Goal, efficiency-based approach to criminal justice in which the sub-systems were placed under the control of the larger system. It established the recognition that the decisions of one agency have implications for others and that interdependence is a necessary reality for criminal justice. The agencies began to co-operate and they became more efficient and accountable and less idiosyncratic. But, although it was once in tune with the times, the limitations of the paradigm, like those of the previous administrative paradigm, became increasingly apparent.

We believe a new paradigm is starting to supersede managerialism. It places emphasis on problem solving rather than on process, on local pluralism rather than on 'the one best way' to do everything, more on dispersed local control and less on hierarchical control, and more on mutual, respect-based networks, less on prescribed systems. This prediction is not just derived from the models described in Chapter 3, for we think we see the first glimpses of the paradigm for the 1990s in certain current (1993) activities in criminal justice. The first instance was the round of 'Ditchling Conferences' in which people from many disciplines and agencies were invited to meet and discuss aspects of the proposed Criminal Justice Act, 1991. Another hint was the development of Statements of Preferred Practice between the judiciary and probation services. The establishment of the Criminal Justice Consultative Council (CJCC) seems to institutionalise the movement.

The CJCC, the first recommendation of the Woolf Enquiry (Woolf, 1991), was set up by the Home Secretary in Autumn 1991. The members of the Enquiry had identified a 'geological fault' between the agencies that should have been involved with prisoners. Members of the health, police, social work, prison, education, court, housing, training, employment and other services were found not to be working together on the problems faced by prisoners. Even those who were included in the 'criminal justice system' were seen not to work well with each other.

At the national level the CJCC comprises two senior judges, the Director of Public Prosecutions, a chief constable, a Queen's counsel, a past president of the Law Society, a senior magistrate, a chief probation officer, the Director General of Prisons, the secretary of the Justices' Clerk's Society, and the permanent secretaries of the Lord Chancellor's Department and of the Home Office. But in addition, there have been established twenty-four local Area Committees, each composed of a magistrate, a chief constable, a director of prisons, a probation officer, a practising barrister and solicitor, and a representative of the Lord Chancellor's Department and of the CPS, and each chaired by a senior Circuit judge.

Significantly, the committees have the power to co-opt members from other disciplines, for example, from the health service, education, and social services, to gain assistance in resolving problems on any specialist topic (Farquharson, 1993). The members of the national forum and of the area committees are not invited as representatives of their organisations or professions, nor are they expected to 'fight their corners'. They are invited to participate in joint problem solving. This should not simply be a high-level co-ordinating committee, nor another forum for court users to be told what is expected of them or to register their complaints. That is the essential difference from the 'system-oriented' forums of the past and from the old managerial paradigm.

10.5 UNDERSTANDING THE CONTEXT

Another aspect of a more mature form of management in criminal justice, the development of which, we argue, should be given emphasis, involves a fuller understanding of the context in which one is working. This demands careful thought and planning. What patterns and profiles of demand can we expect for the future? The reader may recall the impact on the courts of the rise in the number of motor cars in the post-war years. The number of cases brought before the courts in the 1960s and 1970s mirrors the rise of the motor car and in the late 1980s reflects the way motor-related crimes were dealt with - fixed penalties, in particular, having had a profound impact. (Of course, some would argue that the greater social crime is the possession of a motor car, not any particular act done with it.)

What can we say about the demand for adjudication of non-motor related crimes? We note that most defendants are young men, unemployed and living in poverty. (Stewart & Stewart, 1993). What predictions can we make about the future levels of unemployment and impoverishment of our youth? We also note that many of those brought to court have experienced harrowing backgrounds of child abuse, life 'in care' and disrupted schooling (Boswell, 1991). What predictions can we make about the assurance of emotional, physical and financial security for the next generation? We have refrained from discussing social policy, criminology and sociology in this book but, of course, they provide significant contributions to an understanding of the context of the courts. For a moment, though, let us consider the typical young offender who is referred to the probation services and then a raw description of two people brought before the court.

'In all this talk of policy and high level issues, we must remind ourselves of the kind of young people we are working with and the problems they face. By the time they come to the probation service, persistent offending in itself is a major problem, combined in some instances with the aftermath of having served a custodial sentence. They typically have failed all previous attempts to help them, are likely to be alienated from family and social communities, will have dropped out of school early, had very poor experience of employment, no skills, no qualifications. Instead, they will have obtained status, achievement and challenge, and their most satisfactory social contact, around the activity of offending.' (Fullwood, 1989a)

Speaking to another audience, the same author explained:

'Looking at how things actually work in practice, I could do no better than to start with two examples of individual events in my own area which have had a marked impact on me.

a) A single parent mother in her twenties with two pre-school children taken before one of our local courts for non-payment of a fine of a few pounds imposed for the offence, as opposed to the crime, of not paying a 75p bus fare. Living in poverty with all the economic and family pressure on this young mother, one would have hoped that the criminal justice system could have responded with some support and guidance, rather than the decision of the court which was to send her to prison for non-payment of a fine. This was the first offence for which she had appeared before the court and all the complex networks that operate to prevent someone like her ending up in prison did not work, and in fact were clearly spurned by the court. The young woman was taken by the police and the social services department needed to be contacted regarding the care of the two pre-school children. The outraged probation officer in court paid the small fine and was reprimanded by the clerk to the justices who sent a letter of complaint expecting me (the chief probation officer) to discipline him for unprofessional behaviour.

b) My second example is a young man in his late teens who had been through most of the facilities that the criminal justice system has to offer in its attempt to care for and control the wayward. Eventually this man had arrived at one of Greater Manchester Probation day centres for an intensive period of supervision. Included in this were sessions in which the offenders were helped to talk about their offences and their past experiences. It turned out that this young man had been horribly abused as a child... Let me read some of the lines from a poem this young man wrote whilst attending the day centre.

"A little child alone at night,
Dares not sleep, eyes full of fright,
Staring round a small dark room.
Wondering if tonight he'll meet his doom.

Father rages, mother weeps,
Child listens, neighbour sleeps,
Mother screams, then no more,
The child watches an opening door.

'Daddy no please don't hurt me',
cries the child bent over father's knee,
The child cries because of the pain,
Then screams and bawls and is silent again.

No more movement in the child's bed,
As another child now lies dead." (Fullwood, 1989b)

Such a piteous tale serves as a reminder to all involved in the management of criminal justice of the context of their activities. Keeping sight of the context is as important a part of good management in criminal justice as the other aspects which we have discussed in this book.

10.6 COUP D'ÉTAT

As we set our sights on a more mature management of criminal justice, we will end on another solemn note. Let us also remember the frailty of government and the fact that most states this century have experienced martial law.

A leading student of terrorism commented, a few years ago, that, "far from being a fortunately rare exception in an otherwise civilised world, the coup d'état is now the normal model of political change in most member states of the United Nation". "There are now", he continued, "many more military dictatorships in existence than Parliamentary democracies... during the last fifteen years there have been some 120 military coups." These military regimes are a mixed bag, but their effect on systems of criminal justice is uniformly devastating, reducing them to the lowest common denominator of arbitrary repression. (Radzinowicz, 1991, p. 428)

We must manage criminal justice in a way that also preserves what we value about the process, especially the independence of the judiciary. In the urgency to address present concerns, we must beware of compromising our future.

BIBLIOGRAPHY

Ashworth, A (1988), Re-aligning the criminal process, in Harrison, A & J Gretton (eds) *Crime UK 1988: An economic, social and policy audit*, Newbury: Policy Journals, pp 49-54.

Ashworth, A (1984), *Sentencing in the Crown Court*, Occasional Paper No. 10, Oxford: Centre for Criminological Research, University of Oxford.

Audit Commission (1989), *The Probation Service: Promoting value for money*, London: HMSO.

Audit Commission (1990), *The Police Service*, Reports 8, 9, & 10, London: HMSO.

Bacon, R W & W Eltis (1976), *Britain's Economic Problem: Too few producers*, London: Macmillan.

Baddeley, S (1990), The power of innocence: from politeness to politics, *Management Education & Development*, 22, 2, pp. 106-116.

Baldwin, J & M McConville (1977), *Negotiated Justice*, Oxford: Martin Robertson.

Barclay, G (1993), *The Criminal Justice System in England & Wales*, London: Home Office.

Benson, J K (1975), The inter-organisational network as a political economy, *Administrative Science Quarterly*, 20, pp. 229-249.

Boswell, G (1991), *Waiting for Change: Section 53 offenders*, London: Prince's Trust.

Burney, E (1979), *JP, Magistrate, Court and Community*, London: Hutchinson.

Byers, P (1993), Survey reported in *The Independent*, Feb 4th.

Cabinet Office (1988), *Improving Management in Government: The next steps*, London: HMSO.

Cabinet Office (1991), *The Citizen's Charter*, Cm 1599, London: HMSO.

Carlen, P (1976), *Magistrates' Justice*, London: Croom Helm.

Celnick, A (1976), *A Study of the Sheffield Impact Unit*, Sheffield: South Yorkshire Probation Service Research Unit.

Checkland, P (1981), *Systems Thinking, Systems Practice*, London: Wiley.

Church, T (1982), *Examining Local Legal Culture: Practitioner attitudes in four criminal courts*, Washington: National Institute of Justice.

Coote, A (1993), *The Independent*, Jan 17th.

Darbyshire, P (1984), *The Magistrates' Clerk*, Chichester: Barry Rose.

Dunleavy, P J (1989), Bureaucrats, budgets and the growth of the state, *British Journal of Political Science*, 5, pp. 229-238.

Dunn, D (1993), Improving information within magistrates' courts, *The Magistrate*, 49, 2, pp. 33-36.

Dunsire, A & C Hood (1989), *Cutback Management in Public Bureaucracies*, Cambridge: Cambridge University Press.

Elmore, R (1977), Organisational models of social programme implementation, *Public Policy*, 26, 2, pp. 186-228.

Evan, W M (1972), An organisation-set model, in, Evan, W M (ed), 1976, *Inter-organisational Relations: selected readings*, Harmondsworth: Penguin, pp. 78-90.

Farquharson, Lord Justice (1993), The Criminal Justice Consultative Council, *The Magistrate*, 49, 2, p. 26.

French, J R P & B Raven (1960), The basis of social power, in Cartwright, D (ed) *Studies in Social Power*, pp. 83-104, Ann Arbor: University of Michigan.

Fullwood, C (1989a), *The Young Offender: Historical and current perspectives*, Manchester: Manchester Statistical Society.

Fullwood, C (1989b), *Bringing It All Back Home - A personal view of the criminal justice scene*, Address to International Halfway House Association Conference and Probation & Bail Hostels National Conference, Manchester.

Gifford, A M (1986), *Where's the Justice? A manifesto of law reform*, Harmondsworth: Penguin.

Gottfredson, M R and D M Gottfredson (1980), *Decision Making in Criminal Justice: Toward the rational exercise of discretion*, Cambridge, Mass.: Ballinger.

Green, J D (1992), *A Response to a New Framework for Local Justice*, St Helens: The Magistrates' Court.

Gutch, R (1992), *Contracting Lessons from the US*, London: National Council for Voluntary Organisations.

Hart, H L A (1968), *Punishment and Responsibility*, Oxford: Clarendon Press.

Hedderman C & D Moxon, (1992), *Research Findings No. 1, Magistrates' Court or Crown Court? Mode of Trial and impact on Sentencing*, Home Office Research and Statistics Department, London: Home Office.

Heydebrand, W & C Seron (1990), *The Rationalisation of Justice: The political economy of federal district courts*, Albany: State of New York Press.

HM Treasury (1979), *The Government's Expenditure Plans, 1979-80 to 1982-83*, Cmnd 7746, London: HMSO.

HM Treasury (1992), *Autumn Statement, 1992*, Cm 2096, London: HMSO.

Home Office (1982), *Magistrates' Courts: report of a working party*, London: Home Office.

Home Office (1983), *Circular to Police Forces on Cautioning*, London: Home Office.

Home Office (1984), *Circular 66/84, Efficiency and Effectiveness in the Magistrates' Courts*, London: Home Office.

Home Office (1986), *Consultation Paper on size of Benches*, London: Home Office.

Home Office (1989a), *Magistrates' Courts: report of a scrutiny*, London: HMSO.

Home Office (1989b), *Report of the Advisory Group on Video Evidence (Pigot Committee)*, London: HMSO.

Home Office (1990a), *Crime, Justice and Protecting the Public: The Government's proposals for legislation*, Cm 965, London: HMSO.

Home Office (1990b), *Supervision & Punishment in the Community: A framework for action*, Cm 966, London: HMSO.

Home Office (1990c), *Victim's Charter: A statement of the rights of victims of crime*, London: Home Office.

Home Office (1990d), *Report of the Working Group on Pre-Trial Issues*, London: Home Office.

Home Office (1991a), *A Digest of Information on the Criminal Justice System*, Home Office Research & Statistics Department, London: Home Office.

Home Office (1991b), *Listing: Best Practice Advisory Group report*, London: Home Office.

Home Office (1991c), Annual Report, Cm 1509, London: HMSO.

Home Office (1992), Annual Report, London: Home Office.

Hood, C (1991), A public management for all seasons, *Public Administration*, 69, pp. 3-19.

Hood, C and G Schuppert (eds) (1988), *Delivering public services in Western Europe: sharing Western European experiences of para-government organisation*, London: Sage.

Hood, R (1992), *Race and Sentencing*, Oxford: Clarendon Press.

House of Commons (1969), *Children & Young Persons Act (1969)*, London: HMSO.

House of Commons (1980), *The Magistrates' Courts Act (1980)*, London: HMSO.

House of Commons (1982), *Transport Act (1982)*, London: HMSO.

House of Commons (1984a), *The Probation Rules 1984*, London: HMSO.

House of Commons (1984b), *Home Secretary's Evidence to the House of Commons Home Affairs Select Committee*, Jan 23rd.

House of Commons (1993), *Statement by the Home Secretary on the Police* March 23rd.

Huxham, C (1992), *Collaborative Capability: An inter-organisational perspective on collaborative advantage*, Paper presented at the British Academy of Management Conference, Bradford University.

Jackson, E (1992), Catherine Mackinna and feminist jurisprudence: a critical appraisal, *Journal of Law & Society*, 19, 2, pp. 195-213.

James Committee (1975), *Report of the inter-departmental committee on the distribution of criminal business between the Crown Court and magistrates' courts*, Cmnd 6323, London: HMSO.

Jones, C (1991), *Auditing Criminal Justice*, paper presented to the Annual Conference of the British Criminological Society, York.

Jones, C (1993), Auditing Criminal Justice, *British Journal of Criminology*, 33, 2, pp. 187-202.

Kast, F E & J E Rosenzweig (1971), *Contingency Views of Organisations and Management*, New York: Science Research Associates.

King, M (1981), *The Framework of Criminal Justice*, London: Croom Helm.

King, M & C May (1985), *Black Magistrates*, London: Cobden Trust.

LAG (Legal Action Group) (1992), *A Strategy for Justice: Publicly funded legal services in the 1990s*, London: Legal Action Group.

Lane, Lord Chief Justice (1988), Court of Appeal judgement, 28th January.

Liberty (1991), *Evidence submitted to the Royal Commission on Criminal Justice*, London: Liberty.

Local Government Management Board (1992), Building Effective Partnerships, Luton: LGMB.

Lord Chancellor's Department (1948), *Guidance to Advisory Committees on the Appointment of Justices*, London: Lord Chancellor's Department.

Lord Chancellor's Department (1988), The qualities looked for in a Justice of the Peace, *The Magistrate*, 3, p. 78.

Lord Chancellor's Department (1989), *Legal Services: A framework for the future*, Cm 740, London: HMSO.

Lord Chancellor's Department (1990), *Judicial Appointments: The Lord Chancellor's policies and procedures*, London: Lord Chancellor's Department.

Lord Chancellor's Department (1992a), *Lord Chancellor's Department Court Service, Annual Report, 1991-92*, London: HMSO.

Lord Chancellor's Department (1992b), *The Courts Charter*, London: Lord Chancellor's Department.

Lord Chancellor's Department (1992c), *A New Framework for Local Justice*, Cm 1829, London: HMSO.

Magistrates' Association (1992), *Sentencing Guidelines*, London: The Magistrates' Association.

May, T (1992), *Power, Transformation and Identity: a study in human service organisation*, Working paper, Durham University.

Mayhew P, Elliott D & L Dowds (1988), *1988 British Crime Survey*, Home Office Research Studies No. 111, London: Home Office.

McBarnet, D J (1981), *Conviction*, London: Macmillan.

McConville, M & J Baldwin (1982), The influence of race on sentencing in England, *Criminal Law Review*, pp. 652-658.

McGuire, M (1992), *Unequal before the Law*, London: National Council for Civil Liberties.

Mills, B (1992), Comments reported in *The Independent*, Dec 13th.

Mintzberg, H (1983), *Structures in Fives*, New York: Prentice Hall.

Morgan, G (1986), *Images of Organisation*, Beverley Hills: Sage.

Morgan, P (1985), *Modelling the Criminal Justice System*, Home Office Research & Planning Unit Paper No. 35, London: Home Office.

Mowlan, M (1993), Comments reported in *The Independent*, Feb 12th.

Moxon, D (1988), *Sentencing Practice in the Crown Court*, Home Office Research Study No. 103, London: Home Office.

Moxon, D et al (1985), *Juvenile Sentencing: Is there a tariff?* Home Office Research & Planning Unit Paper No. 32, London: Home Office.

National Association of Victim Support Schemes (1988), *The Victim in Court: Report of a working party*, London: NAVSS.

National Audit Office (1990), *Review of the Crown Prosecution Service*, Cm 345, London: HMSO.

Newburn, T & S Merry (1990), *Keeping in Touch: Police: victim communication in two areas*, Home Office Research Study 116, London: HMSO.

Pannick, D (1988), *Judges*, Oxford: Clarendon Press.

Police (1990), CPS has damaged public's confidence in criminal justice, *Police*, Editorial, 22, 5, p. 18.

Pullinger, H (1985), *The Criminal Justice System: The flow model*, Home Office Research & Planning Unit Paper No. 36, London: Home Office.

Quinn, R (1988), *Beyond Rational Management*, New York: Josey Bass.

Radzinowicz, L (1991), Penal regressions, *Cambridge Law Journal*, 50, pp. 422-444.

Raine, J W (1989a), *The organisation of the Wiltshire Magistrates' Courts*, Birmingham: Public Service Management Centre, University of Birmingham.

Raine, J W (1989b), *Local Justice, Ideals and Realities*, Edinburgh: T & T Clark.

Raine, J W & L Henshaw (1985), *Value for Money in the Magistrates' Courts*, London: Home Office.

Raine, J W & R Smith (1991), *The Victim and Witness in Court Project*, London: Victim Support.

Raine, J W and M J Willson (1992), *The CDE of Scheduling in Magistrates' Courts*, London: Home Office.

Raine, J W and M J Willson (1993), Organisational culture and the scheduling of court appearances, *Journal of Law and Society*, 20, 2, pp. 237-252.

Richards, S (1992), *Who Defines the Public Good? Changing the rules of the game*, Project Report, London: Office for Public Management.

Roberts N & Bradley RT(1991), *Stakeholder Collaboration and Innovation*: paper presented to the Annual Conference of the Association of Public Policy and Management, Washington DC.

Rock, P (1991), Witnesses and space in a Crown Court, *British Journal of Criminology*, 81, pp. 266-279.

Rozenberg, J (1992), Miscarriages of justice, in Stockdale E & S Casale (eds) *Criminal Justice under Stress*, London: Blackstone Press, pp. 91-117.

Runciman, Viscount of Doxford (1993), *Report of the Royal Commission on Criminal Justice*, Cm 2263, London: HMSO.

Saville, Lord Justice (1992), Report in *The Independent*, Dec 19th .

Scarman, Lord (1982), *The Scarman Report: The Brixton Disorders 10-12 April, 1981*, Harmondsworth: Penguin.

Shapland, J; Willmore J & P Duff (1985), *Victims in the Criminal Justice System*, Aldershot: Gower.

Smart, J J C & B Williams (1973), *Utilitarianism: for and against*, London: Cambridge University Press.

Smith, D D; Folard M S & D E Smith (1976), *Impact, Intensive Matched Probation and After-care Treatment: The results of an experiment*, Home Office Research Study No. 36, London: HMSO.

Spencer, J (1993), Quality Advice, *The Justices' Clerk*, 149, pp. 74-80.

Spencer, K M & C Kunz (1992), *Building Effective Partnerships*, Arndale Centre, Luton: Local Government Management Board.

Sprack, J (1992), The trial process, in Stockdale E & S Casale (eds) *Criminal Justice under Stress*, London: Blackstone Press, pp. 64-90.

Stewart, G & J Stewart (1993), *Social Circumstances of Younger Offenders under Supervision*, London: Association of Chief Officers of Probation.

Tarling, R (1979), *Sentencing Practice in Magistrates' Courts*, Home Office Research Study No. 56, London: Home Office.

Taylor, Lord Chief Justice (1992), *The Richard Dimbleby Lecture, The Judiciary in the Nineties*, London: BBC.

Taylor, Lord Chief Justice (1993), Address to the Annual Conference of the Law Society of Scotland, Edinburgh.

Tumim, Lord Justice (1993), Report in *The Guardian*, Mar 9th .

United Nations Inter-Regional Crime and Justice Research Institute (UNICRI) (1971), *Public et Justice: Une etude-pilote en Tunisie*, Geneva:United Nations.

Victim Support (1991), *Royal Commission on Criminal Justice: Response by Victim Support*, London:Victim Support.

Victim Support (1992), *Annual Report 1991-92*, London: Victim Support.

Von Hirsch, A (1976), *Doing Justice: The choice of punishments*, New York:Hill & Wang.

Von Hirsch, A (1986), *Past or Future Crimes*, Manchester: Manchester University Press.

Wadham, J (1992), Letter to *The Independent*, Dec 15th.

Walklate, S (1988), *Victimology*, London: Unwin Hyman.

Walmsley, R and K White (1979), *Sexual Offences, Consent and Sentencing*, Home Office Research Study No. 54, London: HMSO.

Wasik, M (1992), Sentencing: a fresh look at aims and objectives, in, Stockdale, E and S Casale (eds), *Criminal Justice Under Stress*, London: Blackstone, pp. 118-141.

White, R C (1991), *The Administration of Justice*, Oxford: Blackwell.

Willson, M (1986), The changing environment of the professional worker, *Probation Journal*, 33, 2, pp. 54-58.

Willson, M (1991), Contracting Corruption, *Local Government Studies*, 17, 3, pp. 1-6.

Winkel, F W (1991), Police, Victims, and Crime Prevention: some research-based recommendations on victim-oriented interventions, *British Journal of Criminology*, 31, 3, pp. 250-265.

Winkel, F W & L Koppelaar (1988), Police Information for Victims of Crime: A research and training perspective from the Netherlands, *Police Studies*, 11, 2, pp. 73-81.

Woolf, Lord Justice (1991), *Prison disturbances, April 1990: Report of an enquiry*, Cm 1456, London: HMSO.

INDEX